Essential Do's
and Taboos

Other books by Roger E. Axtell

Do's & Taboos Around the World: A Guide to International Behavior

Gestures: Do's & Taboos of Body Language Around the World

Do's & Taboos of International Trade: A Small Business Primer

Do's & Taboos of Hosting International Visitors

Do's & Taboos of Public Speaking: How to Get Those Butterflies Flying in Formation

Do's & Taboos of Using English Around the World

Do's & Taboos of Humor Around the World

Do's & Taboos of Preparing for Your Trip Abroad with John P. Healy

Do's & Taboos Around the World for Women in Business with Tami Briggs, Margaret Corcoran, and Mary Beth Lamb

Essential Do's and Taboos

The Complete Guide to International Business and Leisure Travel

Roger E. Axtell

John Wiley & Sons, Inc.

For Mitzi

There are truths on one side of Pyrenees which are falsehoods on the other side.

— Blaise Pascal, seventeenth-century philosopher

Contents

Preface

A man's feet must be planted in his country,
but his eyes should survey the world.

—George Santayana

Early in my business career, the president of The Parker Pen Company, where I worked, decided that I should be assigned to our London offices in order to broaden my value to the firm.

As it happened, I was the first American to be sent to our English subsidiary and, understandably, my British coworkers were hesitant and uncertain about how to deal with me. They wondered, Why is he being posted there? Is he a spy? I also learned later that at the time our British colleagues suffered from an inferiority complex as a result of constantly being told how successful and how advanced American marketing methods were.

The irony of this last circumstance was that, in truth, our U.K. subsidiary had been more successful in establishing the company's brand in that marketplace than we Americans were in the United States. In the United Kingdom, the Parker brand name was so highly valued and respected that people actually aspired to own our products. There, the Parker name was equivalent to Tiffany or Rolex.

So there I was, a very junior manager, assigned to an office where people were guardedly suspicious of me and reluctantly expected to hear over and over again how successfully we marketed our products back in the United States.

Furthermore, one of my first shocks was that British English could be quite different from American English. Even though I had been trained as a journalist in college, many of my attempts at clever communication were lost on my British colleagues. My American witticisms were met with blank stares, my grammar and pronunciation sounded faulty to them, and, according to their standards, even my spelling was incorrect.

Next, I began to realize how much we Americans tend to relish superlatives like *first, best, largest, greatest,* and *grandest*. Not so with the British. They are much more self-deprecating. For example, where a reasonably skilled American tennis player might establish that he had been the club champion at home, his British counterpart might casually comment, "Oh, yes. I managed to play a bit." Only later would the American learn that the Brit had competed at Wimbledon. As another example, I worked with a British colleague for twenty years before accidentally finding out that he had been awarded one of the highest medals of merit while in the army in World War II. During those twenty years, he never once mentioned that to me.

Therefore, one of my new and constant guidelines became "understatement." To deal with the local inferiority complex, I decided to counter any of their beliefs that I considered myself better or smarter than the rest of them. For example, at that time the United Kingdom was experiencing a worrisome "brain drain" among its youngest and brightest. Many of the most talented young people had left the Mother Isle to emigrate elsewhere. So, I often mentioned that my coming to England must have represented a "drained brain," meaning that I considered myself something of an empty-headed type and I had been sent there to soak up all the local knowledge. I also readily agreed to take on any task assigned to me, no matter how trivial, messy, or lowly it might be.

Months passed and I soon received more responsibility, along with less suspicion and more acceptance. Meanwhile, I gained a whole new education. As one example, an early assignment in 1964 was to phone our distributors in Copenhagen, Amsterdam, Brussels, and Rome to advise them of a certain procedural change. In those days, I was so nervous at the prospect of actually phoning these major international capitals that I wrote down every word I was instructed to say, rehearsed them, and then quickly delivered my speech in order to save on long distance expenses. Later, I learned that phone calls to those locales from London were similar, back in the United States, to my calling St. Louis, Denver, Los Angeles, and Seattle.

I also learned to be cautious with my vocabulary, and I studied the intricacies of British English, especially in areas where pitfalls awaited me. For instance, in England a *scheme* is simply a "plan," whereas in the United States, we consider a *scheme* to be something slightly devious.

On another occasion I commented to a British colleague that I considered him "very sharp," but then I detected a change in his demeanor. It turned out he was highly offended because in British English, *sharp* implies being "crafty and unprincipled," whereas in America we define it as "bright and alert."

One year passed. Then two. Then three. And, finally, four years had elapsed. During that time, my duties were expanded to cover other regions outside the United Kingdom. I found myself traveling throughout Western Europe, the Middle East, and Africa. For me, it was an incomparable apprenticeship, like on-the-job training and graduate school all wrapped into one.

During this time, I also adopted the practice of keeping small notebooks in my suit coat pocket to record things I learned, such as important dates, various holidays, the rules of toasting, the full names and birthdays of clients and colleagues, tricky word differences, tips on protocol, dining habits, gestures and body language, the role of women in business, and so on.

When my superiors in the United States finally decided it was time for me to return and become the head of the home office's international marketing department, I departed England with many regrets.

Several months later, I learned that the head of the British subsidiary had written to the U.S. president of the company headquarters to give the following short evaluation of my tour of duty in England. "You sent us a nice American boy. We are now returning to you a proper English gentleman."

For me, there was no finer tribute . . . then or since. I had learned the supreme importance of showing respect for other cultures and, most important, how to adapt and gain acceptance.

I later coined the phrase *chameleon management,* meaning that the wise international manager learns to go from culture to culture adopting some of the local coloration, some of the local values, and some of the local behavior. I don't mean to suggest that we should lose our own nationalism, but we should simply show respect for the way others live.

That's what this book is all about: acquiring respect for and awareness of behavior and protocol in other cultures, no matter how much they differ from our own.

It's what Blaise Pascal warned about centuries ago—we need to realize that "there are truths on one side of the Pyrenees which are falsehoods on the other." He was referring, of course, to the Pyrenees mountain region that separates Spain from France, but, more important, to a third culture—the Basques—that resided in between. Thus, among the three regions, there were many inconsistencies in behavior, beliefs, and lifestyles.

Acknowledgments

Arch Ward, the late popular sportswriter for the *Chicago Tribune*, regularly ended his daily column, "In the Wake of the News," with these simple words: "The Wake depends upon its friends."

I'm sure that expression would be echoed by almost every writer, because we all rely on a myriad of sources for assistance and inspiration. Here are the names of just some of those invaluable friends who helped me in the compilation of this book.

Alex Durtka is considered by many to be the "hostmeister" of the city of Milwaukee and its environs. He is the longtime president and CEO of the International Institute of Milwaukee and the executive vice president of the Friends of the International Institute of Wisconsin, and he serves on the boards of a host of other internationally related organizations in that state. Furthermore, Milwaukee is truly a multiethnic city. In fact, the entire state of Wisconsin is historically unique because from 1840 to 1890, no less than thirty-four different ethnic groups immigrated there, mainly from Europe, and many of those enclaves can still be identified. Old World Wisconsin is the largest outdoor museum in the United States dedicated to Wisconsin's multiple ethnicity. Alex's organization annually receives hundreds of guests, especially government and other political figures, from overseas. Alex is indeed an expert on how to host international visitors, and he aided me greatly by vetting chapter 3, "Essential Tips for Hosting International Visitors."

Mary Regel is the director of International Development within the Wisconsin Department of Commerce. She has been a valued friend for more than twenty years and has assisted me in all my writing. Mary also leads a talented group of trade directors scattered around the world. Five of them were gracious enough to vet segments in chapter 8 of this book:

Vincent Lencioni is the director of the LGA Consulting/Wisconsin Trade Office in Mexico. Vince kindly read my segment on Mexico and provided some valuable corrections and additions for a country that hosts more and more Americans each year. *Salud y gracias,* Vince.

Kara H. Smith is the director of the State of Wisconsin Department of Commerce European Trade Office. Kara took the time and patience to proofread and amend the segments on Germany, France, Italy, and the United Kingdom. These are indeed diverse but highly important regions for any American visitor, and I thank Kara for her vast knowledge and support.

Paul Swenson is the director of the Council of Great Lakes Governors Trade Office, located in Shanghai. With China predicted to perhaps equal the economic power of the United States by the year 2020, learning about that remarkable country is essential for anyone traveling overseas on business or pleasure. Thank you, Paul, for reviewing and improving my words and advice on China.

Nancy Ward is the director of the Wisconsin representation in Canada. One of the two closest neighbors to the United States, with one of the longest international borders in the world, it is essential for all U.S. citizens to understand and respect the wonderful people of Canada. Nancy added some helpful insights to the segment on Canada. My thanks to you, Nancy.

Takahiro Hagisako is the Japan External Trade Organization (JETRO) business adviser to the state of Wisconsin, stationed in Madison. JETRO is Japan's official agency for assisting

American companies to do business in that important trade destination. Takahiro kindly reviewed my section on Japan, for which I thank him most sincerely.

Paul D. Churchill is another friend of more than twenty years who heads the important Export Assistance Center in Wisconsin for the U.S. Department of Commerce. His office counsels all types of Wisconsin businesses, whether it be on a one-to-one basis or before an audience of hundreds. He represents the single most important channel for help from the U.S. government. His patience and wide knowledge were invaluable to me for chapter 9, "Essential Things to Know about Taking Your Show on the Road."

Dan McGinnity is vice president of communications for the Noel Group, one of the country's largest providers of all forms of travel assistance, both domestically and internationally. Dan supplied the details and advice on travel insurance for chapter 7, "Essential Things to Know When Preparing for Travel Abroad." The Noel Group provides, shall we say, "a parachute" full of aids for anyone planning to travel abroad. More information can be found at www.noelgroup.com.

Crista Larson is a graduate student in the Business School of the University of Wisconsin—Milwaukee. Over a period of six months, Crista searched the Net for background information and facts about the Internet for chapter 6, "Essential Things to Know about Using the Internet Internationally." It was a specialized task, and she accomplished it beautifully. Many thanks, Crista, and good luck on your business career.

Ed Meachen, Ph.D., is the associate vice president for Learning and Information Technology for the University of Wisconsin System. That system consists of 160,000 students enrolled on twenty-six campuses across Wisconsin. In 1990, Ed helped to create and lead the Academic Advanced Distributed Learning Co-Lab. It is now one of the nation's premier labs for "next-generation learning," utilizing new technologies in Wisconsin. I turned to Ed to help me with chapter 6, "Essential Things to Know about Using the Internet Internationally."

Patty O'Brien is a computer whiz who not only can help those of us belonging to an earlier generation as we navigate around hard drives but can do it with grace and patience. It will, of course, be difficult for any reader of this book to discern how much Patty helped me to accomplish its writing, but I am aware of her hard work and greatly appreciate it.

Tom Miller, the executive editor at John Wiley & Sons, had the courage to entrust me with writing the last five of my books. His suggestions for improvement were always irritatingly correct, but, of course, that's his job. And since I am now in the three-score-and-fifteen mark of my life, it is unlikely there will be another opportunity for collaboration. But, as I wrote in the chapter on the future of the Internet, only time will tell. I want to thank Tom most sincerely.

I owe special and genuine thanks to Sally Wecksler, who served as my literary agent starting in 1986. She successfully negotiated contracts for nine of my books (including this one) with John Wiley & Sons until her death in January 2005. Sally was also a specialist in foreign-translation versions for many of her clients and succeeded in selling foreign-language versions of my books as follows: eleven foreign-language versions for *Gestures: Do's & Taboos of Body Language Around the World*; six foreign-language versions of *Do's & Taboos Around the World*; three foreign-language editions of *Do's & Taboos of Public Speaking*; plus foreign-language versions of *Do's & Taboos of Hosting International Visitors* and *Do's & Taboos of Using English Around the World*. She was kind, gracious, thorough, and—it should be obvious—a talented businesswoman. How can I eulogize her? To meet that challenge, I happened upon a story involving Joyce Hall, the founder of the Hallmark Company. In his lifetime, Mr. Hall must have read hundreds of thousands of sentimental expressions for every occasion. When asked "Do you have one favorite sentiment that stands out?" he replied, "Yes." And I have chosen that single expression to thank Sally. It is simply this: "I wish I could be the friend you've been to me."

To all of these fine people, I offer my thanks for their contributions.

Essential Do's and Taboos

Introduction

This book is a compendium of helpful things to know about international business, protocol, etiquette, customs, behavior, gestures and body language, and other related topics.

In addition, it contains separate chapters on (1) how to expand your business into overseas markets, (2) how women can carve out careers in international business, (3) how to prepare for a trip overseas, (4) how to host international visitors, (5) what the Internet and e-commerce mean in international business, and (6) some essentials to know about eleven popular international destinations: Canada, Mexico, Japan, China, Germany, France, Italy, Brazil, Russia, India, and the United Kingdom.

It is a potpourri of information on how to successfully travel overseas, whether you are a tourist, a student, or a businessperson.

The word *essential* appears not only in the title of this book but often in the chapter headings and throughout the text. Synonyms for *essential* are words such as *basic, necessary,* and *fundamental.*

Another synonym could be *indispensable,* but I shy away from that rather lofty and egotistical term because this book does not deal in such absolutes. Cultural differences are a complex and fickle business. A certain cultural practice that might be common in one part of a country may not necessarily occur in another area of that same country. Codifying rules for behavior is never easy because behavior is a moving target.

Therefore, consider my use of the word *essential* in this book to mean "very useful," "helpful," and "important," but not "ironclad" or "absolute."

Why Might This Book Be Timely and Helpful?

A number of years ago, *Scientific American* proclaimed that "the future is international." The *New York Times* writer and author Thomas L. Friedman has written extensively on the tectonic movement toward "globalization." One of his first books on globalization was the popular *The Lexus and the Olive Tree,* subtitled *Understanding Globalization.* He claimed that the age of globalization began the year the Berlin Wall was taken down, which signaled the end of the Cold War and the beginning of the globalization period.

The August 1999 issue of *National Geographic* magazine's cover declared that we are in the midst of a "Global Culture," that is "linked by jets, e-mail, cell phones, and films, [and] we are all in each other's backyard." In August 2005, Clyde Prestowitz, a former economic adviser in the Reagan administration and currently the founder and president of the Economic Strategic Institute, a Washington think tank that's influential in international areas, stated on public television that "the Internet and FedEx have brought us in touch globally faster than ever before. In just two seconds, the Internet can connect each of us with every corner of the world . . . and FedEx can deliver a package or parcel almost anywhere within thirty-six hours."

This obliges us to learn more about the world around us. It has been described by some people as "lifeboat earth" or "spaceship earth," and we are all passengers who must try to exist peaceably together.

How This Book Is Organized

The contents and the chapters are arranged so that it's not necessary to read them in consecutive order. You can choose the topics that interest you most. Then perhaps at a later time, you can examine the other chapters for your general edification. Each chapter concludes with a summary of important things to remember.

Chapter 1 deals with—for me, at least—one of the most intriguing aspects of communicating with other people around the world: gestures and body language. As you will discover, we all owe a great debt to the English anthropologist Desmond Morris, who is indisputably the most knowledgeable expert on that subject. As I tell audiences wherever I speak, "You are going to learn how to make rude gestures in more than a dozen different countries . . . without realizing you are being rude."

Chapter 2 concerns protocol. Awareness of international protocol is rapidly becoming an essential skill throughout the business world. Note the following quote from a comprehensive reference manual published by the Convention Industry Council (CIC). This is a federation of leading national and international organizations comprised of 100,000 individuals and 15,000 firms involved in the staging of meetings, conventions, and exhibitions around the world. In 2005, the CIC published its manual to "take the mystique out of international event planning and provide a work of reference that event professionals everywhere will find helpful." According to the CIC, "Protocol is commonly described as a set of international courtesy rules. These well-established and time-honoured [sic] rules based on principles of civility have made it possible for people to live and work together for centuries." Chapter 2 will equip you with a basic guide on the various attitudes and practices around the world concerning punctuality, titles, gift giving, toasting, social dining, social drinking, and conversational taboos.

Chapter 3 unveils the often-underestimated social grace of hosting international visitors. Let's be honest—hosting is done in different ways around the world, so it is important to know how we in the United States host guests, compared to what we might encounter when traveling abroad. Learning the various styles of hosting can be an enlightening discovery whenever we venture outside the United States. For example, we find that some American staples—apple pie, corn on the cob, cooked turkey, and other foods—may be considered weird by our international visitors. Another oddity: why do many American office buildings and hotels not have a thirteenth floor? (You can probably answer that quickly, but a foreign visitor might find it unusual.) Speaking of floor designations, in some countries what we call the "first floor" of a building is often referred to as the "ground floor." Simple enough, until you then discover that their first floor is what we term the *second floor*. Read this chapter for more differences in the seemingly simple task of hosting international visitors.

Chapter 4 deals with what you are reading at this moment—the English language or, more appropriately, the American-English language. We are extremely fortunate that our mother tongue is one of the most widely spoken, if not the dominant, language in the world. Yet there is a paradox. It is also one of the most difficult languages to learn. It is filled with complex grammar, pronunciations, and spelling. Pity the people around the world who have had to learn English as a second language. We speakers of American English must show great patience, respect, and understanding to avoid miscommunication, which can be one of the most damaging and costly aspects of traveling or doing business outside the United States.

Chapter 5 might be considered the "for women only" segment of this book since it speaks entirely to female readers who want to travel abroad comfortably and successfully. For example, what is the greatest fear American women harbor when traveling outside the United States? You'll find the answer in this chapter, as well as a host of suggestions for doing business in male-dominated cultures such as Japan and the Middle East. This chapter is based on interviews with more than a hundred successful businesswomen who offered insights to me and the three women coauthors of *Do's & Taboos around the World for Women in Business*. (I became so immersed in this book that on the speaking circuit, I occasionally made a Freudian slip and said, "I wrote this book with three *other* women.")

Chapter 6 presents a brand-new way to achieve success in international business: the Internet. This chapter addresses the questions "How will the Internet affect the international marketing manager? Will he or she merely sit in front of a computer screen conducting business electronically instead of boarding long transatlantic flights to distant lands?" The Internet will certainly bring a sea-change of improvements in the way we conduct daily communications using our cell phones, hand-held PDAs, video-conferencing, and the like. But wait—an opposing argument says that when it comes to international business, there is no substitute for face-to-face communications and eyeball-to-eyeball understanding.

Chapter 7 will help the tyro—the beginner—to international travel by suggesting ways you can prepare for your trip abroad. It explains the new options for travel agents, plus gives some basic tips for making your overseas voyages more effective and enjoyable.

Chapter 8 zeroes in on eleven of the most popular destinations—Canada, Japan, China, Mexico, England, France, Italy, Brazil, Russia, India, and Germany—and equips you with dozens of tips and bits of background information to help you prepare for your visits.

Chapter 9 is designed for anyone who is doing, or wishes to conduct, business overseas. It begins by outlining basic attitudinal differences toward conducting business in other countries. It then lays out why exporting is easy and profitable and provides a three-step process for entering into business with new customers around the globe. An abundance of low cost assistance—even free assistance—is available from experts at the federal level and within your particular state.

Finally, an epilogue includes the story behind my nine-book "Do's & Taboos" series, plus what I hope will be some amusing stories about my publicity tours, when I appeared on national and international TV shows and did a classic book tour. Accounts of other events that occurred over the last twenty years are also provided.

1

Essential Things to Know about Gestures and Body Language

Sixty percent of our daily communication is nonverbal.
—Edward T. Hall

Are simple hand gestures and body movements important?
Here are some answers:

It's inaugural day in the United States, 2005. President George W. Bush is in the reviewing stand on Washington, D.C.'s Pennsylvania Avenue as the University of Texas marching band passes by. He raises his hand to salute his alma mater with the time-honored "hook 'em horns" sign—fist raised upright, index finger and pinkie sticking up, the sign of the horns of a Texas longhorn steer, the mascot and symbol of the University of Texas. Bush's picture appears on TV screens around the globe . . . and many people in countries around the world are immediately insulted!

That very same gesture—fist upraised, index and little fingers extended upward—is considered rude in certain other countries.

- In Italy, it means "Your wife is cheating on you!" "You are being cuckolded."
- In some parts of Africa, you are issuing a curse.
- In Norway, the Internet newspaper *Nettavisen* expressed outrage that not only Bush, but his wife and two daughters, would issue such an insult.
- Yet the gesture can also have positive meanings. In the Mediterranean Sea, fishing boats may have this symbol painted on their bows to ward off evil, and in Brazil, women often wear gold or silver lockets with this sign as a good luck amulet.
- In the United States, the "hook 'em horns" sign has varied meanings. A baseball player uses it as a signal for "two outs," and in American football, a referee flashes this sign to indicate a "second down." Finally, on the streets of Los Angeles, it is a gangland symbol representing the horns of the devil!

As for poor George Bush, the newly installed president of the United States, he was simply paying tribute to his alma mater, the University of Texas. There are more details on the "hook 'em horns" gesture later in this chapter.

Here are two more examples of how an innocent gesture can become a faux pas: take, for instance, the sole of your shoe.

It's March 2003 in Iraq, and coalition troops are invading Baghdad. People are glued to television sets around the world as U.S. soldiers climb a huge statue of Saddam Hussein and tie a rope to its head. Armored tanks then pull the statue down. Crowds of Iraqis rush forward and *pound the fallen statue with their shoes*! Why? In the Middle East and Southeast Asia, the bottom of the shoe is considered the lowest, dirtiest part of the body; therefore, the crowds were insulting Saddam's likeness with the strongest gesture possible.

It's 1995, and ambassador to the UN Bill Richardson (now governor of New Mexico) is in a negotiating session with Saddam Hussein for the release of American oil workers who were captured after they unintentionally crossed the border into Iraq. Richardson sits down across from Hussein and crosses his legs, inadvertently displaying the sole of his shoe toward the Iraqi leader. One newspaper account reports that Hussein immediately got up and walked out in a huff. In an interview with the *New York Times*, Richardson claims his translator explained that he was expected to apologize, but he decided not to. "I think [Saddam] respected that. When he returned, I saw the glint of a smile when I didn't grovel."

Showing the sole of the shoe is just one of a wide panorama of gestures around the world that is viewed as benign in many cultures but is highly insulting in others. A person using these gestures risks incurring the wrath of onlookers—even to the point of provoking bodily harm.

It's 1988 in Los Angeles, and an entertainer from Thailand is convicted of second-degree murder of a twenty-nine-year-old Laotian. The reason? The entertainer was singing in an after-hours Thai cabaret when the Laotian, a patron sitting in the front row, put his foot on a chair with the sole directed at the singer. When the cabaret closed, the entertainer followed the man outside and shot him dead.

Just how important is this whole realm of gestures and body language? The famous social anthropologist Edward T. Hall wrote that 60 percent of our daily communication is nonverbal. Daniel Goleman, a former science writer for the *New York Times* and the author of the international bestselling book *Emotional Intelligence,* claimed that 90 percent of our emotions are expressed nonverbally.

This chapter will chronicle several dozen signals that can become hidden booby traps in daily discourse with international visitors to the United States or when we travel abroad. This subject is apparently interesting to people in other cultures, too. I am pleased to report that my book *Gestures: Do's & Taboos of Body Language Around the World* has been reprinted in the following foreign languages: Finnish, French, German, Hungarian, Japanese, Korean, Portuguese, Spanish, Swedish, and two separate forms of Chinese for Taiwan and mainland China. Also, at Fort Bragg, North Carolina, where U.S. Army special ops commandos are trained for duty in Iraq, *Gestures* is used to teach soldiers that mistakes can be, if not outright dangerous, at least a serious stumbling block during negotiations and interrogations.

In this chapter, I will arm you (no pun intended) with information on the most commonly misunderstood gestures and will provide material that has been updated since the publication of *Gestures*. You'll see that some gestures date back to ancient times, and others depicted in that book are already out of date and new ones have replaced them. For example, in the world of U.S. sports, the well-known "low five" (i.e., slapping the open palm of a teammate) is, in some circles, now considered passé. It has evolved upward into the "high five," which is still popular. More recently, the bumping of knuckles and of chests has become athletes' signals of congratulation. And in this country, sporting crowds whistle to show approval at sporting events, while in Europe, whistling during a team competition is comparable to booing in the United States.

As an aside, it's important to know that words, as well as gestures, can have different meanings from one country to the next. For example, a *boot* in the United States is a shoe with a high top, whereas a *boot* in England is also the trunk of an automobile. (For more examples, see chapter 4.)

The meaning of gestures can also change from generation to generation within the same country. For example, in Australia, the "thumbs-up" gesture is considered rude by many in the older generation. Younger people there, however, seem to interpret it as we Americans do, meaning "O.K." The supposition is that American movies, plus TV channels like CNN and MTV that are now seen worldwide, have caused this flip-flop in interpretation.

The British anthropologist Desmond Morris is, in my opinion, the world's leading expert in chronicling the meanings of these social gestures. His seminal book *Manwatching* is must-reading for anyone seriously interested in this topic. A later book, *Bodytalk*, is a visual dictionary containing penned drawings and explanations of some six hundred gestures from all over the world. Proof of the fickleness of gestures is evident in *Bodytalk* when Morris indicates which countries a particular gesture is common in and then simply notes "widespread" or "varied locations."

Over the years, these vagaries have been pointed out to me by readers who wrote saying that I was "almost" correct in my definition of a certain gesture or that "They do that in the northern part of my country but not in the south." Or, "That is only done here by the older population." The conclusion is obvious: gestures are elusive and very difficult to codify, so it would be almost impossible to chronicle all of them in each and every country with total accuracy.

Interpreting gestures and body language is like aiming at a moving target, but here is some simple advice you should consider when traveling the world.

- By all means, try to learn some of the basic and more popular gestures before traveling to a country outside the United States, but be aware that this subject is not known for total consistency.

- The best advice is to be aware, respectful, and politely inquisitive when you encounter a gesture that doesn't seem to fit the setting or the context of your conversation.

How Gestures Are Classified

There are three basic types of gestures: (1) instinctive, (2) coded or technical, and (3) social.

1. *Instinctive gestures* are inbred and automatic. For example, Morris points out that when people all around the globe meet one another, there is a tendency to raise the eyebrows and wrinkle the brow. It is called the "eyebrow flash." The theory is that we are opening our eyes wider as a sign of openness and acceptance. A subsection of instinctive gestures is found among certain psychologists who claim that various body movements are clues to what's going on

inside a person's mind. For example, this group suggests that when someone crosses his or her arms across the chest, it is a signal of defensiveness or disapproval. (On the other hand, maybe that person is simply chilly?) These psychologists also suggest that scratching the nose can sometimes be an indicator that a person is telling a lie. (Or, maybe that person's nose just itches?) You have probably read about practitioners of this branch of subconscious body language being hired to interpret what's going on in the minds of jurors at a courtroom trial. If this category of gestures and body language interests you, I suggest that you read Julius Fast's book *Body Language*. More than 3 million copies of this book have been sold.

2. *Coded or technical gestures* are those used by referees, umpires, brokers in trading markets, and, of course, by people using the American Sign Language (ASL) and the Boy Scout semaphore system.

3. *Social gestures*, or acquired gestures, are described in this chapter. These gestures are generated among various societies, often without a logical explanation but with common acceptance of meaning within those societies. For example, we don't know exactly how the "O.K." gesture originated in the United States, but, as you will soon learn, this very same gesture has rude and insulting connotations in other countries.

Fifteen Common Social Gestures—
But with Uncommon Meanings

1. The "O.K." Sign

In 1990, the parlor game–manufacturer Milton Bradley Co. introduced a game called Guesstures, subtitled The Game of Split-Second Charades. As part of the research for the game, Milton Bradley conducted a survey to determine the best-known gestures in the United States. It turned out that the "O.K." sign had 98 percent recognition, greater than any other gesture. (When the game was introduced, I included this finding in my book *Gestures*. Shortly afterward, the then late-night-TV host Arsenio Hall had a segment about it and, referring to my book, kiddingly disputed the "best-known" claim. He proposed that there was another gesture, especially on the freeways of California, that probably had 100 percent recognition and usage! That gesture was, of course, the one-fingered "bird." More on this in a moment.)

Let's analyze the "O.K." sign, its origins and its varied meanings around the world.

In the 1950s, vice president Richard Nixon made a goodwill tour of Latin America. At that time, there was already widespread hostility toward the United States, and Nixon unwittingly added fuel to the fires of resentment with a single, inadvertent act. At the airport in São Paulo, Brazil, he stepped off his airplane and flashed the "A-O.K." sign to the waiting crowd. In fact, he did it with both hands! People responded by booing. In addition, newspapers the next day published large photographs of Nixon making this gesture. Why the boos and the headline news? Because in Brazil, what Nixon had gestured was the symbol for a woman's vagina.

A Frenchman, particularly in the south of France, would read that very same gesture as meaning "zero" or "worthless."

In Japan, the thumb and the forefinger forming a circle is often used as a symbol for money—the fingers creating the round outline of a coin.

It's not definitively known how and why this gesture means "O.K." in the United States; however, the spoken term for "O.K." probably originated here in 1840. At that time, the Democratic Party's "Old Kinderhook" label was given to its presidential candidate Martin Van Buren, who was born in Kinderhook, New York. The nickname was shortened to "O.K. Van Buren" and used as a spoken campaign slogan.

Clearly, the "O.K." gesture, as Americans and many others know it, is "non-O.K." when you communicate with people in certain other cultures. It would be better, perhaps, to quickly learn the words in the local language for "yes" and "fine" and keep your hands to your side.

2. *"Thumbs-Up"*

Pilots do it the world over. Astronauts and cos-
monauts even do it *out* of this world. It has
become an almost universal signal for "Everything's O.K." or "Fine" or "Good going!" and
a dozen other positive messages in that vein.

But watch out! There are some exceptions—important exceptions. Before we get to those, however, let's review the origins of this
gesture. According to Hollywood's portrayal, it goes back to the glad-
iators of Rome who received a "thumbs-up" signal from the emperor
when he thought that a courageous fighter should live or a "thumbs-
down" to signal the opposite, a bloody death sentence for the losing
warrior. It's not the first time Hollywood may be guilty of creating its
own history.

Once again Desmond Morris comes to our rescue. He contends
that recent historians may have confused the Latin phrase *pollice verso*
(meaning a "thumb turned") with the Latin phrase *pollice compresso*
(meaning a "compressed thumb"). Also, there are apparently no
friezes or painted walls from Roman times showing the "thumbs-up"
gesture. Morris theorizes that instead the ancient Romans *compressed
their thumbs by tucking their thumbs inside their fists* to signify "He shall
live." Whereas the "thumbs-down" meant to "plunge the sword into
the victim," just as today in our society where "thumbs-down" means
"no" or "negative" or "bad."

Today in Spain the "thumbs-up" has a strong political meaning
because it is used by the Basque separatist movement from the north
of Spain. Therefore, showing the "thumbs-up" in Spain may bring you
unwanted attention.

In Japan, the upright thumb signals the number five. That is
because when the Japanese count numbers with their fingers, they
start with the upright index finger for "one," then use the middle
finger for "two," add the ring finger to make "three." The little finger
signals "four." Then, when those four fingers are closed into the
palm, the upright thumb stands for "five." The number six is represented by the upright thumb and the upright little finger, and so on.

To confuse this issue even more, in Germany, the upright thumb
signals "one." So in Germany when you want to order one beer, don't

use the upright index finger, as we would in the United States. Instead, show the fist closed with the upright thumb protruding. As we pointed out earlier, however, in Australia, especially among the older generation, this is considered a rude gesture, meaning "Up yours!"—especially if the thumb is jerked upward.

Another locale where the thumb is problematic is Nigeria. Reports have been published telling of Americans walking along Nigerian roads using the hitch hiking motion (thumb jerked up and back), only to have cars stop and the passengers jump out and rough them up because it has rude connotations in that country.

If and when the "thumbs-up" is used around the world with the same positive connotation as in the United States, it has probably been observed in U.S. movies and television. A word to the wise, however—be careful of indiscriminate use of the upright thumb.

3. "V" for Victory or Peace

This well-known gesture has an interesting history. During World War II, it was popularized by England's prime minister Winston Churchill. It signaled "victory" and became a powerful rallying symbol during that war. But—pay close attention—it was done with the palm facing outward. If the palm faces inward (as shown here), it is comparable to signaling "Up yours!"

Now go back five hundred years to the battle of Agincourt when the English longbow archers were considered the most powerful military adversaries on earth. Consequently, if an English bowman was captured by the enemy—in this case, the French—the captors would cut off the forefinger and the middle finger, thus effectively disarming or, in this case, disfingering, the bowman. However—and here's the point—the English won that war, and, consequently, when the French prisoners were paraded away in defeat, the surviving English bowmen would raise those two fingers in triumph, as if to say, "See! I still have mine." But—and once again, pay close attention—they would give the gesture with the *palm facing inward*.

Thus, to this very day, in all of Great Britain and many of the former British colonies (e.g., Australia, South Africa, etc.), when the two fingers are raised upward with the palm facing inward, it is a sign of insult and derision.

Two other anecdotes about the "V" for victory sign come to mind. The former president George H. W. Bush once flashed that "V" signal to nearby journalists and impishly asked, "Do you know what this means? It's Julius Caesar ordering five beers in Roman numerals."

In 1995, during a visit to the Portuguese island of Madeira, I casually asked our guide what the "V" signal meant there. She looked at me strangely and said, "It's simple. It means 'two.'"

Finally, the gesture is also well known in the United States from the days of the antiwar demonstrators in the 1960s, when it did not signal "victory" but instead meant "peace."

4. "Hook 'em Horns," "Hang Loose," "I Love You"

A. Fist closed, index and little fingers extended—"hook 'em horns"

B. Fist closed, thumb and little finger extended—"hang loose"

C. Fist closed, with thumb, index finger, and little finger extended—American Sign Language shorthand for "I love you"

These three gestures, very similar in nature, are often confused with one another:

A. *"Hook 'em Horns."* As we learned at the beginning of this chapter, "hook 'em horns" comes from the University of Texas at Austin, where the longhorn steer with its huge, widespread set of horns is the school mascot and symbol. According to press reports, it was a University of Texas student, H. K. Pitts, class of '73, who fashioned the signal. In the Texas football stadium on Saturday afternoons in the fall, you'll see thousands of students thrusting their hands upward and shouting, "Hook 'em horns!" But when in Italy— caution!—this is the sign for the *cornuto*, which refers to the "horns of a bull" and is an insulting signal that means you are being cuckolded or says, in effect, "Your spouse is cheating on you." Press reports tell us that University of Texas alumni serving in the U.S. military forces in Italy have innocently flashed this sign to fellow alumni in restaurants and other public places, which actually provoked fistfights with native Italian men who view it as insult to their manhood and honor.

And there are other meanings for this gesture. Fishing boats in the Mediterranean Sea carry this sign painted on the bows of their boats because it signifies warding off evil. In parts of Africa, when pointed downward at another person's feet, it signals a curse. In Brazil and Venezuela, it carries the meaning "good luck," and women often wear it as a charm around the neck.

When an American baseball player or umpire gives this signal, it tells teammates that there are "two outs." In American football, a referee uses it to indicate the "second down."

And in Milwaukee, Wisconsin, the home of many metal-fabricating companies, the gesture signifies slightly coarse barroom humor because it supposedly identifies a long-suffering punch-press operator ordering "four beers."

B. "*Hang loose.*" In the Hawaiian Islands, "hang loose" is a signal for "Take it easy." It is called the "shaka" and sends the message "Hang loose, brah!" (for "brother"). It should be done with a twist from the wrist or the elbow. Its origins are unclear. One version of the story is that it comes from a plantation guard, Hanmana Kalili, who had lost his three middle fingers in an accident and afterward worked as a guard in the sugarcane fields. Kalili apparently used his disabled hand to wave off local youths who tried to steal sugarcane. Other youths repeated the gesture to warn their friends that Kalili was nearby. Another explanation is that the Kahuku high school football team is said to have adopted it as a pep signal when breaking from the huddle. In other regions of the islands, it became a neighborhood greeting. Today, it simply means "Relax, brother," and is unique to the Hawaiian Islands.

C. *"I love you."* The origin and explanation for this gesture is simple. In American Sign Language (the third-most-popular language in the United States, after English and Spanish), it is a shorthand signal for the words *I love you*. Rock and heavy metal musical groups have adopted it and often flash it to their cheering fans.

5. Touching and Space

Wherever Americans travel, they are each accompanied by an imaginary bubble of air around them, measuring about eighteen inches. This is called our "territorial imperative" or "our personal space." We Americans value our personal space. When Americans meet one another in social or business situations, note that there will be about thirty-six inches between them (eighteen inches of space per person). That's just about the distance of extending your arm and putting your thumb in the other person's ear. In other words, in public situations it's a symbolic "arm's length" relationship. That's how we are comfortable—and, heaven forbid, not any closer!

In Latin America and much of the Middle East, however, the "bubbles" are much smaller. People there will often stand just inches apart. Friends may grasp each other's elbows or forearms and might even touch the lapel of the other person's suit jacket (though not with women, of course).

Observers in those regions have noticed a mythical dance called the "conversational tango." That occurs when American and Latin men meet each other and the Latin steps forward, not realizing he is entering the American's space. The American, naturally, takes a step backward. The Latin thinks, "Where's he going?" and steps forward; the American steps backward; the Latin steps forward; and . . . there you have it—the conversational tango.

The famed American anthropologist Edward T. Hall posits that there are four distinctive spatial zones:

1. The *intimate zone* is eighteen inches of space extending outward from the body. This is the zone for lovers and parents holding infants. In this zone, the sense of smell and awareness of radiated warmth also comes into play.

2. The *personal zone* is the "arm's length" distance described previously. In this zone, the facial expressions of the other person are clearer. But even here, there are incongruities. When seated in the economy class on airplanes, we accept and permit elbow touching and even possible knee-to-knee touching. This same anomaly is true in wide spacing–conscious Japan where touching is uncommon, yet we see photos of Japanese office workers packed tightly together on commuter trains.

3. The *social-consultative zone* extends outward from, say, four feet to eight or ten feet and often occurs in ordinary daily conversation. It's at this distance that we acknowledge other people and include them in our conversations.

4. The *public zone* is a ten- to thirty-foot space extending outward from the body, or the outer boundary for acknowledgment—a professor standing in front of a class, for instance.

Many of the same variations apply to touching. Americans avoid casual touching in business and social situations, unless the two parties are very close friends. We may, on occasion, pat shoulders, slap a back or two, and hold the other person's elbow when shaking hands. But this is usually taboo in most of Asia, the United Kingdom, and Northern Europe. Even between cities such as London and Paris, there are differences in touch patterns. Richard Gesteland's wonderful book *Cross-Cultural Business Behavior* describes how hidden cameras recorded the number of times casual touching occurred in social situations such as during lunch. In Paris, about a hundred touches took place. In London, zero.

The ultimate act of social touching may occur when two men walk down the street holding hands. My first encounter with that behavior occurred in Saudi Arabia. My male customer and I were walking down a street in Jeddah, he in his long, flowing robe, when he silently reached over and took my hand . . . and we continued down the street holding hands. I was stunned, but I just hung on. Very quickly, however, my palm became very sweaty. Later, I found out I was shot with luck. In his country this was merely a sign of friendship and respect—there were no sexual overtones in the least. If I had abruptly pulled away, I would have risked insulting the man. This same sign of friendship might be seen—and experienced!—in Bombay or in parts of Southeast Asia. In Latin America, two male friends may stroll down the street arm in arm, with no message intended other than general friendship.

Another example of this was cited in the summer of 2004 when terrorists in Saudi Arabia targeted Westerners employed there. Americans were encouraged to grow beards and don the traditional ankle-length robes worn by Saudi men in order to look less conspicuous. But there was more. According to a July 2004 issue of *Time* magazine, Westerners were cautioned, "Don't walk like you are going somewhere. Here (in Saudi Arabia) we walk like we're not going anywhere. We saunter as if we have nowhere to go." Furthermore, Americans were advised, "When walking with another man, hold hands, like Saudis do. That makes you look more authentic."

6. Greetings

You will learn in chapter 2 that while there are many forms of greeting, the most common is the handshake, which is also the most common type of touching. With thanks again to my friend, the author and world traveler Dick Gesteland, here is a list of variations around the world for the ubiquitous handshake:

Germans	Firm, brisk, and frequent
French	Light, quick, and frequent
British	Moderate
Latin Americans	Firm and frequent
North Americans	Firm and infrequent (compared to France and Latin America)
Arabs	Gentle, repeated, and lingering
South Asians	Gentle, often lingering
Koreans	Moderately firm
Most other Asians	Very gentle and infrequent

That last version is particularly true in Japan because the traditional greeting there is, of course, the bow. When the Japanese offer their hands for handshakes, they are simply showing knowledge of and respect for the Western custom of shaking hands. In Japan, bowing involves many nuances that most Westerners find difficult to comprehend. In brief, the higher the stature of the person you're meeting, the lower you bow. But in general, a slight bob of the head is sufficient for most of us. I've heard Americans complain, "You want me to bow? I'm an American! I don't bow to anyone!" In Japan, however, bowing does not imply subservience or subordination—it is an act of humility and respect. Personally, I don't find anything objectionable in being humble and gracious and respecting the cultural mannerisms of others.

In places like Thailand and India, the traditional greeting involves pressing the palms together at chest height, as in a prayerful position, and bowing the head slightly. When this is done, the person is saying, in effect, "I am praying to the God in you." Top that for an impressive greeting!

As for other forms of greetings, in parts of the Middle East, you might observe the other person placing the right hand over his heart. In New Zealand, among the Maori ethnic group, using your nose to rub the nose of the other person is the customary greeting. In certain parts of Africa, tribal people actually spit at one another's feet. And in Siberia, they may open their mouths and repeatedly stick out their tongues.

What about shaking hands with women? In American business and even social circles, it has become more common to exchange handshakes man to woman or among women themselves. That is also the case in many European countries. But, in general, one cautionary rule is to wait and see if the woman extends her hand first.

And what about cheek-kissing and the embrace, or *abrazo*, so common throughout Latin America and popular in countries like Italy, France, Russia, and many Middle Eastern locales? First, as a general rule, this is not usually done among strangers or at first greetings. It is said to have originated in ancient times when everyone wore robes or gowns and a body hug was a quick way to determine whether the other person had any weapons hidden beneath. As for so-called cheek kissing, these are usually not lip-smacking kisses but instead are called "lip brushes to the cheek" or "air kisses."

How can you tell when a hug is appropriate? First, it is likely reserved for people who have become fairly good friends. Second, and this is especially helpful when meeting women in another country, if you extend your hand and she takes it, and then you feel a slight tug on your hand, this signals that she is expecting a friendly hug—not a full-body hug, but only one from the shoulders up.

Finally, for the definitive word on handshaking, check out *The Power of Handshaking for Peak Performance Worldwide*. The coauthor, Robert E. Brown, says, "Handshaking is a method and process for communicating that we've had with us since the beginning of time. It is extraordinarily important. It seals the deal."

Brown wrote that handshaking originated during the Roman Empire, about two thousand years ago. Then, when a man met another man, he had to make sure he wouldn't be attacked, so the two either laid down their weapons or showed the empty palms of their right hands. To ensure that neither would go for the sword or lunge, the two men grasped hands.

There are twelve basic handshakes, according to Brown. They range from the finger squeeze to the water pump (an enthusiastic, rapid movement), to the "dead fish" (limp, effeminate), to the two-handed shake (one hand doing the shake, and the other covering the two clasped hands). Brown claims the "all-American" shake is a warm, firm, palm-to-palm shake that a confident person gives with no hidden agenda. One could also add to that list the finger-busting "Texas" grip.

In summary, the handshake is both varied and ubiquitous . . . so, let's shake on that!

7. Eye Contact

Most Americans, starting as youths, are told by parents, teachers, and other superiors, "Look me in the eye when you speak to me." It's clear that we Americans favor direct eye contact. But around the world, other parents and superiors teach just the opposite. In most of Asia, and especially in Japan, direct eye contact is considered inappropriate, too forward, and impolite. In the Native American culture, staring directly into the eyes of another—especially of an elderly person—was also considered rude and impolite.

On the other hand, strong, direct eye contact is especially important in Latin America and the Middle East. In places like South Korea and the central African countries, eye contact is termed "moderate" by Gesteland, and, of course, throughout Northern Europe the practice is very similar to that in the United States.

8. Beckoning

As you read this, imagine that another person walks into the room and you want him or her to come toward you. What will you do? The natural American gesture is to raise one hand, with the palm inward, and move the upright fingers toward you. Or, a second acceptable gesture is to raise the hand, palm inward, with the index finger upright and curling back and forth. But in countries as widespread as the former Yugoslavia and Malaysia, the curled finger gesture is used only for animals. Therefore, using it to beckon a person would be terribly impolite. Incidentally, in Australia and Indonesia it might also be used for beckoning "ladies of the night." But in most of Europe, if you wish to beckon someone to come toward you, the proper gesture is to extend the arm, *palm downward*, and make a "scratching" motion downward with all the fingers.

Here are some other forms of "beckoning": in France, the preferred way to call a waiter to your table is simply to catch his eye and then perhaps quickly nod your head backward. In Colombia, one way to get a waiter's attention is to clap your hands lightly. In China, to beckon a waiter to refill your tea, simply turn your empty cup upside down in its saucer or leave the lid of the teapot off or open. In Spain, Mexico, Haiti, and a sprinkling of other countries, when calling a waiter, restaurant patrons can be heard issuing a noise with the lips, something like "hsssst" or "psssst," or even a kissing noise. Don't, however, try the kissing sound to call a waiter or a waitress at your nearest American truck stop.

9. Kissing

How did the act of kissing begin? Anthropologists are unsure. Desmond Morris called it a "relic gesture" that probably originated when mothers passed chewed food, mouth-to-mouth, to their infants.

In recent years, the kiss has reached—shall we say—new dimensions. Britney Spears and Madonna were shown at the 2003 MTV Video Music Awards on national television giving each other an open-mouthed, tongue-to-tongue kiss that was rehashed and replayed on TV countless times.

Good male friends in many Eastern European and Middle Eastern countries greet one another with kisses to the cheek, often as many as three times, alternating the cheeks.

The French seem to idolize the kiss. In the nineteenth century, the French had a kissing game called *maraichinage* that involved deep-tongue kissing among ten or more couples who changed partners weekly. In some parts of France, this "tongue dueling" was conducted in parks and even in churches. It was banned by the clergy in 1864. Two years later the French sculptor Auguste Rodin created one of the world's most famous sculptures, *The Kiss*. The French are famous today for the "air kiss" to the cheek and sometimes to the back of a woman's hand. This means the lips do not actually touch the skin.

Finally, I was told that among some women in Brazil, a common greeting among good friends and relatives is to kiss the cheeks alternately, three times. "Why three times?" I asked. My source explained that the first cheek kiss signifies "I hope you get married." The kiss to the other cheek sends a second message, "And I hope you have children," and the final kiss on the original cheek says, "And I hope your mother-in-law does not come to live with you." Truth or myth? I'm not sure.

10. "I See a Pretty Girl"

How do we signal this in the United States? One would think that whistling while raising the eyebrows would be the answer, and that such a signal would be universal. Not so. Here are ways that people in other cultures send that message:

1. The French, of course, kiss the fingertips and then wave the hand outward. This is a special Gallic gesture for praise, whether it be for beauty or a memorable wine.
2. An Arab may stroke his beard.

3. Many South American men will place a forefinger against the lower eyelid and pull down slightly, in effect saying, "That's an eyeful."

4. An Italian gesture, used in old American silent movies, was twisting the mustache, as if a man were preening himself to prepare for his advances toward a girl.

5. An Italian man might also place his forefinger against his cheek and make a screwing motion, as if he were creating a dimple.

6. A Greek man may stroke his cheeks with one hand because in ancient times an egg-shaped face was considered especially beautiful.

7. But it is in Brazil where there is a unique but clearly indicative gesture that sends the message "I see a pretty girl." The man forms two tubes with his hands and brings them up to one eye as if peering through a telescope.

11. Applauding

One would think that the act of applauding would be duplicated the world over. Well, almost. Try this experiment first. Go ahead. Applaud. Just applaud, right now. You've probably never thought of it or noticed before, but if you are right-handed, you are probably pounding the right hand down into the left palm. And if you are left-handed, vice versa.

Hearing-impaired people cannot, obviously, hear the gratifying sound of applause. So how do they substitute? They raise both open hands head-high, one on either side of the head, palms outward, and waggle them vigorously. Picture an entire audience doing this signal, and you can understand why it sends a powerful message of thanks and gratification.

Also, the timing for applause varies from country to country. In Russia and China, groups may use applause to greet someone. If you are fortunate enough to visit young children at schools in China, you will probably be greeted by line after line of small children standing and applauding your arrival. Performers in Chinese and Russian theaters also will often applaud back to an audience at the end of their performances.

Finally, applauding does not automatically mean approval. In many European countries, audiences frequently clap in rhythm as a sign of approval, whereas in North America, slow rhythmic clapping signals impatience. Similarly, in the United States, when spectators whistle at sporting events, it means approbation and encouragement. But in many parts of Europe, whistling is tantamount to booing by American audiences.

12. The "Fist Slap"

For many years, Johnny Carson did it during his late-night-TV opening monologue. His successor, Jay Leno, continues to do it. In fact, many of us do it on occasion. It's the "fist slap"—when we might be standing on a corner and casually swing our arms and slap the closed fist into the palm of the other hand. In Chile and parts of France, however, this motion is tantamount to saying, "Up yours." In Chile, it is called the *tapa*. An abbreviated version in Chile is done by a person who simply makes a fist, knuckles pointing outward, and taps the thumb up and down into the top of the fist; that's called the *tapita* in Spanish.

13. The "Ear Waggle" and the "Thumbing of the Nose"

These are two acts of derision that schoolchildren all over the world seem to learn instinctively. With the ear waggle, one places the hands at either side of the head, with the thumbs at the temples or the ears, and then flaps the hand back and forth. Morris claims that this is probably an imitation of the long, floppy ears of a donkey, an animal usually depicted as lazy and stupid. With the thumbing of the nose, the person places the thumb of one hand on the tip of the nose with the other fingers splayed outward and makes a wiggling motion. It is thought that this represents the hostile, erect comb of a fighting cock.

14. The "Forearm Jerk"

This powerful and well-known gesture is done by raising the fist upward and outward and then, with the other hand, cutting down sharply into the crook of the elbow. It is a strong, sexual, and insulting gesture, and in American street language it signifies "Up yours!" The upright arm represents the phallus—which allows us to segue into the final and perhaps the most ubiquitous gesture of all.

15. The "One-Finger Salute"

We should fittingly end this tutorial with one of the most famous and best-known gestures of all: it's sometimes called "the bird" or "flipping off." On highways and expressways, it is occasionally referred to as "the expressway digit." In Latin, it is the *digitus impudicus* (translation: "the indecent digit"). Or, we simply call it "the finger."

It sends a powerful, insulting message with little leeway for misunderstanding. It may interest you to know that it has been used for more than two thousand years. Desmond Morris wrote that "The [Roman] Emperor Caligula is thought to have used the extended middle finger as a substitute for the phallus when offering his hand to be kissed, as a deliberately scandalous act." In other words, a demeaning act to people beneath him.

Arabs have reshaped the upright finger into a downturned finger, with the hand extended outward, the palm facing down, and the middle finger dangling downward. When this is done, the finger also represents the phallus.

This ubiquitous gesture has even been lionized with its own Web site (www.ooze.com). According to this site, "By jabbing a threatening phallus at your enemy like a wild animal, you aren't just belittling him, but also making him your sexual inferior."

And finally, there are other, more benign, variations of upright-finger gestures: "The three-finger salute" has had two disparate uses. In Yugoslavia and Serbia, it is a nationalistic salute used by ethnic groups in that region. A second and quite different use appeared in the 2004 presidential election when George W. Bush adopted the upright three-fingered gesture to depict his middle initial—"W"—which represented his name as distinguished from his father's: George H. W. Bush.

A Summary of Essentials to Know about Gestures

Here is a short list of gestures and examples of body language most commonly used by North Americans that have other meanings elsewhere.

1. Shaking Hands

Here: As children, North Americans are taught to do this with a firm, solid grip.

There: While hand clasping as a greeting has generally been adopted around the world, the Japanese prefer bowing but will quickly cater to Westerners by shaking hands. Southeast Asians prefer to press their own palms together in a praying motion. And if and when Middle Easterners and Asians do shake hands, they favor a gentle grip because in their cultures a firm grip suggests aggressiveness.

2. Eye Contact

Here: When greeting and conversing with others, North American children are taught to look people directly in the eyes. To do otherwise is often regarded as a sign of shyness, as a lack of warmth, or—even worse—as weakness.

There: In Japan and certain other Asian countries, parents train their children to avert their eyes and avoid direct eye contact, which is considered intimidating or may have sexual overtones. Interestingly, among Native American tribes, it was consider disrespectful to stare directly into an elder's eyes.

3. Waving

Here: Whether a North American is signaling "hello" or "good-bye" or simply trying to get the attention of some distant person, he or she raises the arm and waggles the open hand back and forth.

There: Throughout much of Europe, waving back and forth signals "No!" To signal a greeting or a farewell, a European customarily raises the arm and bobs the hand up and down at the wrist, similar to the wrist action when dribbling a basketball. And Italians may use an entirely different version: palm up, fingers curling inward, back and forth in a scratching motion.

4. Beckoning

Here: A North American will often summon another person by waving to get his or her attention and then turning the hand to make hand scoops inward. Another beckoning motion an American might use is to raise the index finger (the palm toward one's face) and make a curling motion with that finger.

There: Both of these beckoning gestures may be misunderstood in other parts of the world. Throughout Europe, the gesture that says "Come here" is done by raising the arm, palm down, and then making a scratching motion with the fingers. As for curling only the index finger, in places like Australia and Indonesia, it is used only for beckoning animals and never for humans.

5. "V" for Victory

Here: Display the index and the middle finger in the shape of a V with the palm facing outward, and virtually all over the world it is understood to mean "victory" or "peace."

There: Be careful, however, in England, Australia, South Africa, and other former members of the British Commonwealth. In these countries, when this same gesture is done with the *palm facing inward toward the face*, it is tantamount to signaling "Up yours!"

6. The "O.K." Gesture

Here: In a national survey, this proved to be the single best-known gesture in the United States, with 98 percent recognition. North Americans flash this gesture frequently and enthusiastically: it's done by forming a circle with the thumb and the forefinger, with the other three fingers splayed upward.

There: Take care in France, however, where it can mean "zero" or "worthless," or in Japan where it can mean "money," as if making the shape of a coin. In places as disparate as Brazil, Russia, and Germany, it is the signal for a very private bodily orifice. So, in these countries, the American signal for "O.K." is definitely not.

7. Thumbs-Up

Here: North Americans and people in many other cultures flash this nearly ubiquitous gesture when they want to silently say, "Good job," "O.K.," "Great!" or a dozen other expressions, all of which demonstrate support and approval.

There: In certain locales, however, it can carry completely different meanings. Among the older generations in Australia, if the upright thumb is pumped up and down, it is the equivalent of saying "Up yours!" Where Americans may use the upright thumb when hitchhiking, in Nigeria it is considered a rude gesture and should be avoided. In Japan and Germany, the upraised thumb is also used when counting: in Japan it signifies "five," but in Germany it means "one."

8. "Hook 'em Horns"

Here: Most Texans will recognize this gesture (the fist raised with the index and the little finger extended) as a rallying call at the University of Texas because it mimics the horns of the school's symbol and mascot, the famous Texas longhorn steer.

There: In Italy, this same gesture says that someone is being cuckolded. In Africa, when pointed downward, it can mean placing a curse on someone. And in Brazil and Venezuela, the same gesture (pointed upward) is considered a good luck sign to ward off evil.

9. Spatial Relationships

Here: In normal social situations, North Americans generally stand about thirty inches apart from one another. That's considered the personal comfort zone and is equal to about an arm's length.

There: Asians, however, tend to stand farther apart. In contrast, Latins and Middle Easterners often stand much closer—sometimes even toe-to-toe or side by side, brushing elbows. As a result, North Americans need to steel themselves for such close encounters because to move away sends an unfriendly message.

10. Touching

Here: North Americans are not touch-oriented. With good friends, they may occasionally touch a forearm or an elbow, and with very good friends they may go so far as to place an arm around a shoulder. But hugging is almost never done among casual acquaintances.

There: While Asians join Americans in shunning such bodily contact, Latins who are good friends seem to dote on it, with hearty embraces and warm pats on the back. In the Middle East, two Arab male friends may even be seen walking down the street hand in hand, and all it signifies is friendship.

11. Kissing

Here: Among North Americans, kissing is usually reserved for sweethearts, one's spouse, and one's mother and can occur among close female relatives, friends, and acquaintances, but rarely between two men.

There: Among Latins, southern Europeans, and Russians, both male and female acquaintances will commonly greet one another with kisses to the cheeks. These are more likely feigned kisses to one cheek, sometimes to both cheeks. Incidentally, the continental practice of kissing a lady's hand has almost disappeared—except among a few pockets of gallant gentlemen in Italy and other Romance-language cultures.

From the various forms of body language and gestures, we move now to the types of ceremony and etiquette that are common among various peoples of the world. In one word, it's called *protocol*. This is probably even more complex than all the silent signals we send to one another because social behavior varies so much in both form and content, depending upon where you are on this diverse globe. Is there any rational person who does not want to know the rules for proper behavior? Read on.

2

Essential Things to Know about General Protocol

Protocol is knowing how to yawn with your mouth closed.

—Anonymous

The word *protocol* actually comes from the Greek word *protokollon*, meaning the first sheet glued to a papyrus roll bearing a table of contents. Thus, "to glue together" has morphed into "agreed behavior." In more recent centuries it has come to mean "the agreed forms of ceremony or etiquette observed by diplomats, heads of state, and other officials."

Time magazine has reported, "As anti-Americanism has grown in a post-9/11 world, firms that teach good manners . . . have flourished. A once fledgling industry of protocol schools and etiquette consultants now serves a growing list of corporate clients that pay $10,000 or more a day to learn the cultural sensitivities of far-flung regions."

In Washington, D.C., an umbrella organization called the International Association of Protocol Consultants (IAPC) (www .protocolconsultants.org) has been formed by Alinda Lewris to recognize these far-flung experts and trainers as true accredited professionals.

Today, public libraries and bookstores carry numerous volumes dealing with protocol and etiquette. Internet booksellers such as www.amazon.com and www.bn.com can also quickly provide long lists of books on this subject. Articles by Letitia Baldrige and Judith Martin (Miss Manners) are featured daily in our newspapers.

The message is that whether you are a student, a businessperson, a tourist, a government official, a member of the military, or whatever, to get along in this world, it has become increasingly essential to understand international protocol (read here "proper behavior").

This chapter deals with important subsections of general protocol, such as punctuality, titles, gift giving, toasting, social dining, social drinking, and conversational taboos.

Following are some essential tips about these key areas of protocol.

As you learned in chapter 1, the customary handshake is not the universally acceptable way of greeting people. Read chapters 1 and 8 for details.

Punctuality

Here are some essentials regarding punctuality around the world:

- Punctuality is highly valued, even at times a way of life, in Australia, Bangladesh, Chile, China, Denmark, Germany, Iran, Japan, Luxembourg, Malaysia, the Netherlands, New Zealand, Norway, South Africa, Sweden, Switzerland, Thailand, and Venezuela.

- Punctuality is important, expected, and appreciated in Austria, Bahrain, Belgium, Bulgaria, Canada, Costa Rica, the Czech Republic, El Salvador, England, Fiji, Finland, Hungary, India, Italy (northern), Ivory Coast, Qatar, Scotland, the Sultanate of Oman, Turkey, Uganda, the United Arab Emirates, the United States, Wales, and Yugoslavia.

- Punctuality is expected, but locals may arrive late in Argentina, Bolivia, Brazil, Chile, Colombia, France (northern and central), Ghana, Greece, Guatemala, Honduras, Iraq, Ireland, Israel, Italy (southern), Jordan, Kuwait, Libya, Mexico, Nicaragua, Panama, Pakistan, Paraguay, Peru, Poland, Portugal, Saudi Arabia, Senegal, South Korea, Spain, Sri Lanka, Syria, Taiwan, and Zambia.

- Punctuality is more laissez-faire in Algeria, the Caribbean, France (southern), Greece, Iceland, Lebanon, Morocco, Nigeria, and Spain.

And here are some tips about attitudes toward time around the world:

- In Saudi Arabia, locals often wear two timepieces. One is set to the worldwide system established by Greenwich Mean Time zones, and the other is set to the time of the rising and the setting sun.

- Saudi Arabia also uses two types of calendars: one is the Gregorian calendar that is followed in most other parts of the world, and one that is based on the lunar calendar and that counts the years since the birth of the founder of Islam, Mohammed, in A.D. 622.

- Devout Muslims are required to kneel in prayer five times each day—sunrise, sunset, and three times during the day. They must face the direction of their holy city, Mecca, and bow, kneel, and bend forward.

- People in Islamic countries commonly work on Sundays but not on Fridays or Saturdays.

- In Islamic countries, the month of Ramadan is a holy period established as the ninth month of the Islamic calendar. Ramadan requires prayer and fasting by Muslims, and its date varies in the Gregorian calendar. This is not a good time to visit Islamic countries, so check in advance when Ramadan will occur according to the Western calendar.

- In Latin countries, Carnival is the period preceding Lent. It is similar to Mardi Gras in the United States and can have as much as a two-week impact on efforts to do business. If you're visiting for pleasure, however, Carnival time in Latin America might be very enjoyable.

- In Chinese and Southeast Asian countries with substantial Chinese populations, Chinese New Year is also established by the lunar calendar. It usually occurs sometime during the first two months of our Western calendar, and it, too, is not a good time for business travel.

- Throughout much of Europe, the months of July and August are considered vacation months, meaning it is very difficult to conduct business then, and popular tourist destinations will be crowded by locals, as well as by international visitors.

Titles

My father once told me that three benefits come from reaching the age of seventy-five: (1) you can be crabbier and people will understand, (2) you can call your doctor by his or her first name, and (3) you can flirt with younger women and they know you aren't serious.

Personally, I would still have trouble with the doctor thing. It seems so ingrained. But this underscores the point that titles are indeed important whether you are traveling overseas on business or as a tourist.

In Germany, for instance, titles are highly respected and should be recognized and used. "Doctor" and "Professor" are two easy examples. In fact, when greeting someone for the first time, it is considered impolite to address the person by his or her first name. The same would be true in Switzerland, Austria, France, and similar European countries. It is best to wait to be invited to use first names.

In Asian countries, the title on one's business card carries great importance. It establishes where you stand in the pecking order. Yet certain American-type titles—like Associate Vice President or First

Vice President—only create confusion. The same is true of American designations such as CEO, COO, CFO, CIO, and so on.

In Spanish-speaking countries, an elderly or accomplished man might be addressed as "Don." This is used before the Christian name, but it is purely a courtesy title conveying respect and status.

In the United Kingdom, "honors" are bestowed each year by the Crown. A "knight" earns the title of "Sir." "O.B.E." following one's name is a lesser honor, signifying "Order of the British Empire." One American, however, seeing the "O.B.E." on a visitor's business card, mistook it for that person's last name and spent the whole day referring to him as Mr. Obee.

Speaking of business cards, carry plenty of them when traveling abroad. They are exchanged more often and more formally than in the United States. Japan is probably the premier country for formal exchanges of business cards. There, it is a ritual more than a passing courtesy. When two Japanese businessmen meet, each one offers his business card with a slight bow; it's important to hold the card outward in both hands using the thumbs and the forefingers. Then each person takes the time to read the other's card . . . carefully. That's because in status-conscious Japan, this card tells exactly who you are: your name, your title in the organization, the name of your company, and its location. Then, where appropriate, they carefully place the other person's card on the table for further reference. Americans tend to glance at the card and quickly slip it into a shirt or suit coat pocket. I've seen an American take his Japanese counterpart's card, glance at it quickly, and stuff it away. Later, he may take it out and write on it . . . in the eyes of the Japanese, this is tantamount to graffiti. One American who was bored during a meeting even took out the Japanese person's card and picked his teeth with it!

Incidentally, when traveling to markets where English is uncommon, you should have all the information on the English side translated into the local language and printed on the opposite side. Be careful to have that printing done with the same quality as on the English side, lest you imply that the other country's language is second class to English.

In the Middle East and Southeast Asia, always present business cards with the *right hand*. As you will read in chapter 7, in a section titled "Bathrooms of the World," the use of the left hand is considered impolite because it is the "unclean" hand, meaning that it is generally used for bodily hygiene.

Finally, don't be tempted to fabricate your own titles in hopes that your international visitor or counterpart abroad will treat you with more respect. The problem is that if your puffery is discovered, your credibility will be undermined, doing more damage in the long run.

Gift Giving

In North America, gift giving, especially in business, has certain distinct characteristics: (1) gifts are never lavish, lest they hint of a bribe; (2) they are usually viewed more as mementos, or they bear company logos and are thus subtle bits of advertising, (3) there are tax limits on deducting the dollar value of gifts as a cost of doing business, and (4) they may more often take the form of entertainment—a dinner, a play, a sporting event, and so on.

When traveling for pleasure, it may be appropriate to pack a few modest gifts in your baggage to present to people who extend special hospitality to you, but the value should usually be modest—a picture book from your home locale, rather than a gold watch. Here are a few more gift-giving rules to observe:

- Japan is probably the most gift-oriented culture in the world. The Japanese are a very generous, gracious people. Gift giving is ingrained in their culture. In past centuries, each prominent Japanese family actually retained a functionary to do nothing but determine and keep track of who gave what to whom. Today in Japan, when and if gifts are exchanged, the local custom is to have them wrapped (pastel-colored papers, but never white—white is for funerals) and without fancy bows. Don't open the gift immediately; save that for later, in private. Never give four of anything because the word *four* in Japanese is *shi*, which also means "death."

- Countries in the Middle East, East Asia, and Latin America stand right below the Japanese on the gift-giving chart. In China, gift giving is appropriate and appreciated but not necessarily required.

- The main trick in exchanging gifts is not to embarrass the other person. One way to do this is to say it is a "memento" or a "thank you" or a "gift for the family."

- The best gift of all, in almost any circumstance, is the gift of thoughtfulness. This can take many forms. If you have happened to observe that your hosts have special collections—stamps, coins, a brand of candy, cut glass, and so on—or if they have children who enjoy North American music or sports, then you can either send something appropriate to their interests on your return home or bring a sample on your next visit. Just make certain it is a gift of quality.

- Whenever in doubt about the appropriateness of a specific gift for a certain culture, call directory assistance for the 202 area code (Washington, D.C.) and ask for the telephone number of the embassy for the country in question. Then ask to speak to the cultural attaché or the information officer, and ask your question.

Social Dining

The first thing you've probably learned about dining in other countries is that not everyone dines when, where, and how we do in the United States.

The most common difference is that, in many countries, the main meal of the day is taken at midday. Then, in the evening, a light snack is provided. On the other hand, you might also find yourself at a monstrous-size lunch and may then repeat the adventure all over again in the evening. An extreme variation on that is found in Spain. Dinner, or the evening meal, is often served at a very late hour compared to dinner in the United States. In Spain, it is not uncommon to sit down for dinner at 10:30 p.m. or later.

By the second week of such high living, if your clothes start to feel tight around the middle, here's a suggestion: order two appetizers—one to be served as your first course and the other as your main course.

As for *how* we eat, international observers can spot Americans in a restaurant simply by watching us eat: we hold the fork in the right hand, of course, but when we cut something we deftly flip the fork into the left hand, replacing it with the knife; then we switch the fork back to the right hand to pick up the food. In contrast to our style, in the so-called continental style of eating the fork remains in the left hand. From a standpoint of etiquette, either style is acceptable. Another bit of etiquette to keep in mind is that in much of Europe, both hands should be kept above (or on) the table. Forget what your American mother told you about keeping your left hand in your lap. The European custom goes back many centuries to a time when diners feared that a hand under the table meant either a weapon or some hanky-panky with their tablemates.

As for eating with chopsticks, no book can teach you how to do it. You must struggle through it yourself. Watch other people, or good-naturedly ask for lessons. Your hosts will probably enjoy tutoring you. Be sure to observe how and where others place their sticks, though; this often sends a signal, such as "I'm done" or "I'd like more." And never put the chopsticks upright in rice or other food—it's considered bad luck, even an omen of death. Ask your hosts about the local customs.

Now, let's deal with *what* we eat. Probably the most distressing part of dining in a foreign land occurs when strange foods are offered or served to you. For example, raw fish is very common in Japan. This prompted one guest from Ecuador to comment to me at a Japanese dinner, "You say this is considered a delicacy here? In my country we call it 'bait.'"

Yet there are even more startling foods you might encounter around the world: bear's paw soup, chocolate-covered grasshoppers, seaweed, shark's fin soup, reindeer tongue, sheep testicles, and even cooked scorpions. On my first trip to Saudi Arabia, we sat one evening cross-legged on a beautiful carpet in an outdoor courtyard, and an entire roasted lamb was laid before us. As the guest of honor, I was offered the delicacy: the eyeballs. Yes, I swallowed them, but so quickly I can't tell you how they tasted. And in Southeast Asia, the counterpart to sheep's eyeballs might be monkey brains.

Your natural first reaction may be to look for help, push it aside, or, worse, let your stomach do what it demands, and empty itself. But before resorting to any of these possible reactions, consider two facts:

1. You are the guest of honor; your hosts are favoring you with what is probably a national delicacy. It could be taken as an insult to refuse.

2. Also, remember that people in that country have been eating this specialty for centuries with complete impunity.

Remember, too, that when international visitors come to North America, they encounter the same problem. Here, certain North American favorites might be regarded by our visitors as disgusting. Such things as roast turkey, gravy, peanut butter, root beer, ketchup, grits, pecan pie, corn on the cob, pumpkin pie, rare steaks, popcorn, many fast foods, and even hot dogs are a few examples.

Toasting

One of the least-known social graces—at least, among Americans—is how and when to propose a memorable toast.

> On one of my very first visits to Hong Kong, I was treated to a formal full-course Chinese dinner. In this case, "full-course" literally means eight, nine, or even ten separate courses ranging from appetizers to desserts. Guests are seated at round tables with large revolving platforms in the center—we would call them "lazy susans."
>
> Each course is laid out in a large bowl or on a plate, one by one, on the revolving platform and then slowly turned around so that each person at the table can reach in with chopsticks (of course) to take a portion to his or her plate.

In the middle of this palatable parade, my host turned to me and quietly whispered, "Now!"

I looked back, totally confused, and asked, "Now . . . what?" He replied, "Now would be the proper time to make a toast."

It seemed that the apex of the meal had just been served—the shark's fin soup, considered a true delicacy in East Asia.

Of course, I was totally unprepared and stumbled through without a clue about whether I was coherent.

After that unpleasant experience, I began to compile notes on napkins, matchbox covers, or even facial tissues on the various customs and ways to make toasts around the world.

Here are some of the things I learned:

- The host usually makes the first toast, and the guest of honor is expected to respond.

- Toasts should be kept memorably short, never more than a moment or two.

- Stand or, if in a small group, gather everyone's attention and direct the toast to the senior guest; then make eye contact with all the guests.

- This is an occasion where you can say truly gracious things about the present company, about the host, about the friendship and joy present at the table . . . you get the idea.

- Short Ogden Nash–type poetic quips are often used; Irish toasts are common; profound philosophical statements are good, too. In other words, it's wise to collect these and memorize them in advance.

- *Never* use off-color words or comments, and do nothing that would embarrass anyone at the table (unless the occasion is a "roast").

- Ask your host what the proper words are for a toast in the language of the country you are visiting. In the United

States and Great Britain, this means, of course, "Cheers!" or "To your health." Others around the world are *"Sante"* (French), *"Salud"* (Spanish), *"Prosit"* (German), *"L'chayim"* (Hebrew), and so on. As I said, just ask your host.

One toast that has served me well for almost any occasion purportedly has both old German and old Chinese origins. I've never learned which one—if either—is correct, but here it is:

This is a toast on "How to enjoy life."
To enjoy life for one hour—get drunk.
To enjoy life for one day—play golf.
To enjoy life for one week—kill a pig (i.e., you'll eat well for one week).
To enjoy life for one month—get married.
To enjoy life for one year—inherit a million dollars (i.e., then it will be gone).
But to enjoy life for a lifetime . . . have good friends!
Here's to good friends!

Another very short toast comes from the Swedish poet and architect Piet Hein:

Live while you have life to live.
Love while you have love to give.

While traveling in China, Allen Fredericks, the associate editor of *Travel* magazine, encountered a Chinese host who was much more pointed than philosophical. At the end of the meal, he rose, thanked his guests, raised his glass in a toast, drank, and then said, "Now go home!"

Visit your local library, where you'll undoubtedly find numerous books on toasts and toasting. One toast that you probably won't find I heard at a dinner several years ago:

A government official from Colombia once visited my company, and, after a delightful day of visiting, sports activities, and socializing, he turned to me at dinner and said in Spanish, "I wish to make a toast to our group, which I will try to translate into English. Is that okay?"

I assured him that it was. He rose and said with a mischievous twinkle in his eye, "This is the most fun I have ever had . . . dressed!"

Protocol and the Story of Parker Pen

I first became interested in the subject of protocol as a matter of personal survival in business. In 1956, I started working for The Parker Pen Company in the Public Relations Department, and, to my good fortune, it was already an internationally known company. In fact, in the 1950s, a popular trade magazine of the time, *Printer's Ink*, conducted a survey of the "five best-known American brand names in the international market place." Parker Pen was ranked third on that list.

I remember learning that fact in 1950 when I was a student at the University of Wisconsin. At dinner one evening, a business school student who had heard about the list asked whether we could guess the top five names. Several people correctly guessed "Coca-Cola" and "Kodak" but failed to go further. That was when I found out that "Parker Pen" was so well known. At that time, little did I realize that I would eventually have a thirty-year career with Parker. Incidentally, another company name on that list would be difficult, if not impossible, to guess today. It was the Singer Sewing Machine Company. The logic of Singer's high international ranking became clear when our business school colleague explained that in the fifties, in every urban city and remote village in the developing world, one could find the original pedal-powered Singer sewing machines creating one of life's essentials—clothing. In later years, this was proved to me as I walked down dusty streets in East Asia or saw women in open doorways in Africa huddled over their Singer sewing machines, pedaling furiously while the needle flew along almost invisibly.

There are several reasons for the lofty brand positioning of Parker. George S. Parker founded his company in 1888 in the small town of Janesville, Wisconsin. He had come to Janesville to attend a school of telegraphy, which was a booming profession in the 1880s as railroad networks marched across the United States. He stayed on at the school to teach, and to augment his meager income he sold pens to his students. Soon he learned that the pens did not work well, so he repaired them. In the process, he decided that he could make a better pen—and he did.

In 1902, he sold his first overseas allotment of pens to a stationer in Denmark who had seen a Parker advertisement in the *Saturday Evening Post* magazine. This caused Parker to realize, "My pens can write in any language." He appointed the stationer as his exclusive distributor for all of Scandinavia, and later, in 1911, he identified a dealer in Thailand who became The Parker Pen Company's second international distributor. World War I interrupted Parker's appointment of overseas distributors, but even in wartime he still managed to sell pens in a unique way. He designed a pen called the "Parker Trench Pen." One of the most treasured personal possessions of an American doughboy was a pen because that allowed him to stay in touch with his relatives at home. The design of the pen was simple, but the issue became "How to supply fluid ink?" To solve that problem, instead of having the pen require fragile glass bottles of ink, Parker supplied small pellets of concentrated ink powder. All the user had to do was put the pellet into the pen's reservoir and fill it with water. The result: instant ink.

After World War I, Mr. Parker continued his expansion overseas, and during the 1920s he traveled the world, carefully researching every new market, locating a trustworthy tradesman who knew the pen business in each country, and appointing him "exclusive distributor."

Then, just before World War II, George S. Parker's son Kenneth designed a modernistic new fountain pen with a metal cap and a sleek hooded nib that he dubbed the "51." He used a numeral because he realized that numbers were recognizable in just about every language. The "51" was an instant success, but production was eventually halted by the war. However, once again, the "51" fountain pens already in the marketplace became a favorite of soldiers, sailors, marines, and aviators in the U.S. military. The reason was the same as in WWI . . . the pen was a small but sentimental personal possession that symbolized contact with home. It was reported back to Parker that, so treasured were their pens, aviators who were forced to bail out of their airplanes would actually step back into the cockpit just to retrieve their Parker "51s."

The "51" pen established Parker as a major American brand all around the world.

In 1963, I made my first business trip overseas. That was my baptism into other cultures.

A year later, I was assigned to our London office where I stayed for four years, while also traveling throughout Europe and parts of Africa. This was my introduction to the diverse world of protocol.

In 1967, I was posted back in the United States and for the next ten years traveled extensively to the Far East and the Middle East. In 1978, I was named vice president and area manager for all of Latin America, where I served for four years. During all of these years and wherever I traveled, I formed a habit of keeping notebooks and journals, filling them with bits and pieces of information about international holidays, distributors' birthdays (along with their children's), methods of proper toasting, key English words that were misunderstood in other languages, and a host of other helpful facts about customs, behavior, and etiquette.

In 1984, I decided that Parker should publish a book to be titled *Do's & Taboos around the World—A Guide to International Behavior.* This was, in reality, a public relations and marketing tool for Parker because we included a chapter on gift-giving practices around the world. And since Parker pens made excellent gifts (remember "They write in any language"?), the book was a thinly veiled pitch to American businesspeople who traveled to pack their bags with Parker pens. At the time we published that book, we thought the audience would be relatively small—hard working, hard-traveling cadres of American businessmen (they were almost all men in those days— refer to chapter 6 for more on women in international business). But, amazingly, we soon learned that the book had a much wider appeal. Thanks to a skilled PR person named Ian Kerr, I found myself booked on NBC's *Today Show* and two days later on the *David Letterman Show* (only to be bumped that night because the TV news personality Connie Chung spent too much time trying to crack three walnuts in one hand).

On September 16, 1985, the *New Yorker* magazine did a feature story about the book and described me as "an international Emily Post." Publicity spread and within six months we received seventeen thousand individual letters from people wanting to purchase the book. That paid for all of the editing, design, and printing, along with the PR costs.

Distribution rights for bookstores were subsequently obtained by the publisher John Wiley & Sons. Three revised editions have followed, along with six foreign-language versions, with total copies now in print exceeding three hundred thousand.

Meanwhile, in the mid-1970s, Parker purchased Manpower Inc., the temporary help firm headquartered in Milwaukee, Wisconsin. From a business standpoint, it turned out to be a golden idea. Manpower grew to a point where today it is the world's largest supplier of temporary help. Sadly for Parker, Manpower eclipsed the pen business, and in 1986 the directors of the parent company decided to sell the assets of Parker to a group of British investors. Several years later, the British sold Parker to the Gillette Company, which subsequently sold it to the Newell Rubbermaid Company, where it now resides and still holds an enviable position in international sales.

I retired from Parker in 1986 after thirty years. My last position was vice president, worldwide marketing. Having written one book, I decided I should try another. I did, and eight more books followed. (For more about how this "Do's & Taboos" series was developed, including some—I hope—amusing stories from the publicity tours and the speaking platform, see the epilogue.)

A Summary of Essentials about General Protocol

It's obvious there are hundreds, if not thousands, of facets to protocol. Here are just a few to emphasize.

- The teaching and training of protocol is becoming a full-fledged profession. At a minimum, it is now considered an important business skill. And as a tourist, the more you know about protocol in countries you visit, the greater the chance that you will enjoy your visit and be respected.

- Punctuality is not necessarily practiced the same way around the world. Learn what the rules are in your destinations *before*, not after, your visit.

- Knowing when national holidays occur in the countries you visit is essential.

- Titles—Mister, Mrs., Ms., Doctor, Professor, and so on—are more important in some countries than in others. When introduced to someone, don't jump immediately to a first-name basis, as we do in the United States.

- Gift-giving practices around the world vary from country to country. There are definitely "good" gifts and "bad" gifts. The best gift of all is thoughtfulness.

- Social dining—when, where, and what you eat—can vary dramatically from country to country.

- Toasting is done more often overseas than in the United States. It's wise to have a few memorable toasts in your hip pocket.

You've just had a short course on protocol and now realize that protocol is much more than learning to yawn with your mouth closed. So ask yourself, "Where am I likely to be tested on my awareness of gestures, body language, and general protocol?" One plausible answer is "The next time I host international visitors . . . in my home, my community, or wherever."

Good answer. Read on.

3

Essential Tips for Hosting International Visitors

*What the United States does best is to understand itself. What
it does worst is understand others.*

—Carlos Fuentes, Mexican novelist

Stewart S. was a vice president and area manager for his company's
Latin American business when he decided to invite the top two managers from his Argentina factory to visit the home office, located in a
small town a hundred miles north of Chicago. In later years, Stewart
would call it "the visit to hell." Here's what happened.

Juan and Enrique, the two executives from Argentina, spoke little
or no English, so when they arrived at Chicago's O'Hare Airport late
on a Saturday afternoon, they expected to be met at the airport.

Stewart had indeed retained a limousine and a driver . . . but the
driver could not locate the Argentine pair. That's when the first mistake occurred. The driver simply left!

Juan and Enrique sat on their luggage in the baggage claim area for several hours, patiently waiting for their driver. And they waited and waited. Neither had Stewart's phone number, but amid their business papers they located a number for one of his staff members whose name was Luis and who spoke Spanish. Luis gave them the only advice he could: call a taxi.

Using gestures and with the help of some Spanish-speaking people in the terminal, they found a taxi willing to make the 200-mile-round-trip journey. Cost: $250 plus tip. It was midnight when the weary pair arrived at their destination, only to learn that since they had not arrived before 6 p.m., as scheduled, their rooms had been rented to others.

They were finally sent to another hotel, one substandard to the first, and they settled in.

But that was just the beginning of this ill-fated attempt at hospitality.

The next morning, Stewart learned that the day of the mishap had been Juan's birthday. What a way to celebrate a birthday! But it didn't stop there.

Luis phoned Stewart early Sunday morning, saying, "Don't you realize what day this is in Argentina?" "Yes," said Stewart. "It's Juan's birthday. I feel terrible about that." Luis replied, "No, no, no! Today is the World Cup [Soccer] final match." Stewart knew that among Europeans and Latins, the World Cup final championship match was comparable to the United States' Super Bowl and the World Series . . . *combined*!

"Oh," said Stewart. "Well, they'll be able to watch it on TV." "But don't you understand?" Luis asked excitedly. "The two finalists are Argentina and Brazil!" It quickly dawned on Stewart that there was hardly a more fierce rivalry in the world of soccer than Argentina versus Brazil, and he immediately felt like he'd swallowed a huge lead weight. "And furthermore," Luis said, "the final match is being played in Buenos Aires . . . this afternoon!"

The full impact finally hit Stewart. Unthinkingly, he had invited his two managers to fly thousands of miles north, only to be stranded at O'Hare for hours. They arrived at their destination late and were shuffled from one hotel to another. Even worse, not only was one of the managers forced to miss celebrating his birthday, but they had been asked to be absent from their home city on the day when one of the greatest sporting rivalries ever was taking place! The rivalry between Argentina and Brazil exceeds that of the New York Yankees and the Boston Red Sox—and it's not one city competing against another, it's two huge *countries* competing head to head.

There was a slight redeeming footnote in this sad story. Thinking quickly, Luis realized that the World Cup match was being shown live on a large-screen projection TV in a theater in nearby Milwaukee. He drove the two managers to the theater and they saw the match . . . but, as the saying goes, "It was nothing like being there in person."

> *Helpful hint:* On a recent trip to Chicago's O'Hare Airport to meet visitors from Denmark, I waited in the baggage reception area to greet them. While waiting, I glanced around and couldn't help but notice a heavyset man sitting on a bench wearing a bright green clown's wig, covered with curls. Curious, I asked him, "May I ask why the electric-green wig?"
>
> He replied, "I'm a driver for a local limousine service sent to meet some business visitors who do not speak English. My client simply told his guests, "There will be a driver in the baggage area waiting to meet you and take you to your hotel. Look for a man with bright green hair. That's your driver.'"
>
> Moments later, a gentleman approached us, walked directly toward the man with the wig, shook hands, and off they went.

The moral of this story is that hosting international visitors can be fraught with mishaps and land mines, but there are ways to avoid them. In this chapter we will show you how. First, though, some statistics.

Since 2003, the number of international visitors to the United States has increased every year. In fact, according to the Department of Commerce's International Trade Association's Office of Travel and Tourism, in 2007 there will be a greater than 20 percent increase over the last few years.

Another set of statistics provides evidence of growing numbers of international visitors coming to our shores. Approximately 150,000 American college students study abroad each year, and every year, that figure increases . . . despite the threats of terrorism. But consider this fact—more than 500,000 international students are studying in the United States. That is certainly a compliment to the American education system. More and more young people want to study here and learn about American culture. These figures also suggest that we should encourage more of our young people to do the same—learn about other cultures.

This, however, is a chapter about hosting. Few, if any, of us would claim to be poor hosts. Yet in the business world, as you will learn in chapter 9 on the business of exporting, we are considered to be "deal focused." This means our business managers are taught that "time is money" and that they must focus on accomplishing the deal, or the sale. In other cultures—primarily in Asian countries, the Middle East, and Latin America—business is "relationship focused." This means the relationship between the two parties is extremely important. Mutual respect must be acquired slowly but steadily. Businesspeople in these areas take more time than we might in socializing . . . getting to know one another, building mutual trust and integrity. This leads us to the skill of hosting, and the first element of becoming a better host of international visitors is to know how we are different from people in other cultures.

How Others View the United States

The U.S. International Association of Convention and Visitor Bureaus, in its annual report, listed the following strange and amusing questions from visitors, as gathered by its state affiliates:

- From Florida: Which beach is closest to the water?
- From Arizona: Have we made peace with the Indians?
- From Pennsylvania: Where can we find Amish hookers?
- From Alaska: What is the official language of Alaska?
- From Georgia: Where are Scarlett and Rhett buried?

- From Idaho: If you go into a restaurant in Idaho and don't want any kind of potato with your meal, will they ask you to leave?
- From Colorado: What's the best time of the year to watch a deer turn into an elk?
- From California: I am trying to build a flying saucer; where do I go for help?

And get this: these questions were posed by Americans, not international visitors! Imagine the questions international visitors might ask. Here are some examples I've collected over the years:

- Why must each state have its own automobile license plate?
- Why are the TV channel numbers different for each network, depending on the city you're in?
- Why are your plumbing fixtures so different from place to place?
- Why do all your police officers carry pistols?
- Why are Americans so hooked on junk food?
- Why don't your hotels have a thirteenth floor?
- Why do you have different speed limits on major highways in different states?
- Why do you have four-way stops at some of your intersections? In my country that would lead to chaos. Everyone wants to be first.
- Why, on so many of your college campuses, do the students get involved in binge drinking? What is binge drinking?
- Why do I see signs on city streets that simply say, "Slow Children"? Are those for schools for slow-minded children or what?

What are some of the basic impressions international visitors have of the United States? In 1990, for my book *Do's & Taboos of Hosting International Visitors*, I determined that there are three basic impressions international visitors have when they come to the United States.

1. The United States is *vast*. It is among the largest countries in the world, spanning four different time zones, with mountains and prairies and deserts and forests, not to forget two distinctively different states that are not even attached to the American mainland. Just take any long-distance airplane ride and look out the window. It's especially noticeable when flying over the Great Plains states—hundreds and hundreds of miles with only widespread evidence of agriculture and large stretches with no houses or major byways. In contrast, if a visitor from London travels eastward for four hundred miles, he or she can traverse several different countries. For us, that's the distance from Chicago to St. Louis. Some visitors, accustomed to comfortably touring all of Europe by bus, come to the United States and sign up for a sixty-day unlimited travel ticket by bus, thinking they can experience all of the United States via one four-wheeled caravan. All they experience is a permanently numbed bum.

2. Americans are—to be polite—*plump*. The U.S. secretary of health and human services Tommy Thompson put it much more bluntly when he left office in 2004. "We're just too darn fat!" Thompson said. Sixty percent of Americans are either overweight or obese. In addition, according to a March 2004 *Knight Ridder Tribune* news article, "Obesity-related deaths rose by 33 percent over the past decade and obesity may soon overtake tobacco as a leading preventable cause of death in the United States, the government said in a [recent] study." Governor Jim Doyle of Wisconsin declared that "Obesity is a growing epidemic, not only in Wisconsin, but also across the nation. Children who are overweight have a 70 percent chance of becoming overweight or obese adults. There is a proven link between a lack of nutrition and proper fitness and health problems like diabetes, cancer, and heart disease." He made these statements in launching

a program called "Lighten Up Wisconsin 2005." So, maybe our international visitors have a point.

3. Americans are *friendly*. In more than thirty years of hosting international visitors in my Midwestern city, that is the single most common adjective I heard. Americans usually treat foreign visitors with curiosity, respect, and a desire to assist. Americans, it is widely said, want to be liked, and this is noted and appreciated by most visitors. Oh, yes, there are the unfortunate and even ugly incidents—robberies, muggings, curses—but they happen in all large populations everywhere around the globe. The friendly side of the United States is everywhere, though. Waitresses smile and chat with customers, people wave freely and call one another by their first names. The Soviet radio reporter Irina Simonova commented at a Midwestern backyard picnic, "I knew about the style of life [in America] and I knew about the friendliness and the attitude—but you can actually feel it here."

It's not all good news, though. In September 2005, a nine-member advisory committee headed by Bill Smullen, former secretary of state Colin Powell's chief of staff, found contrasting views of the United States. The harshest views came from the Middle East, where the United States is considered "less a beacon of hope than a dangerous force to be countered because of its policies, especially because of the occupation of Iraq." While U.S. policies in the Middle East were condemned, the American systems of higher education, science, and technology were praised, as were the values of freedom, democracy, and individual dignity, according to the advisory committee. "America is still seen as a place where things can happen, where change is not feared; a land of diversity, openness, candor and generosity," the report said.

Dining Differences

Dawn appears exactly the same way every place in the world, but from that moment on, eating patterns and customs around the world may vary as much as the weather. At one extreme, for example, in the Western provinces of China a routine daily greeting is "Have you eaten today?" Note that the question is not "Have you had breakfast or lunch or supper today?"

Throughout history, we have not always eaten three meals a day: morning, noon, and night. In the Middle Ages, the custom was to take only two meals per day, interrupted by a period of fasting. However, for extra nourishment the very young and the very old were allowed to "break the fast" by having a third meal, hence our word *breakfast*.

We in the United States customarily call the midday meal lunch, and it is normally a light meal. Again, throughout history it was not always the same. In early agricultural America, the main meal was taken at midday. That changed as the faster pace of an urbanized and industrialized America emerged. Today, many Americans seem to breeze through light lunches, preferring instead to linger at the dinner table over a large meal in the evening.

Speaking of breakfasts, many Europeans prefer cheese, cold cuts, and fruit, along with bread or hard rolls. In Germany, honey is often served as well. Hotels around the world that cater to international guests have buffets with something to please everyone, and many American hotels have followed suit.

In chapter 2 on general protocol, you learned that in many countries the main meal of the day is taken at midday so the considerate thing to do with your international visitors is to take them to restaurants with full menus and not just fast-food offerings. Once inside the restaurant, your guests will often note the ubiquitous glass of water, filled with ice. In many other countries, ice is less common and bottled mineral water is provided instead.

> Ian Kerr, a British-born public relations executive, once visited the headquarters of his client in a small Midwestern city. Dining at the local hotel one evening, he finished his meal and the waitress politely asked, "Coffee?" "Yes," he replied, "but I'd like a demitasse, please." Without missing a beat, the waitress replied, "Oh, I'm afraid we only have regular or decaf."

It is also essential to be aware of dietary differences. At the outset, you should probably inquire of your guests whether they have any dietary requirements. For example, for Muslims, pork is absolutely forbidden. To be more precise, any animal that scavenges (pigs, goats, dogs, various birds, and shellfish) is forbidden. This includes patés, terrines, and frankfurters if pork is used in them. Food cooked in alcohol also falls into this category. Some American hosts will be sensitive to these strictures even to the point of questioning restaurant chefs about the forbidden ingredients. For example, "Is your filet mignon cooked with bacon wrapped around it?"

Visitors from India, Pakistan, and Bangladesh are often vegetarians. Buddhism has no dietary restrictions, but because Buddhists abhor killing, some do not eat meat. Orthodox Jews do not eat pork or shellfish, nor do they eat certain parts of the cow, and milk and meat should not be served together.

For the Japanese, the appearance of food on a plate is just as important as the quality and the taste. For Italians and French, salads are often served and eaten after the main course, rather than before. Visitors are often overwhelmed by the quantity of food served in American restaurants. In most other countries, smaller portions are the norm.

Even the menus might confuse visitors because we begin with appetizers and the main dish is called an "entrée." In Europe and many other countries, however, the "entrée" is the starting course, not the main item.

A Rockford, Illinois, woman wrote to me about a college student from Iceland they had hosted. When she was helping him get settled, she noted that in his suitcase was a collection of dinner forks, each different from the first. She asked him whether he was a collector of forks, and he explained, "No, but I've noticed an unusual custom here in the United States. Near the end of the meal when hostesses clear the dishes from the dinner table, they always say, 'Keep your fork,' . . . so I do."

Entertaining Visitors

Ideas for places to go and things to do with your visitors are limited only by your own imagination. I collected the following suggestions from my audiences at seminars around the country.

- Heading the list is a simple tip: invite them into your home for an American-style dinner. We are all interested in seeing how others live. It is usually an enlightening and enjoyable experience to see how others live.

- The same rule applies to taking your guests to ethnic restaurants. If they are German, your first inclination is to take them to the nearest German restaurant. But that's not always the best idea. German food cooked in the United States usually doesn't compare to the real thing in Germany. On the other hand, if they have been in the States for a week or more, they may appreciate tasting their own style of cooking . . . even if it is slightly below par.

- Obviously, the normal sight-seeing places and events in your region should be considered—museums, historic sites, state and national parks, and so on.

- Rodeos—or anything having to do with cowboys and Indians—are very popular, especially among the French and the Germans.

- State and county fairs—animal judging, sulky racing, crafts and dressmaking, Country Western music—fairs are often unique sites for visitors.

- Boat tours on major rivers and lakes may be just as interesting to tourists as voyages on the Amazon and the Yangtze are for us.

- Fall colors—only a few countries can rival the annual coloramas that stretch across the northern half of the United States each autumn.

- A local grocery store can actually provide a rare experience for some visitors. While giant supermarkets are perhaps the best, whatever the size of the store, visitors love to compare packaging, sizes, varieties, and prices.

- A local courtroom may be an unexpected attraction to catch the interest of business visitors because law, justice, and order are important in every country.

- An obvious choice would be an American sporting event, especially baseball and American football. But be prepared for the almost impossible task of explaining such things as innings, outs, downs, scrimmage line, and why there are only three strikes in baseball, yet four balls. Tennis is played all over the world and, with its simplified scoring system, you don't even have to know your opponent's language. The Japanese enjoy baseball and golf and have a growing interest in American football. Swimming is another universal sport. We Americans are known as sports enthusiasts, and if our games are foreign and complex to visitors, "Don't worry," advises one British publication dryly, "any one of 200 million Americans will be glad to explain them."

- Stock car races are somewhat unique to the United States, as are demolition derbies—called, less kindly, "conspicuous destruction" by some visitors.

- Auto shows—Europeans are usually very automobile conscious and knowledgeable about horsepower, displacement, and design features. In places like the United Kingdom and Germany, the type of car driven by a company executive is a direct reflection of his or her status within the company.

- State capitols help to emphasize the separation we have in this country between federal and state's rights.

- Local amusement parks are another obvious consideration.

- Local schools, local factories, local colleges and universities . . . any of these might be a good choice.

While on a Mediterranean cruise, John and Freda struck up a close acquaintanceship with a fellow passenger, a widow from

Europe. As is so common with shipboard friendships, at the end of the cruise they said to the woman, "You must come and visit us in America some day."

Several months later, the widow wrote advising that she was indeed planning a trip to the United States and would enjoy seeing them again. John and Freda immediately renewed their invitation, and the lady arrived on the first of May. As it happened, John and Freda were known for their warm congeniality so they threw themselves into creating a memorable entertainment schedule for the lady, who was obviously delighted over such hospitality. Finally, after three weeks of nonstop partying and touring and with the month of June approaching, the American couple was near exhaustion. They ventured to ask, "Well, is there anything else you would like to see?"

Pausing just a beat or two, the matron replied, "Yes, there is. I think I would like to see the Fourth of July."

Social Drinking

An American businessman who had lived in Japan for several years once told me, "In Japan they call social drinking *the water business—* that is actually the Japanese term for the popularity and even necessity of social drinking in that country. In my terms, it's neither 'water' nor a 'business.' It's downright two-fisted, long-term drinking."

Halfway across the world, the national drink in Peru is called a Pisco Sour. This is an innocent-looking, limeade-tasting drink found, to my knowledge, only in Peru. It slides down easily, even innocuously, but it hits bottom and bounces back to the head with the force of an Incan war club. A relative of the Pisco Sour might be the margarita. The manager of the American Chamber of Commerce in Lima, the capital city of Peru, told me this story about Pisco Sours:

An American businessman attending a large, formal event in Lima downed one too many Pisco Sours. After dinner, he staggered out of the dining room into the ballroom. As the music began, the American turned to a distinguished-looking person with flowing gray hair, wearing a long, bright-red robe, and asked for the first dance. "Thank you, señor," the person responded, "but the orchestra happens to be playing the Peruvian national anthem . . . and I happen to be the Archbishop of Lima."

Entertaining and hosting in the United States almost invariably lead to the bar. Let's begin by examining some common imbibing habits in the United States that your international visitors may find new and strange.

The United States is identified with the cocktail hour—an hour-long before-dinner ritual—recognized more here than in any other country. Some visitors are startled to see signs in cocktail lounges advertising this social curiosity as "Happy Hour," "Two-for-One Time," "Double Bubble Huddle," or—according to one sign—"Animal Hour."

The American cocktail hour stems from the Roaring Twenties and Prohibition, when Americans began drinking in their own homes because it was the only legal place they could drink. Now we stage cocktail parties, which Judith Martin, also known as "Miss Manners," waspishly defines as an event when you get to meet "all the people your host didn't like well enough to invite to dinner."

Another expert on proper etiquette, Letitia Baldrige, reports that when she asked an Italian industrialist what bothered him most about doing business with Americans, he replied, "The length of your cocktail hour before dinner. I meet my American friends in a restaurant or at their home and they keep ordering drinks before we can order the meal. It exhausts us all. One cocktail before dinner is enough—maybe two at the most, and then we should move to the dinner table where wine will be served."

Here are some more Americanisms concerning social drinking:

- We mentioned it before, but it's worth repeating. We seem to have a love affair with ice.
- Order whiskey in the United States, and you'll be served bourbon; order a whisky (note the different spelling) in the United Kingdom, and you'll be served scotch.

- Brandy may come next in popularity, but, of course, beer and wine are also ubiquitous.

- Gin and vodka rank equally with all of the previous.

I once entertained two Argentine gentlemen in a rural road-side restaurant that could have come right out of a Norman Rockwell painting—very simple, rustic, and filled with American rural types. The Argentines spoke little English, so when I asked what they wished to drink, they naturally requested the national staple in Argentina, red wine. The waitress, who was rather uncosmopolitan, to say the least, asked, "Do they want that straight up or on the rocks?" When I translated, the Argentines were shocked. Wine over ice cubes? But there was more to come. At the conclusion of the meal, I asked whether they would like a "digestif," or after-dinner drink. They asked for cognac, a fine after-dinner brandy. Expecting the brandies to arrive in snifter-type glasses, they were equally shocked to be served, first, a shot glass full of brandy, and, second, a beer "chaser." I'm certain they talked about that evening over and over again when they returned home.

In general, when hosting guests from overseas, you can hardly go wrong offering the following: wine, beer, scotch, gin, or vodka, along with, of course, mineral water, soft drinks, and fruit juices. After-dinner liqueurs—or "cordials," as they are called in England—are popular among Europeans and Latin Americans but not so much among Asians, with the exception of the Japanese, who favor cognac or a comparable fine brandy.

I'm often asked "But what if I don't like or don't drink alcoholic beverages?" There are several solutions at hand:

- Ask for a glass of tonic water with a slice of lemon or lime, or a glass of ginger ale. Both resemble a mixed drink.

- If you believe an explanation is necessary, just tell your guests that for personal reasons, you don't drink alcohol, but do add that you have no objection whatsoever if others do.

- Another option is to explain that, for medical reasons, you don't drink alcohol or say that you are taking a certain medication that does not permit mixing with alcohol. The problem with that gambit is that your guests may then want to know what type of medication you are taking or what type of illness you have.

- Finally, when toasts are offered, there is no discourtesy in using water for a toast or merely lifting a glass of wine to your lips and no farther.

Hotels

The first rule for hosting international visitors is determining who will pay the hotel bill. My company policy was this: if the guests were important customers from overseas, we expected them to pay for their transportation to the United States, but once they were in our home city, all other expenses were paid by our company.

This checklist will identify you as a considerate host:

- Determine in advance what type of accommodations your guests prefer: single, double, smoking or nonsmoking, lower floor or not, suite, and the price.

- Can you preregister the guest? This small, often-forgotten gesture signals that you planned ahead. You might also be able to obtain a corporate rate.

- Does this visitor warrant gifts of flowers, candy, a fruit basket, liquor, or soft drinks placed in the room in advance? The visitor may already know about the exorbitant prices for items in the minibar, but it's best to explain that.

- Most of your guests will probably be hotel savvy but still may have questions regarding tip rates, thermostats, ice machines, room service, house doctors, laundry services, and so on. If there is no concierge available, personnel at the registration desk may be able to answer those questions.

- Another example of endearing yourself in the eyes of your guest, especially if he or she comes from Germany, France, Scandinavia, and such European countries, is to ask whether the hotel can provide a "duvet." That is what we Americans might call a down comforter.

- And what about your visitor's spouse? Will he or she require separate hosting during the stay?

- What about language services? Will they be needed? Or, you might explain to your guest that a custom that some American hotels have adopted is to provide members of their staff with lapel pins in the color and shape of country flags, and this designates that the staff member speaks the language of that country.

- Provide a list of telephone numbers for you and your associates; a tin of homemade cookies for that personal, homey touch; a copy of the business or touring agenda for the duration of the visit; a list of names, titles, and addresses of the people your guest will meet; and historical information about your company and your city.

- Finally, there are unexpected problems. Ken Kirkpatrick, a Nashville international business executive, reported that his French visitors invariably commented about American washcloths. In France, he learned, two washcloths are sewn together to form a mitt, or a glove, so that scrubbing can be done more efficiently. "Your washcloths come in a single piece," a French visitor complained. "How do you make them work? They either slip out of my hand or it takes two hands."

Colors Matter

Americans "see red" when they're angry; jealousy is green; blue signifies coolness and placidness; black is morbid . . . and so it goes in our culture. In other cultures, however, the symbolism among colors can vary as much as sushi differs from succotash.

Let's start with a seemingly safe one: white. In early history, white signified purity or virginity. Remember the Roman vestal virgins cloaked in white? Yet today for the Japanese, white is used at both funerals and weddings as a symbolic representation of hope and rebirth. Therefore, white chrysanthemums are the flower of death, much like our white lily, but they also represent the imperial family. Therefore, when giving gifts in Japan, never use white paper; use pastel colors without bold colors or patterns.

White is right for brides in the United States, but not in India. There, they prefer red or yellow wedding gowns. In the Middle Ages, the more colorful the wedding dresses, the better. Medieval brides often wore red wedding dresses, and in Victorian days, brides usually wore their brightest finery, no matter what the color.

Here is a spectrum of color tips for American hosts:

- The French, the Dutch, and the Swedes associate green with cosmetics and toiletries, yet it is considered the national color of Egypt and should not be used for packaging there.

- In Malaysia, consumers complained about a green product because the color is associated with the jungle and disease.

- In the Orient, green symbolizes exuberance and youth, but in some parts of China, men should not casually wear green hats. An associate of mine took green baseball caps as gifts for people he met there and quickly noted that the recipients would not wear them. Reason? In those regions of China, a man wearing a green hat is advertising that his wife or sister is available for sex.

- Green, as in shamrock green, is the national color of Ireland, but in Northern Ireland, orange is the national symbol.

- In England, red is regarded as an "old" color, but in Japan, the combination of red and white is widely regarded as appropriate for happy and pleasant occasions, and the national flag there is red and white, symbolizing the rising sun. In the United States and many other countries, the "red light" district, red hearts, and a red nose (as in Rudolph) all have different and special meanings.

- In Hong Kong, during the Chinese New Year, bright red envelopes are used to hold money and are handed to others as presents.

- In England, yellow connotes youth and humor, but in the Orient, yellow is often considered the imperial color because it suggests grandeur and mystery. And in Mexico, don't bring yellow marigolds to the home of your hostess, since that is considered the flower for funerals.

- In Brazil and Mexico, purple is the color of death so avoid bringing purple flowers as a gift. Brown, as seen in withered leaves, is the funeral color in Iran, and blue (for heaven) is used for funerals in Syria.

- Gold and its various hues have symbolism, too. Just about everywhere it signifies wealth, even though platinum and iridium are both rarer and more useful. If you are considering gifts with gold plating or content, in the Far East, "dark" or "orange" gold shades are preferred. In the United States, more "champagne" or "light" gold colors are preferred. Bear in mind that gold can come in many forms and colors: white, rose, dark, light, and so on, depending on other metals that are mixed with it. The Japanese generally dislike gold jewelry and personal accessories, regarding gold as "flashy." They seem to prefer products with white precious metals, such as sterling silver or white gold. Yet the reverse is true in Hong Kong, the Middle East, and most of Latin America.

- In England, black cats are considered lucky.

- Blue suggests high achievement (as in "blue ribbon") in most countries.

Finally, here are some commonly accepted color symbols from around the world: the white flag of truce, which goes back to the eleventh century; red-letter days, which come from hand-lettered medieval calendars when feast days were printed in red; and the red-yellow-green combination used on traffic lights around the world, which is standard.

A Summary of Essentials for Hosting

1. The art of entertaining foreign visitors deserves research, thought, and a touch of courage. Done well, it brings a warm reward akin to finding the perfect gift. Done poorly, and you may risk losing an important friend or business contact.

2. The best gift of all is the gift of thoughtfulness. Examples: you notice that your hosts overseas have an interest in such things as stamps, cut glass, baseball, or even a special brand of candy. Show your thoughtfulness by presenting something from those categories when they visit your home. Another example of thoughtfulness is to assist someone from their family if and when they come to the United States; such things as helping the person rent a car, open a bank account, receive medical care, or solve some other chore that is routine for us but new to that person.

3. If you wish to demonstrate special interest in and care for your guests, try to meet them at the airport and usher them through the baggage area and into your car for the trip to your home or their hotel. One of the most pleasant moments when traveling is to be met at an airport by smiling, welcoming hosts.

4. Women should not be afraid to invite their female guests into the kitchen (unless it is for a very formal dining occasion). Similarly, men who host should not hesitate to show male guests their woodworking equipment or hobby rooms down in the basement. And take note— many, many homes around the world do not even have basements. I took my closest British friend downstairs to

my basement, and he was fascinated by, of all things, the central heating. He was also curious why we had a stove, a refrigerator, and a sink there. I explained it was for canning. He said, "Where is your tinning machine?" "We don't have tinning machines," I said and showed him the shelves lined with preserves in mason jars. "My good friend," he said, "you don't do canning . . . you do bottling!" . . . which is what canning is called in the United Kingdom.

5. Don't rush to the nearest restaurant that specializes in ethnic foods from your guests' home countries. The quality of the fare is usually not up to par. The best place to entertain is in your own home. But, if your guests are here for prolonged periods, they might enjoy a respite by visiting their own special ethnic type of restaurant once in a while.

6. Don't hesitate to ask your guests what they find different, strange, confusing, or agreeable in the United States. If you see one of them flash a strange gesture, don't hesitate to inquire—gently—what it means. Or, better yet, start the conversation about gestures by asking, "How would you call a waiter to your table in your country?" Then, to keep the conversation alive, ask about customs for calling waiters in other countries.

7. Watch the eyes. The eyes of your guest will give you clues as to whether there is comprehension behind them. One of my best friends from Denmark said he could tell that someone he was conversing with was uninterested in what he was saying when "his mind would disappear from behind his eyes."

8. By all means inquire—discreetly—about dietary restrictions, likes, and dislikes. Explain in advance whether you are having a light lunch or are eating at a restaurant with a full menu. You might even review in advance the menu you plan for that evening just to be certain it is acceptable and agreeable to your guest.

9. If languages interest you, inquire about a few common phrases in the language of your guest, and try to learn and use them. Also, ask your guest whether he or she has encountered any confusing American English words.

10. One final tip—in American homes, we usually leave the bathroom doors open to show they are unoccupied. In some European countries, bathroom doors are kept closed so one always gently raps on the door before entering. And remember to use the word *toilet* instead of our many other labels for it.

On your journey through the "Do's & Taboos" around the world, you might logically ask, "Now that I've learned some rules about body language, protocol, and hosting, what about language? What should I know about some of the basic differences between American English and other languages?"

Once again, good questions. Read on.

4

Essentials Things to Know about Using English around the World

A very great part of the mischiefs that vex this world arises from words.

—Edmund Burke, British statesman (1729–1797)

We Americans are lucky. There are about five thousand different languages in the world, but English is considered the most widley used language in business and tourism.

That's the good news. The bad news is that we've messed it up! We use metaphors, analogies, idioms, jargon, buzzwords, slang, oxymorons, lingo, axioms, acronyms, metaphors, contractions, and so on. Then we mix in military and sports terminology. If that isn't bad enough, our grammar and pronunciation are terribly complex and inconsistent. Our vocabulary is huge! When you consider there are 2,231 different words and phrases in English just for the word *drunk*, pity the poor person who has learned English from a textbook or has learned British English. Our cousins in England, Ireland, Australia,

New Zealand, and South Africa speak a form of English that can sometimes be as strange to our ears as American English is to theirs. More on that in a moment.

This chapter will make you more aware of some of these variations and pitfalls. You'll learn that words are like hand grenades— handled carelessly, they can blow up in your face. After reading it, you will, it is hoped, become a better communicator with your international contacts and guests.

Let's start with an examination of the history of the English language.

The History of English

English, of course, comes from the motherland, England. But the well-spring of English first bubbled up in the Dark Ages when Germanic tribes in the fifth century invaded what we now call Great Britain. The next seminal event occurred in the year 1066, well-known to school boys and girls as the year of the Norman Conquest, or, more precisely, when the Normans from the Continent crossed the English Channel and defeated the resident Saxons. That's when the Old English period ended and the Middle English period commenced, with an infusion of French influences.

For example, the Normans spoke a version of French, which helps to explain why today sheep's meat is called *mutton* (from *mouton*, the French word for "sheep"), beef (or *boeuf* in French) comes from oxen, veal is the meat of calves, and venison is the meat of deer.

Between 1476 and 1776, written English became more prevalent, and during this time more French, Italian, and Latin words were added. In 1776, American English veered off in its own direction, adding more prefixes and suffixes, changing nouns into verbs, creating slang and idioms, and producing a dizzying number of other mutations.

According to the fascinating book *The Story of English*, by Robert McCrum, William Cran, and Robert MacNeil, plus *U.S. News & World Report*, today there are about 500,000 English words in common usage and another 500,000 in technical lingo. Another source, *The*

Global Language Monitor, claims there are 804,000 words in English. By comparison, the German language has about 185,000 words, and French about 100,000.

American English versus British English

Now, what about differences within English? Thick reference books are available listing the differences between American English and British English. Here's just one example from my own experience:

> I have an American friend who said, "I won't have any problems. I'm going to England for a vacation; I'll rent a car and tour around the countryside and be able to communicate perfectly well. I know they drive on the left side of the road, but I can adjust to that."
>
> My answer was, "Wait a moment. In the first place, in England you don't 'rent' a car, you 'hire' a car. And then once you get inside that car, many of the common terms you use for parts of that car are different in England. For example, the *hood* is called the *bonnet.* The *dashboard* is called the *fascia.* The *muffler* is called the *silencer*, and the *trunk* is called the *boot.*"
>
> On one of these occasions, a gentleman from Sri Lanka was present, so I added, "You use these same British English terms in your country, don't you?" He replied that he did but then quickly added, "Oh, by the way, we don't call the trunk the *boot*. We call it the *dickey*." When I asked why, he said, "I really don't know . . . but that's what we do." I followed with, "Has this ever caused you any difficulty?" He said, "Well, yes. I was in New York City one time. I hailed a taxicab at the airport, put my luggage in the 'dickey,' and we proceeded into Manhattan to my hotel. As we drove up in front of the hotel entrance, I could see my friends waiting for me, so I said to the taxi driver, 'Quick! Quick! Open your dickey! Open your dickey!" (Long pause) "I won't tell you what that taxi driver told *me* to do!"
>
> Since I first heard this story, I learned that generations ago in England the word *dickey* was used for what we

Americans called the "rumble seat." For those of you unacquainted with that term, during the 1920s and '30s, in the back of a two-door coupe automobile, there was a hatch where the trunk would be, but the hatch opened up and tilted backward to serve as a back rest for a two-passenger bench seat area, and it could also be used to store or carry luggage. I was told that in England this was called the *dickey* and also the *mother-in-law seat*, presumably meaning the inglorious spot to carry one's mother-in-law. As a further historical note, my older brother's first car was a 1936 Pontiac coupe outfitted with a rumble seat, and in 1943 it was where I sat on my very first boy-girl date!

In this short segment, we can provide only a sampling of differences. Your local library or bookstore very likely has numerous dictionaries and reference books devoted to inventorying thousands of contrasting American and English words.

You should also be aware of certain double-meaning words that are innocent to American ears but would cause the British to suffer embarrassment. And then, vice versa, benign words for the British that would raise alarms to an American.

First, here are some relatively harmless words in an American conversation that might be considered "#!*@#%" to a British person:

stuffed	fanny
randy	buggered
sharp	vest
napkins	on the job

Here are the translations when used in British discourse:

stuffed: This is vulgar slang for "having sex with a woman," or if used as "Get stuffed!" it means "Go to hell!" Another bit of slang meaning "to engage in sex" is *to bonk*.

fanny: In England, this does not refer to a person's derriere but instead to a woman's genitalia. Similarly, a *willie* is, for an Englishman, his penis (also called his *roger*).

randy: This is not the familiar or diminutive form of the name Randolph; in England it is synonymous with our word *horny*.

buggered: An American might say, "I'll be buggered," meaning confused or confounded, or we might refer to a cute child or animal as a *cute little bugger*. But in England, to *bugger* is to commit sodomy.

sharp: If an American describes a colleague as *sharp*, it is a compliment, meaning that a person is quick, intelligent, and able, but in England, especially among the older generation, it means the person is devious and unprincipled.

vest: The wife of my American boss once commented to a British gentleman, "That is an attractive vest you are wearing." What the British person heard, according to his definition, was "That is an attractive *undershirt* you are wearing."

napkins: These are diapers, or *nappies*, to a British mother. A table napkin in England is referred to as a *serviette*.

on the job: In some parts of England this is a slang expression for "having sex," which explains why one British gentleman expressed delight when an American acquaintance casually mentioned that his father "was eighty years old when he died on the job."

Now, let's turn the tables. Here are a dozen common, harmless words in the British vocabulary that would get immediate attention from an American listener:

pecker	bangers	to knock up
rubber	pissed	scheme
cheap	homely	to bomb
vet	tinkle	spotted dick

Translate these from American to British English, and here's the result:

Pecker refers to the chin, so don't be surprised if a Britisher says to you, in an attempt to perk up your spirits, "Keep your pecker up."

Bangers are sausages in Great Britain, which means you might easily hear a pub patron order, "A beer and a banger, please."

To knock up can be used with complete impunity in several ways in England because it does not have the American meaning "to impregnate." In England, it can mean "to phone or wake me up," or, in a game of tennis, it can mean rallying the ball back and forth in practice before starting a game. (On my first trip to England I was invited to play tennis with a charming young lass who coolly inquired, "Would you like to knock up first?")

Rubber is the word for "eraser." You can therefore understand why the Florida PR executive Gary Stogner was shocked on hearing an English architect friend cry out, "Who nicked my rubber? It was my favorite rubber. I had it for over two years!" Later, Stogner deciphered his friend's complaint to mean "Who stole my eraser?"

Pissed is not only an expression of anger, as it is in the United States; in England, it usually means someone is very drunk.

Scheme, for many Americans, is a negative word, because it suggests something that is a bit sly and slick; in England, however, it is just a synonym for the word *plan*.

Cheap, for Americans, connotes something of poor quality; in England, however, it is used more often to refer to something inexpensive, as in a cheap day ticket on the railroad.

Homely does not mean "unattractive," as it would to Americans; rather, in England, it is a positive word suggesting "homelike" or meaning a warm and comfortable person around the house.

To bomb in England means almost the exact opposite as in America. In England, it means to "succeed" or that something is a "large triumph." Whereas, to many Americans, it would mean to fail or flop.

Vet in England means to "thoroughly check something out" as in the statement "Let me vet your proposal before we send it out." In the United States, it could be taken as referring to a veterinarian. It should be noted, however, that to "vet" something in the English sense is creeping into American terminology more frequently.

Tinkle is used by American parents of young children to refer to "urinating," whereas in England it means to call someone on the telephone, as in "I'll give you a tinkle tomorrow morning."

Spotted dick is an English dessert pudding, and the "spots" are ordinary raisins.

British grammar, pronunciations, and spelling can also differ from American English.

Here are just a few differences in spelling:

American	British
color	colour
honor	honour
humor	humour
center	centre
jewelry	jewellery
traveling	travelling
skeptical	sceptical
aluminum	aluminium
inflection	inflexion
check	cheque
jail	gaol
whisky	whiskey

(I should mention, that as I write this, the "spell check" feature of my Word program is going crazy.)

We'll finish this brief exposition on American English versus British English with a short commentary on two well-known British words—*bloody* and *blimey*—that Americans hear often and identify with British speak and might like to know the derivations of.

In years past, a woman in England might be considered rather crude to bandy the term *bloody* around frequently, but that is not as true today in British society. It might be compared with the American slang word *darn*, which some stiff-backs among us regard as a slippery way to say "damn." There are two supposed origins for the word *bloody*. First, that it is a slang contraction of *by our lady*, and second, that it is a vestige from the reign of Mary Tudor, who was known as Bloody Mary because of her short but violent monarchy in the sixteenth century.

The English exclamation *blimey* is a contraction from the longer exclamation "*God blind me!*"

"*A dog's breakfast*" in England means a mixture, mélange, or conglomeration of things . . . like the leftovers from yesterday's meal that are scraped into a dog's bowl. So, fittingly, here is a "dog's breakfast" of common British terms that are uncommon to Americans:

- The letters "WC" on a door in some public buildings refer to "Water Closet," a British term for the "bathroom."

- One common problem for many Americans is realizing that the label "Great Britain" refers to the three individual but united countries of England, Scotland, and Wales, all located on the famous island, whereas "United Kingdom" includes Northern Ireland.

- What's the difference between *Scots*, *Scotch*, *Scottish*, and *Scotland*? The answer: the people who live in Scotland are Scots who drink Scotch and who wear Scottish tartans. Also, a *plaid* is not a pattern but an item of clothing.

- As in many other countries around the world, what we would call the "first floor" of a building is called the "ground floor" in the United Kingdom. And therefore, what we Americans would call the "second floor" is what our cousins would call the "first floor." This could be perplexing if and when you agree to meet someone on "the first floor."

- What we refer to as "electrical wires" are called *flexes* in England, and what we call "plugs" are called *points* over there.

- In the theater (often spelled "theatre" outside the United States), a pantomime is not a soundless performance but instead a traditional form of entertainment for children at Christmas, usually based on a famous nursery rhyme. Also, the person we call the "master of ceremonies" is called a *compere*, and a magician is called a *conjurer*.

- Santa Claus is known as "Father Christmas" throughout the United Kingdom.

- What we in the United States call the "backyard" of our homes is, in England, the small paved area where the *dustbins* (or garbage cans) are stored. The entire area with grass and flowers behind a British person's home is called the *garden*.

After that conglomeration—or what you can now call "a dog's breakfast"—we will table that subject and move on. But wait! In England, "to table" something means just the opposite of the American definition. In American English, to "table" something means, according to parliamentary rules, "to delay, by setting it aside." In England, to "table" means to "lay a subject on the table for *immediate* discussion."

Finally, many Americans have learned, via George Bernard Shaw's now-famous observation, that "America and Great Britain are two great nations separated by a common language."

Pronunciation and Vocabulary in American English

As a youngster I moved from Wisconsin to Louisiana, as my family followed my father who was called up in the military just before World War II and sent to the South for training. My mother enrolled me in the public schools in Alexandria, Louisiana, where culture shock hit me directly between my two Yankee eyes. Each day after school, I came back to our trailer camp in tears. "What's wrong?" my mother wanted to know. "I can't understand the teachers," I cried. I simply could not comprehend the Southern accents.

One example I remember most vividly was during a spelling test. The teacher read a list of words aloud, and we were supposed to write them out. "Lather," she intoned. I wrote "l-a-t-h-e-r," only to have it marked wrong on the test paper. It seemed she wanted the word *leather*. Situations like that seemed to occur every few moments. In desperation, I usually jabbed the shoulder of the girl sitting in front of me and asked, "What did she say?" But that only made it worse. The teacher thought I was cheating. In fact, on one occasion she berated me in front of the entire class: "Rahger! Are y'll cheaten'?"

My older brother had it even worse. He often came home bruised and scratched from playground dust-ups because of his Yankee accent.

Interestingly, many decades later, Robert MacNeil, the coauthor of the landmark book *The Story of English*, wrote that here in the United States deep-rooted local dialects and rapidly evolving subcultural slang not only still exist but seem to be more prevalent. Instead of our language usage and pronunciation becoming more homogeneous, it's becoming more diverse.

As examples of this, in a PBS documentary titled *Do You Speak American?*, the television reviewer Kevin McDonough explained that MacNeil "cites hip-hop slang, Internet and instant-messaging jargon, Appalachian mountain talk, unique Southern phrases, Cajun words, Spanish-influenced cowboy terminology and 'Spanglish,' meaning the evolving hybrid of English and Spanish."

McDonough continued, "MacNeil [tells us] about a coastal island off South Carolina, where speech patterns from West Africa still endure. And Pittsburgh has its own local patois, dating to its early Scot-Irish settlers where some Pittsburgh slang is identical to street-talk in Belfast, Northern Ireland."

Take that most Southern of all expressions, "y'all." Linguists tell us that its usage has, in the last fifty years, spread well beyond the Deep South. They say that the dynamic causing this is the increasing geographic mobility of our population. And they go one step further: ever since English converted *thee* and *thou* into one word—*you*—for both second-person singular and plural, American speakers have improvised, turning it into *youse* (Northeast), *yunz* or *yinz* (around Pittsburgh), and finally the ubiquitous "you guys" scattered across the country. And since the word *guys* suggests only the masculine gender (but increasingly includes young women), "y'all" resolves all of those variations and seems particularly popular among hip-hoppers.

For still another perspective, put yourself in the shoes of a person from outside the United States endeavoring to learn our brand of English. One particular problem comes from our use of contractions—that is, shortening words by omitting or combining letters or sounds. For example, shortening "is not" to "isn't" or the ubiquitous "ain't." Or worse, changing "going to" into "gonna."

The Anglo-American PR executive and my good friend Ian Kerr has often questioned our fickleness when pronouncing the names of certain states in the United States. As examples, he points out that Louisiana is *Looze-iana* by residents there. And Missouri comes out as *Miz-oorah*. But what really baffles him is why Arkansas is called *Ar-kan-saw* when Kansas is pronounced with the final s-a-s fully intact.

> We had visitors from Argentina in our home recently. Four of them did not speak any English. After a few days, we noticed that they greeted Americans by saying, "Machu Picchu," which is, of course, the famous Incan fortress built many centuries ago high in the mountains of Peru. We didn't say anything at the time, other than wonder if it was some type of colloquial greeting. But it continued—each time they met one of us, they shook hands and said, "Machu Picchu." Finally, one of the brighter members of our group shouted out, "I've got it!" He explained, "They are using our American greeting 'Nice to meetchew.'"

> A similar confusion is suffered by Danes who have nothing in their language that corresponds to the English greeting "How are you?" The Danes don't know how to reply . . . unless you want them to reply literally and say something like, "Well, if you must know, my aunt is not well, the dog died recently, and we had a cold, cold winter."

> An Iranian professor confessed to me that he was completely baffled when Americans said to him, "See you later." He

usually paused for a second or two and simply responded, "Well . . . when?"

Then there was the case of the student from South Korea who studied English for nine years in preparation for enrolling at the University of Illinois. On his first day on campus, an American student approached him and said, "Hi! What's the good word?" Stunned, the Korean thought to himself, "My goodness, I've studied English for so many years . . . and no one taught me what 'the good word' is." So, later in the day, he tried the phrase out on an American, saying, "What's the good word?" The student simply replied, "Oh, not much.")

Then there's *popspeak*. That word was coined by the *New York Times* writer Leslie Savan to refer to pop phrases of the day, sometimes strange inventions of phrases that are au courant but soon fall out of favor and disappear. Such things as "Saddam is *toast!*" Then there are catchphrases like "Don't even think about it" or "It's show time!" How about announcers at soccer games screaming, "Scooooooorrre!"? Recently, the term *blog* was invented to describe what self-determined commentators do on the Internet. If these phrases interest you, look for Ms. Savan's book *Slam Dunks and No-Brainers*.

To dramatize how English is inconsistent in both spelling and pronunciation, read the following poem, appropriately titled "English Is Tough Stuff." It was sent to me by an engineer in Portugal who had read my book *Do's & Taboos of Using English Around the World*. He sent me this poem as graphic evidence of how difficult English is for others to learn.

(This can also become an amusing parlor game. Ask each person in your conversational circle, one by one, to read it aloud—very carefully—without making a mistake. The winner(s) will be those who can do this successfully. It's a challenge even for people who have English as their first language.)

English Is Tough Stuff

Dearest creature in creation,
Study English pronunciation;

I will teach you in my verse
Sounds like corpse, corps, hearse, and worse.
I will keep you, Suzy, busy,
Make your head with heat grow dizzy.
Tear in eye, your dress will tear;
So shall I! Oh, fare well, fair.
Just compare heart, beard, and heard,
Dies and diet, Lord and word,
Sword and award, retain and Britain
(Mind the latter, how it's written).

Now I surely will not plague you
With such words as vague and ague,
But be careful how you speak:
Say break and steak, but bleak and streak,
Cloven, oven, how and low;
Script, receipt; shoe, poem, toe.
Hear me say (naught here is trickery)
Daughter, laughter, and Terpsichore;
Typhoid, stoic; topsails, aisles;
Exiles, similes, and reviles;
Scholar, vicar, and cigar;
Solar, mica; war and far;
One, anemone; Balmoral,
Kitchen, lichen; trauma, laurel;
Gertrude, German, wind and mind;
Scene, Melpomene, seen, and signed;
Billet scarcely discards ballet;
Bouquet, wallet; mallet, chalet;
Blood and food are not like stood,
Nor is mould like ghoul and would;
Viscous, viscount; load and broad;
Toward, too forward to reward.

Bard leads his leaden tongue among
His Muse's mews, is lead unstrung.
Pain reigns unreined—just ask your psyche:
Is a paling stout and spiky?
Won't it make you lose your wits,

Writing "groats" and saying "grits"?
It's a dark abyss or tunnel,
Fraught with rot like rowlock, gunwale;
Islington, but Isle of Wight,
Housewife, verdict and indict.
Tell me: which rhymes with "enough":
Though, through, plough, cough, thorough, tough?
Hiccough has the sound of "cup,"
Enough of this stuff—give it up.

And if that doesn't convince you that English is tough stuff, consider these head-scratchers from the World Wide Web:

- Why is the third hand on a watch called the second hand?
- If a word is misspelled in the dictionary, how would we ever know?
- Why do we say something is out of whack? What is a whack?
- Why do "fat chance" and "slim chance" mean the same thing?
- Why do we sing "Take me out to the ball game" when we are already there?
- Why are they called "stands" when they are made for sitting?

The Tower of Business Babel

The American business sector ranks high on the list of creating new and confusing terminology. "Shareholders" become "stakeholders," and when discussing interest or commission rates, "basis points" (the three numbers that come after a decimal point that we used to refer to as tenths, hundredths, or thousandths) become essential to know.

Football seems to breed much of this jargon. "When in doubt, punt" is one example. Another that has gained recent favor is "We've got to move the chains more often," referring to the sideline chain that marks the first-down distance.

And how about "That's not on our radar screen" or "It crept in under our radar" or "We've picked all the low-hanging fruit"? Meaning, respectively, "It's not on our agenda," "We missed seeing that," and "We've collected all the easy items."

Brian Fugere, Chelsea Hardaway, and Jon Warshawsky have authored an entertaining book titled *A Bullfighter's Guide: Why Business People Speak Like Idiots*. The book resulted from focus groups that were formed to learn what clients of Fugere's firm, Deloitte Consulting, wanted for assistance. The answer was "less double-speak and gobbledygook."

Here are more examples:

- "Thanks for giving me a heads-up," meaning thanks for the warning or notice of something coming up.
- "I just wanted to touch base with you," meaning I wanted to tell you something.
- "We've experienced a sea change," meaning a large, major change.
- "Mission critical" means an important topic or project.
- "Thinking outside the box" means thinking outside normal boundaries.
- To "reengineer" simply means to change.
- "Client focused" and "result driven" are almost meaningless, because when wouldn't the client and the results be important?
- I'm told the phrase "that dog won't hunt," meaning something won't work, is from the Deep South of the United States, referring to hound dogs used for hunting.
- "Let me pick your brain" means, of course, to get some ideas from you.

One bright Sunday morning, sitting with my German manager in the manicured garden of his home in Baden-Baden, we were discussing ideas for the next year's marketing plan. Midway through our conversation my German host, Willi S., turned abruptly toward me and said, "Here. Let me pull some worms from your nose." My gasp caused Willi to sit bolt upright up and ask, "What's wrong?" "What did you say about worms?" I asked. Confused, Willi replied, "I said, 'Let me pull some worms from your nose.'" And then, rather defiantly, he added, "What's wrong with that? You say that in English, too." After some further probing we discovered that "picking worms from your nose" was an actual German phrase more akin to the English metaphors "harder than picking hen's teeth" or "picking one's brain."

Here are some more common business terms that, when taken literally, can be confusing:

Snail mail—Is there bird mail?

Legal eagle—Are there legal beagles?

Downtime—Is there *up* time?

Will it float?—Why is that important?

Shotgun approach—Shotguns hurt people.

The bottom line—Bottom of what?

Pigeonholed—Are pigeonholes different?

Dog and pony show—Just slides will do.

A catch-22 situation—What happened to catch-21?

Now let's move from the boardroom to that equally ubiquitous quarter called the bathroom. Have you ever considered the multiple euphemisms we Americans use just to designate the toilet? Here is a partial list. (Precede each word with the phrase "I have to go to the _____.")

washroom	men's room/ladies' room
sandbox	boys' room/girls' room
restroom	WC (British for "water closet")
throne	commode
conveniences	facilities

gentlemen/ladies	lads/lassies
used beer department	altar
biffy	cloakroom
indoor plumbing	john
can	gents
lavatory	head (U.S. Navy and Marines term)
powder room	outhouse

And when we wish to *use* the bathroom, we have a separate collection of masked words and phrases. Again, precede each with "I have to _____":

wash my hands	visit the restroom
take a tinkle	use the facilities
have a wash (British)	spend a penny (British)
use the plumbing	make a pit stop
hit the head	powder my nose
make a call of nature	take a pee
stop my back teeth from floating	go number one/number two
go wee wee	

A Houston businessman told me about an occasion when he and an American associate were visiting oil-drilling customers in Saudi Arabia. The Houstonian's associate was experiencing digestive problems and, during the meetings and later at dinner, frequently excused himself, asking, "Where's the little boys' room?" Toward the end of the evening, when one of these absences occurred, the Saudi host turned to the Houstonian and gently inquired, "Am I to take it that your friend likes little boys?"

Some Essential Tips for Using Interpreters

One of the fastest-growing professions in the United States is that of a courtroom interpreter. This is because of the many Asians, Hispanics, and other nationalities who have emigrated here, and their numbers will only increase.

Nowhere is that more evident than in the state of Arizona. According to the *Arizona Republic* newspaper, "[W]orking as an interpreter involves more than just knowing the basics of a language. An interpreter must know technical terms in various vocations (medicine, the law, science, engineering, etc.). Also, Spanish is spoken with different slang, accents, and regional words depending on where one was raised in Latin America."

For example, in Mexico, if you want to take a taxi, you would say in Spanish "*coger un taxi.*" But if you are in Argentina, *coger un taxi* means "to fornicate a taxi." Also, insults in English tend to refer to body parts, whereas in Spanish they may refer to someone's mother.

According to the *Republic,* an attorney, with his incomplete Spanish, tried to ask a defendant to fill in a box on a form, but he inadvertently told the defendant to mark his private parts. Another attorney was trying to say *peña de muerte,* meaning "death penalty," but it came out *piña de muerte,* "pineapple of death."

The word *translator* usually refers to a person translating from one written language into another. *Interpreter* is typically used for someone translating the *spoken word.* Whichever specialist you use, here are some tips when you are overseas.

- Ask for help from your hotel concierge or, if you are traveling on business and need a true professional, check in with your home country's consulate or embassy. It can often supply a list of competent professionals.

- If you are only going sightseeing, no problem. But if your concern is business, try to meet with the interpreter in advance to get acquainted. Explain something about yourself and your business. During this breaking-in period, the interpreter will be listening to your pronunciation, accent, pace, modulation, and word emphasis.

- There are two types of interpretation: simultaneous and consecutive. Simultaneous is the type used at the United Nations, where some of the finest interpreters in the world operate in soundproof rooms, listening to a speaker and then quickly—very quickly!—converting the words or, more likely, the content of what you are saying into another language. When you work with simultaneous interpreters, it is helpful to provide either a full text in writing or some type of outline in advance. On the other hand, consecutive interpreters ask you to speak in groupings of one, two, or three sentences . . . and then to pause, to allow him or her to convert your thoughts into the desired language. Obviously, this takes time—almost *double* the time it would take you to present the speech in English—so be sure to take that into account when delivering your speech or comments.

- Try to review any technical terminology you may use. Each business has its own lingo.

For example, an American metal company executive used the word *pickling* to describe a chemical process for treating metal. His interpreter stopped and checked his dictionary. Finding the definition, he passed it along to the German customer, who responded through the interpreter, "Why does your chemical treating process use cucumbers?"

- Speak clearly and slowly. It is said you can detect veteran American international travelers and business people by the pace of their speech—they tend to speak slowly. Construct your message in groups of short, compact sentences. Repeat and explain your points in several different ways.

- Use visual aids wherever possible. Educators advise that we learn more from what we see than from what we hear.

- Don't interrupt the interpreter. That can be jarring. And don't be concerned if the interpreter seems to spend a longer time repeating your point than you did in presenting it.

- If confusion arises during your discussions, ask the interpreter for advice. A good interpreter knows more than merely how to translate from one language to another. He or she may detect other problems or misunderstandings from the tone or reaction of the other person.

On one occasion, Daniel Parker, the president of my former company, The Parker Pen Company, hosted a distinguished head of a competitive Japanese pen company. During lunch, Mr. Parker asked a rather pointed question: "When will your government reduce the unusually high duties on pen imports into your country to allow us to compete better?" The interpreter repeated the question in Japanese, and the visitor started talking . . . and talking . . . and talking some more. When he finally finished, the interpreter simply turned to us and said, "He doesn't know!"

Examples of Common Misunderstandings

In the 1980s and 1990s, Thomas Loftus was the second-most-powerful man in Wisconsin politics when he served as majority leader in the Wisconsin state senate. He also ran for governor in 1990 but was defeated by the incumbent Tommy Thompson. During the Clinton presidential administration, Loftus was being considered for an appointment as U.S. ambassador to Norway. A key juncture occurred when he was called to the White House for a personal meeting and interview with President Clinton.

Afterward, Loftus thought the meeting had gone very nicely. Several weeks went by, however, with no notification of the results. Then more time went by. Finally, worried and frustrated, he asked some of his friends in the White House to investigate what had happened.

A few days later, a very relieved aide to the president explained to Loftus that Clinton had scribbled a note on the top of Loftus's resume. The note said, "Not a bad idea." Unfortunately, the first people who read the note did not decipher the writing correctly. They interpreted the comment as "No. A bad idea." The confusion was cleared up, and Loftus spent a long and successful term in Oslo as the U.S. ambassador.

High school and college essays are a great source for malaprops and mishearings. According to Richard Nilsen of the *Arizona Republic* newspaper, one student wrote that Julius Caesar was killed on the "yikes of March," and he uttered the famous words "I came, I saw, I went."

Another offering from the Internet deals with double negatives. A linguist teaching a class explained that in English "a double negative forms a positive." Furthermore, that "in some languages, a double negative is still a negative. However, there is no language in which a double positive forms a negative." But then a voice in the back of the room said, "Yeah, right."

And what about plurals?

- The plural of box is boxes. But the plural of ox is oxen.
- One fowl is a goose and two are called geese. Yet the plural of moose is never meese.
- You might find a lone mouse or a nest of mice. But the plural of house is houses, not hice.
- The plural of man is always men; then why shouldn't the plural of pan be call pen?
- "One" may be "that," and "three" would be "those," yet the word "hat" in the plural would never be "hose."

More things you can learn from the Internet:

- In the 1500s, most people got married in June because they took their yearly baths in May and still smelled pretty good by June. Baths consisted of a big tub filled with hot water. The man of the house had the privilege of the nice clean water; next, all the other sons and men took baths; then the women; and finally the children. Last of all the babies. By then the water was so dirty you could actually lose someone in it. Hence the saying: "Don't throw the baby out with the bath water."

- Houses had thatched roofs piled high with straw, with no wood underneath. It was the only place for animals to get warm, so all the cats and other small animals (mice, bugs) lived in the roof. When it rained, it became slippery and sometimes the animals slipped off the roof. Hence the saying: "It's raining cats and dogs."

    That phrase is particularly confusing for people from certain Asian countries where dog meat is considered a delicacy. For them, "raining dogs" would be a godsend.

If malaprops like these stimulate your curiosity, I highly recommend reading the *Far Eastern Economic Review*, a weekly magazine published in Hong Kong and widely distributed throughout the Far East. Nury Vittachi is a witty columnist for that magazine who writes a regular page-long article titled "Travellers' Tales." I have a good octogenarian business friend named John Hough who regularly sends me the column, to the extent that I now have a thick pile of individual pages from dozens of issues. Vittachi's collection of mangled misstatements is bound to make you smile, even laugh aloud. He has a particular penchant for unusual signs that suffer from being converted from local Asian languages into English. Here are some examples:

- China Airlines of Taiwan reportedly applies to the doors of their aircraft large, prominent stickers that say, "Do not open door during flight."

- A train in Taipei has a sign printed in both Chinese and English on a diaper-changing unit. Along with the instructions for use, the sign warns that the maximum load is 159 kg, or 350 lb.

- From northern India, a retail store that sells earrings proclaims in English, "We make hole in ears with gun."

And here are more from diverse sources:

- A native of Thailand was driving an auto in Cuba when a police officer stopped him and barked, "This is a one-way street. Can't you see the signs?" The visitor complained that although the sign posts were present, the actual signs were missing. "Well, that's what they would say if they were there," the officer explained. "Don't let me catch you ignoring them again or you'll be in real trouble."

- A roadside sign in Branxton, Australia, provided by the Branxton Lions Club, welcomed drivers to their city with this bit of advice: "We have two cemeteries, no hospital."

- Another roadside sign, this time in Namibia, warns: "Danger ahead. Fasten Safety Belts and Remove Dentures."

- And to prove that we here in the United States are not immune to these types of misstatements, here are two examples:

    1. In a state where the governor had recently vetoed a record number of bills passed by his legislature, a prominent newspaper ran this headline: GOVERNOR'S PEN IS A SWORD. Unfortunately, the space between the second and third words was missing, with the result that readers learned the GOVERNOR'S PENIS A SWORD.

    2. And in Southern Florida, a prominent hotel decided to make its lobby friendlier by producing some of its signage in Japanese because of the increasing number of Japanese visitors. The hotel thought it would begin with the sign at the concierge's desk, since that's where guests could inquire about special services. The hotel management asked one of its Japanese gardeners for the Japanese character for *concierge* and he duly sketched it out on paper. That was transferred onto a neat metal sign. Within days, the hotel management noted considerably more traffic at the concierge's desk from Japanese visitors. It wasn't until several weeks

later that the Americans learned that the word provided by the gardener was actually the Japanese word for "pimp."

- Here's one you can relate during your next cocktail party conversation. Americans are really not very good at cussing. According to the Wisconsin Writers Council, "Americans have, depending on how you define them, only a couple dozen swear words. If you add impolite words to the profane and obscene, you might hit 60. The Romans had more than 800 dirty words. The Japanese, Malayans and most Native American Indians have no swear words." When the Finns want to utter an expletive, they say a term that means "in the restaurant." In Norwegian, "devil" is similar to the use of a four-letter word for copulation. The worst possible slur in Chinese is to be called a turtle. For the Xoxa of South Africa, the term for "your mother's ears" is sure to start a fight.

- *Hemispheres* magazine reports that for the Chinese, Hong Kong means "Fragrant harbor"; for the Japanese, Tokyo means "East capital"; for Argentines, Buenos Aires means "Favorable breezes"; for Thais, Bangkok means "Olive village"; for Hindi speakers, Calcutta means "Kali's dwelling place"; and in Arabic, Cairo means "the Victorious."

A Summary of Essentials for Using English Abroad

1. Be patient. The number-one complaint our international cousins have about Americans is that we are "impatient."

2. Use simple vocabulary. Avoid idioms ("It's raining cats and dogs"), slang ("We don't want any hanky-panky with this deal"), euphemisms ("I need to use the restroom"), sports terminology ("When in doubt, drop back and punt"), acronyms ("We need a reservation ASAP"), and jargon ("We don't have that problem on our radar screen").

3. Enunciate clearly. This means, avoid slurring words together or using words or contractions that Americans seem to prefer: gonna, wanna, wouldja, oughta, shoulda, comin', goin', watcha, saying *ya* instead of *you*, and saying *'em* instead of "them."

4. Watch the eyes. It is said that "The eyes are the windows to the soul." If a person is listening and comprehending, his or her eyes will usually be active and alert. If not . . . well, as a Danish friend of mine explained, "You can see the mind disappear from behind the eyes." In other words, the eyes become dull or blank.

5. Use the "repeat" technique during your conversations. That is, stop the discourse from time to time and say, "Let me make certain we understand each other. What I've heard you say is . . ." And see what happens as a result.

6. After you return home, confirm all the key points in writing.

7. Whenever you visit another country, it is always useful to learn the word for "toilet" in the local language. For example, in French, one of the words is *toilette*, and in Spanish it is *baño*.

8. A *cognate* refers to certain words in different languages that have the same root. For example, the Spanish word *muchas* means "many" or "much," and *numero* means "number." But when dealing with foreign languages, you should be aware of *faux amis*, which means "false friends." Take the French word *demander*, which one would think means *demand*, but it actually means *ask*, which is much weaker than the word *demand*.

Michael P. Wynne is a much-respected consultant on international business from the Chicago area who happens to speak Spanish fluently. On a recent trip to Brazil, he was hosted by a group that took him to a *churrasco*, which is a well-known, fancy barbecue in Brazil.

When his hosts asked him how he liked the food, Wynne, who did not speak Portuguese, drew on his knowledge of Spanish and said, "*exquisito*," which means "exquisite." Wynne noted that his hosts responded with strange looks so later he privately asked what the word *exquisite* meant in Portuguese . . . only to be told in that language it meant "weird."

Next we turn to a subject involving more than half of the world's population: *women*. Sadly, while women hold a majority position in numbers around the globe, they still do not share equality in most countries. Even in advanced cultures where women share the vote and other civil rights, they still do not match men in terms of compensation and the number of high corporate positions they hold.

In the next chapter, you will learn the "Do's & Taboos" for women—whether traveling for business or pleasure. As you'll soon find out, women's greatest fear when traveling abroad is—did you guess it?—*sex*.

5

Essentials Things for Women to Know When Traveling Abroad

In some countries, if I sit in the hotel lobby alone,
I am often approached by men who assume
I'm a hooker looking for business.

—One woman interviewed in a survey

In the 1970s and earlier, there were few American businesswomen traveling abroad in pursuit of international business. It was largely a male monopoly. And I was part of that conspiracy!

The reasons were simple. First, three and four decades ago it was considered too dangerous for American women to travel overseas on business, especially if unescorted. And second, if they did venture into many of the world's male-oriented cultures, they would not be welcomed. Indeed, the only other women they might see in the offices of faraway lands would be serving tea, answering phones, performing secretarial duties, and the like.

Today, all that has changed . . . dramatically. Now it is acknowledged that American women actually make outstanding international business executives. The reasons, according to Professor Robert T. Moran of the famed "Thunderbird" International Graduate School in Glendale, Arizona (now called the Garvin School of International Management), is that women are more respectful of other cultures and therefore more aware of local behaviors. They are less beholden to the win-win agenda of many American men, and thus they make great business negotiators.

Many women are joining the ranks of international business seekers, and their numbers will only grow. The reason? Because morally, legally, and ethically, American women can no longer be barred from seeking assignments that involve traveling overseas on business.

When compared to women in other countries, American women have made huge strides in both domestic and international business. Sadly, when it comes to compensation, they are still not on an equal footing with American men.

In 1997, three women and I authored the book *Do's & Taboos Around the World for Women in Business*. For that book, we interviewed more than a hundred women who had succeeded in American international business. They told us how they prepared, how they succeeded, and what skills it took to break not only the glass ceiling but also the glass walls.

Significantly, the first foreign-language version of that book was published in 2004 . . . in Chinese! For many decades, Chinese women have labored right alongside men in every profession and at every managerial level. When I first visited China in 1976, at a time when the leadership there was hesitantly turning to Western economic theories, we visited factory after factory and farm after farm where we saw both men and women working side by side in key management positions. The same is not yet true in Japan, although, within the last decade or so, liberalization of attitudes about Japanese women in business and other professions has progressed admirably. Japanese women are now seen on TV as commentators and even as elected representatives in the Diet, the Japanese counterpart of our Congress. Regarding much of the Middle East, women do not enjoy equality with men, especially in countries such as Saudi Arabia.

What Women Fear Most

What is the greatest fear experienced by American women when traveling overseas? The answer to that question is fairly obvious. The great majority of American business women we interviewed gave the same answer: fear of sexual advances and encounters.

One woman told us of an experience she had in South Korea that illustrates the predominant attitude toward American women in business. At a formal dinner, the Korean businessman who was her dining partner turned to her and said, "I'm sorry about your husband."

Startled, the woman asked, "What do you mean?"

He replied, "I see by the ring on your finger that you are married, but I assume your husband is deceased. Otherwise, you would not be traveling alone on business."

In the area of sex and sexuality, here are some essential things for American businesswomen to keep in mind when traveling around the world:

- Remember, this is business travel, and in almost all cases it is inappropriate to date international business colleagues or acquaintances. An old Spanish saying explains why: "Don't wash your feet in your drinking water."

- Don't be insulted if and when men make passes at you. In many countries, it is considered a compliment. To deflect passes, be calm, polite, and very firm when you say, "I'm sorry, I'm here on business," or else respond with a plain "no."

- Be prepared for surprising, blunt questions from men you meet, such as, "How old are you?" "How much do you make?" "What kind of birth control do you use?" and "What does your husband do when you are traveling in foreign countries?" Because these questions stem from centuries-old, male-dominated cultures, try not to take immediate offense but instead respond with firmness, patience, and diplomacy.

- Don't flirt with business associates overseas. Avoid giving mixed signals. Dress conservatively. If you are married, be sure to wear your wedding ring. If you are not married but are thinking of wearing a wedding ring to discourage advances, don't do it. If you lie about your marital status and your overseas associates discover the truth, you'll be trapped in a lie. If you are married and have children, ask your host about his children, which then gives you an opening to show photos of your own children.

- Remember that many perceptions of American women come from U.S. movies and TV shows that are exported abroad. These often create an impression that all American women are aggressive, glamorous, sexy, and even promiscuous. To counter this, act professionally in every aspect of your business life. This means dressing conservatively with high necklines, loose-fitting dresses in somber colors, and modest skirt lengths.

- Don't drink or dine alone late in the day. A glass of wine during midday lunches with male business associates is perfectly acceptable, but avoid solo social drinking unless you are part of a large group. Never over-imbibe. If you don't drink, politely tell your host that you don't drink alcohol but have no objections if others do. That way, if your host is male and is considerate, he will ensure that you are offered soft drinks and will protect you if others press you to drink alcohol.

- If you must do business entertaining overseas—for example, hosting male clients or customers for lunch or dinner—explain to your guests in advance that you wish to host them. They will probably protest, but stick to your guns. Then, at the restaurant, to avoid that awkward moment when the check is delivered, inform the maître d' well in advance that you will settle the check later in private.

- Avoid spending long periods of time alone in public places, such as cocktail lounges, restaurant dining rooms, hotel lobbies, or buses unless you are part of an organized tour. If you must dine alone at a restaurant, tell the maître d' that you do not wish to be disturbed. Another trick is to take a book along to signal that you are fully occupied.

- If both you and your male business associate are single and there is a true mutual attraction, try not to succumb to temptation. How you handle this depends, of course, on your own personal interest and ethics. Still, you need to consider the issues of mixing business with pleasure, one-night stands, and long intervals and distances preventing a continuation of the relationship. If Cupid enters the picture, weigh all the risks, especially if it could be just a temporary infatuation.

- What about sexual harassment? There are clearly delineated laws in the United States and certain parts of Europe regarding harassment. Much of the rest of the world, however, does not necessarily follow our rules or laws. While some of us in North America consider casual touching to be a form of sexual harassment, it can also be viewed as normal, acceptable behavior in other countries.

Here are several strategies for dealing with sexual harassment:

Counter offensive sexual remarks by saying coolly and firmly, "Stop. I don't want to hear this."

Keep a written log of incidents of harassment. Jot down the date and a description of each incident.

Report the conduct to a higher-up in your chain of command, following any rules and practices of the organization you work for.

If you are employed by an American company, consult the company's U.S. attorney. Otherwise, consult a local attorney in the country where the offense occurred. In either case, recognize that U.S. laws for harassment probably will not apply abroad.

Gaining Respect and Acceptance in Male-Dominated Societies

There are several simple, clear rules for achieving the respect you deserve when traveling in parts of the Middle East, Asia, Europe, and Latin America where men have dominated the business scene for many decades, if not centuries.

- Know your product or service. Expertise is valued everywhere, so be prepared to demonstrate your technical and commercial competence. This cannot be emphasized enough. The more you know, the less important gender becomes.

- Know the culture. Do your homework before entering any new culture. Twenty years ago, there were precious few resources on cross-cultural protocol, etiquette, and behavior. Today many bookstores and libraries have large sections devoted to these topics. Remember that we Americans follow certain rules of business behavior that other cultures may not consider important. For example, take the respect for punctuality. Our training tells us to "get right down to business" and that "time is money, so let's not waste time with social chit-chat." But not everyone marches in step with that drumbeat.

- Be certain that your business cards clearly state your title or position. Avoid fuzzy words like *assistant* to or *associate director*. The higher the job level, the better. The best title, of course, is "president." Being a "vice president" is very American and is becoming understood elsewhere, but it is not that common overseas. *Director* is a good term, but in the United States it can mean being a member of the board of directors, whereas in the United Kingdom it is tantamount to being a vice president in the United States. Your hosts want to know, as best they can, what your responsibility and authority may be.

- Gain a clear understanding from your employer what parameters you have regarding decision making. Nothing frustrates your overseas business associates more than the excuse "I'll have to check that with the home office." Be able, whenever you can, to make decisions on the spot.

- Don't be afraid to list your professional and academic credentials—the more, the better.

- Know the lingo of your special business. Learn the technical terms, but be careful about using too much purely American or industry-specialized terminology for fear of clouding simple comprehension among people for whom English is a second—or even a third—language.

If you follow these rules, experienced women travelers counsel that your male counterparts will regard you as a "third sex" and will be amenable to conducting business.

Jeane Kirkpatrick, a one-time U.S. ambassador to the United Nations, told me that once while attending an all-male conference in the United Arab Emirates, she was asked by a male counterpart, "Would you mind if we temporarily designated you an official 'male'?" She declined.

Security

Whether you travel on business or for pleasure, be especially cautious about where and how you carry your essential travel documents: passport, credit cards, plane ticket, traveler's checks, vital medications, and prescriptions. The same goes for valuable jewelry. If you carry these items in a handbag, make certain it has a heavy strap that you can hang around your neck, and then carry the bag in front. Even better, invest in a pouch that hangs around your neck and is concealed by loose-fitting clothes.

Make duplicate copies of all valuable documents: credit cards, driver's license, telephone credit cards—everything. Store the copies separately, perhaps in your suitcase. One little-known fact is that if you lose your passport and have a photocopy of it stashed away in your luggage, it will be much easier to obtain another passport at the nearest U.S. embassy or consulate. Also, leave copies of these necessities back at the home office or with close friends or relatives.

Try to travel in small groups on well-traveled routes. Beware of sudden distractions, such as a child crying or tugging on your skirt. This is a common device used by pickpockets who then relieve you of your valuables. Another trick is for a thief to stand behind you on a bus, a subway, or a crowded street and then squirt mustard or a similar substance on the back of your coat. He next offers to help you wipe it off. Once you remove your coat, the bandit can quickly gain access to your inside pockets or even your purse.

Staying Healthy

Preparation is the key word when it comes to staying healthy while traveling abroad.

One of the best resources comes from the Canadian Department of Foreign Affairs, which has published an excellent pamphlet titled "Her Own Way—Advice for the Woman Traveller." It's filled with practical and useful advice for women who travel abroad. (Access to this and other helpful booklets published by the Canadian government can be found at www.voyage.gc.ca, where the information is considered to be in the public domain and can be reproduced without permission.)

For example, the section titled "Staying Healthy" has this advice aimed directly at women:

1. Not all travel books deal with uniquely female health needs. You can augment what you read with the experienced advice of other women travelers.

2. It's a good idea to carry your doctor's phone and fax numbers, as well as copies of prescriptions for medications you might require along the way.

3. You won't always be able to eat properly. Consider carrying multivitamins to supplement your diet. Also, many grocery stores now carry foil-packed seafood (tuna and salmon) that needs no refrigeration until opened and is lightweight and easy to carry.

4. Your regular brand of contraceptive pill may not be available at your destination. Take enough with you to last the whole trip.

5. Major stomach upsets (diarrhea or vomiting) can cause your body to lose its ability to absorb the contraceptive pill. It's wise to use condoms to help guard against unwanted pregnancy.

6. When traveling to developing countries, carry a supply of tampons and sanitary napkins. They may be expensive and difficult to find. (One woman traveler said that she visited a store in France and, not knowing the French phrase for sanitary napkins, was repeatedly referred to the dinner napkin section of the store.)

7. It's not unusual for women to stop menstruating when they travel for long periods of time. If you're concerned that you might be pregnant but there are no other symptoms, don't worry.

8. If you're prone to yeast infections, they're more likely to recur in warm, moist climates. Wearing loose-fitting cotton underwear and skirts rather than pants may help. Carry appropriate medications in your first-aid kit; they might not be available where you're traveling.

9. Cystitis is an infection of the urinary tract and the bladder. Drinking a lot of purified water, especially in hotter climates, may help to reduce your chances of suffering from this problem.

10. If you wear contact lenses, consider using disposables. Storing and cleaning your lenses can become a nuisance if you're going to be on an extended journey.

11. And finally, to minimize unpleasant experiences, if you require medical or dental assistance, contact your nearest home embassy. Its staff can often provide lists of approved doctors and dentists in that country.

To conclude on a lighter note, Lynn Payer has written an engaging book titled *Medicine and Culture*, in which she lightheartedly explains how different cultures view medical treatments. In Germany, she wrote, physicians confronted with general illness are likely to begin by examining the heart and the circulatory system. In France, more emphasis is placed on the liver. In America, a doctor's first suspicion is that "It's probably a virus." As for cholesterol, American doctors measure it to help to determine your chances of a heart attack, whereas in France, cholesterol is checked to see how well a person has lived. In England, the first concern may be constipation, which is "a wastebasket or catch-all" for many maladies there, according to Payer, and the treatment for general illness is often "come back in six months."

Here are some easy preventative measures:

- Wash your hands frequently. Germs are transmitted in unsuspecting ways: on paper currency, on doorknobs, when shaking hands, and so on.

- Drink only purified, bottled water. Never drink directly from faucets. And remember, too, that ice cubes can be made from tainted water.

A professional American meeting planner told me that she had visitors from South America and one of the Latin guests complained to her, "There is no water in my hotel room." The American quickly sought a hotel assistant manager and the two accompanied the Latin guest back to her room. Everything was in order—the faucets all operated perfectly. When this was demonstrated to the Latin lady, she replied indignantly, "Well, you don't expect me to drink directly from the faucet, do you?"

General Travel Tips

Today, with carry-on luggage so popular, it's common to see women manhandling all of their luggage, including lifting it up into overhead compartments on airplanes. Keep in mind that your trip will be less of a struggle if you learn to pack lightly.

Try this good advice, again from the Canadian government:

- A few days before your departure, try some test walks. Pack your bag(s) and make your way around the block with your luggage. Visualize yourself climbing the stairs in a subway or getting on or off a train unassisted. You may find yourself returning home and reducing the bag's contents by half.
- Consider using only a medium-size suitcase with rollers, a backpack, and/or briefcase.
- Avoid an expensive-looking camera bag or computer bags. Use a diaper bag instead.
- Hide your baggage name tags from inquiring eyes.

According to Erin Woodley, Canadian Olympic silver medalist in synchronized swimming, there are three important things about traveling: "Pack light, always wear comfortable shoes, and smile." (But don't smile too much or too broadly, lest it be interpreted as an invitation or a come-on.)

General Protocol

For more information on protocol and behavior—such topics as greetings around the world, social dining, conversational taboos, and gift giving, turn to chapter 2. Most, if not all, of the essential do's and taboos listed there apply to both women and men.

Following are some basic rules for crossing cultures:

- *Be culturally aware.* Observe what's going on around you—in restaurants, offices, and other public places. Look for similarities but also for differences.

- *Don't expect equality.* As explained earlier in this chapter, women around the world have had difficulty reaching equality with men.

- *Prepare.* Do your homework. Your local library and the Internet provide vast resources on countries on your itinerary. Study their histories, heroes, languages, literature, food, economies, demographics, and so on.

- *Build a personal network of international contacts, experts, and resources.* Find a mentor, male or female, who has international business experience.

- *Be professional.* Develop your competency to the highest possible level so that your international colleagues will know they are dealing with the best person for the job. Never fail to act with tact and diplomacy and always exhibit self-confidence and self-control.

- *Be compassionate, patient, tolerant, and flexible.* Remember the fundamental advice given throughout this book: in many parts of the world, international business is built on establishing personal relationships based on trust and integrity.

- *Keep your sense of humor.* When organizations send students abroad for study, one of the chief characteristics they look for is the ability to laugh at oneself. There'll be plenty of mistakes made by those students and they must learn to laugh and learn.

- *Recognize that success lies in humility.* Admit that there's a lot you don't know. Tahirih Lee, a professor of Chinese law at the University of Minnesota, insists, "Humility is a key to overcoming obstacles. Don't ever believe you are better than anyone else because of your job or your education. This always makes communication and trust-building more difficult." One definition of *intelligence* is "knowing how little you know."

- *Learn to distinguish between gender differences and cultural differences.* As a woman, your first reflex may be to conclude that gender differences are the culprit when you and your international male colleague can't work together. The problem could be a result of cultural, gender, or personal differences—or all three. It's your job to analyze the situation, keeping all these factors in mind.

- *Seek training and solid academic credentials.* Today, more and more women are carving out careers in international business. Women in the first wave were generally picked from existing personnel and had to learn the craft while on the job. A new wave of women is currently coming along that has college and university training. The best way to prepare while in school is to take as many courses as possible with the word *international* in the class title.

- *Act with authority.* To earn respect in international business, especially in male-dominated countries, you must (1) have excellent credentials and experience; (2) know your product or service, as well as the attributes of competing firms; (3) have the authority to make business decisions on the spot; and (4) dress very conservatively.

- *Be especially conscious of good safety and health measures.*

The Pathways toward a Career in International Business

How does a woman break that glass ceiling or glass wall to gain entry into the international business arena?

The best way, of course, is to get a degree in international business. Many public universities offer majors in international business. Some schools are known for specializing in this field. For example, the University of South Carolina in Columbia, South Carolina, offers an international master's of business administration degree, formerly known as the MIB program, which stood for master's in international business. The University of Wisconsin–Madison offers a five-year undergraduate degree program in its business school, with one of those years involving an overseas internship position. Another master's degree program is offered by the Garvin School of International

Management, better known as "Thunderbird," mentioned at the beginning of this chapter, located in Glendale, Arizona, a suburb of Phoenix.

Here are ten methods to help you qualify for a job in international business:

1. During your job interviews, ask whether the employer has a training program for international assignments. Many companies, however, will often require a training program in the U.S. market before moving an employee into international training.

2. Develop language skills, credentials, and experience in the business you have targeted. You need to develop concrete skills and experience in a recognized international area, such as marketing, finance, law, engineering, and so on. A love for traveling abroad, plus a few language courses, are insufficient qualifications for an international job.

3. Learn to speak one or more foreign languages. Strive for fluency, not just familiarity. While learning a language, find out everything you can about the business culture and the protocol of the country or countries where your chosen language is spoken.

4. Gain experience in one of the specialties of international business. Some examples are international banking, service companies that offer export shipping and documentation, international insurance, or advertising agencies with international clients.

5. Don't be afraid of working first in U.S. marketing, sales, or customer service. Then, if and when your current employer expands into international sales, you'll be positioned just outside the doorway, waiting to be admitted.

6. Seek out international internships and volunteer opportunities. Also, search the Internet for organizations offering employment in foreign countries.

7. Internationalize yourself. Cultivate traits that make you attractive to employers—a knowledge of world geography

and economics, experience in living abroad, and demonstrated work experience with people from other cultures. Travel overseas at every opportunity, even in high school with two- or three-week trips abroad, and, of course, take part in study-abroad programs at colleges and universities.

8. Lower your expectations for an entry-level job in international business. Clerical positions or translation work are often the best places to learn about international business. Prove that you have the adaptability and the potential, then urge your employer to reward and motivate you through increased international responsibilities.

9. Join local trade clubs and international associations in your area. Attend seminars, community colleges, or universities. This will bring two benefits: it will add to your present store of information and knowledge, and it will also allow you to do valuable networking.

10. Make your current employer aware of your interest in expanding your responsibilities and your career directions into international business.

A word of caution: many young people who have had a brief experience traveling overseas want to immediately step into a job that will allow them to go back. Employers want you to know their business first and are not impressed if you are just looking for a quick excuse to get back overseas. Be patient. You must have a good grounding in the business itself. You'll be more effective that way. Make certain your employer knows that you have ambitions—and qualifications—for an overseas posting, but don't rush it.

A Summary of Essentials for Traveling and Conducting Business Abroad

1. Be cautious about getting involved in a romantic affair while overseas, especially with your business associates.

2. Women should be prepared for men making passes at them and for casual touching.

3. Dress conservatively at all times.

4. Know your product. Know your competition.

5. Do your homework about the country you will be visiting.

6. Make certain that you have decision-making authority so that you won't always be saying, "I'll have to check that with the home office."

7. When preparing for a career in international business, take all the appropriate courses in college. Become as fluent as you can in at least one foreign language.

8. The best single way to avoid illnesses while traveling overseas is to wash your hands as frequently as possible. Try to drink only bottled water that has been sealed.

9. Remember that the United States is still probably one of the most advanced countries in the world when it comes to gender equity.

10. Practice chameleon management—try to adapt to local customs regarding punctuality, dining habits, greetings, and so on.

Clearly, the newest and most significant development in communicating around the globe is the development of the Internet. Change is occurring at exponential rates. The next chapter will examine just one aspect of the phenomenon: e-commerce in international business.

6

Essential Things to Know about Using the Internet Internationally

The Internet has the power to inundate and educate the masses with information not previously available to much of the world's population.

—Stephen Taylor, director, International-Business-Center.com

"The [I]nternet may be the closest thing to a working anarchy the world has ever seen. Nobody owns it, nobody runs it, and most of its 30 million or so citizens get along by dint of on-line etiquette, no rules and regulations." So wrote Donald Ball and Wendell H. McCulloch Jr., in *International Business, the Challenge of Global Competition*.

Actually, since that sweeping description of the Internet was issued, the U.S.-based nonprofit organization the Internet Corporation for Assigned Names and Numbers (ICANN) has managed basic policies concerning Internet addresses. ICANN is in charge of names and addresses but has no control over the Internet. The Internet Engineering Task Force (IETF) is an international agency that comes closest to managing the Internet. In December 2003, when world leaders convened for a World Summit on the Information Society in Geneva, they could not agree on a structure for Internet governance. There are continuing efforts to reach accord on Internet governance, but at this writing nothing significant has developed.

Meanwhile, Stephen Taylor, the director of International-Business-Center.com, adds "e-commerce might better be called 'i-commerce' for *instant commerce*, because that is what cyberspace and the Internet represent. It gives a person or company the ability to instantly access information and services, acquire merchandise, and transfer funds around the globe at the speed of light."

That's the setting for this chapter on how the Internet might affect e-commerce around the world. This chapter is not intended as a primer on the Internet but instead covers that one aspect of the Net called "business-to-business" (B2B).

Therefore, this chapter was written for current and would-be international marketing executives who view the Internet as an electronic pathway to fresh new markets overseas.

Specifically, it is intended for managers in the businesses described in chapter 9 who are eager to export their products outside the United States. The Internet offers a slick method to open new markets, create incremental business, and gather fresh profits.

In this chapter, you will learn the answers to the following questions about using the Internet for international commerce:

- What is meant by "the Information Age?"
- What are "business-to-business (B2B) marketplaces"?
- Is your business "consumer-friendly" for international e-commerce?
- What New Age tools are available for the modern international manager?
- Exactly how will the Internet aid communications in international business?
- How are Internet auctions handled?
- How does online learning help the international business manager?

- What should you know about security checks?
- Will the Internet make the role of the international marketing manager obsolete?
- What are some guidelines for selling over the Internet?

Finally, what does all this portend for the thousands of traditional international marketing managers who are accustomed to regular, lengthy trips overseas in search of new orders? Will they no longer have to travel to distant lands and instead transact their business by simply sitting in home offices in front of computer screens?

This chapter will examine those important questions—and many other related ones—in detail. But first, some background to set the stage.

The Information Age

The definition of "the Information Age" is, according to some experts, the convergence or confluence of the telephone, the television, and the computer. Children today have grown up knowing all three . . . plus more new and exciting electronic devices. People from past generations can remember when telephones had dial systems, when television appeared only in black and white, and when the electronic calculator was the new wizard in technology.

Decades ago, there were demonstrations of the conjoining of telephones and television, where our images would be transported to small screens over telephone lines and the telephone, not our computers, would be the prime carrier of our images. It was first demonstrated at the 1964 New York World's Fair and was called "video telephony." Today video phones are sweeping the market; one example is Motorola's Ojo Personal Video Phone, PVP-100.

Now we have access to the marriage of all three: computers, telephones, and television. Millions of new jobs and new careers have resulted, and individuals and companies can think and work globally instead of only nationally. Just one of the technological advancements of this new age is the GMPCS (Global Mobile Personal Communication Services) satellite system. This constellation of powerful satellites is constantly orbiting the earth offering voice, video, fax, and data transmissions. Almost every corner of the globe is now accessible via instant communications.

One form of fast communication is found in "instant messaging," dubbed "e-mail on steroids" by Stu Durland in the August 2004 issue of *National Underwriter* magazine. The instant message service is offered by major Internet service providers (such as AOL), as well as by individual firms. A user maintains a list of people whom he or she wishes to communicate with by computer. At any time of the day or night, a user can send messages to a compatriot or see who is available to receive a message and with one click start a back-and-forth conversation. One can also have "chat room" conversations among a multitude of users. The advantages are obvious: speedy, real-time communications at low cost. But there are some risks. Messages can be intercepted; workers can do instant messaging with acquaintances and not with fellow employees and business contacts. So, avoid sending sensitive material without encryption or password protection.

B2B Marketplaces

B2B is an important, frequently used term that refers to business-to-business electronic marketplaces that use the Internet to electronically connect with one another. Before the advent of the Internet, the term simply referred to one business directly doing business with another. Today, because of e-commerce, B2Bs are estimated to handle billions of dollars in sales and purchases, and some people estimate that the volume of commerce transacted through B2Bs will amount to trillions of dollars over the next decade.

Consequently, the U.S. Federal Trade Commission (FTC) has conducted extensive research on this enormous trend. Just one conclusion reached in the FTC's study was that "the Internet technology that powers B2Bs is potentially transformative in that it can speed business-to-business communications into 'real-time' transactions, conducted globally, with heightened accuracy and reduced waste, thus increasing the nation's productivity."

B2Bs, according to the FTC, are remarkably diverse. They serve a broad array of industries, from metals to fresh produce, to hotels, to chemicals, to energy, either across various industries or vertically in only one industry. (Parenthetically, my own firm, The Parker Pen

Company, established a business-to-business operation long before the days of electronic commerce. Parker merely sold pens directly to a variety of end users—read "businesses"—that used writing instruments for advertising, for service awards, as premiums, and for corporate gifts; in addition, Parker, of course, sold pens directly to customers via conventional retail channels. Today, the term *B2B* usually refers to *electronic* commerce.)

B2Bs can be organized under a variety of ownership structures; some are founded by the companies that use them; others are founded by third parties that do not plan to buy or sell through them; some are a blend of the two.

Prices in B2Bs can likewise be established in various ways: by auction, catalog, a bid-ask system, or negotiation. B2Bs may earn revenue from multiple sources, including transaction-related fees, membership fees, service fees, and advertising and marketing fees and from sales of data and information.

B2Bs can foster efficiency in a variety of ways. They can reduce administrative costs and search costs and make it easier for buyers to comparison shop. Reduced search costs mean that suppliers can have greater and cheaper access to more potential customers. B2B marketplaces have the potential to win lower prices, improve quality, and result in greater innovation for consumers. According to the FTC, one business analyst commented that "From a very macro perspective, B2B e-commerce is simply the next generation of productivity growth for the U.S. economy."

Furthermore, B2Bs can make it easier for buyers to comparison shop; instead of thumbing through bulky paper catalogs, consumers can search for products quickly and efficiently online.

The FTC survey indicated that B2Bs may raise a variety of antitrust issues; however, the panelists agreed that antitrust concerns are amenable to traditional antitrust analysis.

Is Your Business Consumer-Friendly for International E-Commerce?

The FTC asked this key question of a panel of specialists several years ago in response to the query "What should the competition policies be in the world of B2B electronic marketplaces?" The panelists not only helped to define the parameters of B2B, as laid out previously, but from that conference came the following checklist to help determine whether any specific business was prepared to venture forward.

The checklist consisted of three basic parts:

1. Do you clearly disclose on your Web site a variety of key points?
2. Do you use fair business, advertising, and marketing practices?
3. Do you use fair information practices?

Here is a more detailed checklist for each question:

DO YOU CLEARLY DISCLOSE ON YOUR WEB SITE THE FOLLOWING KEY INFORMATION:

ABOUT YOURSELF:

- What kind of business you operate?
- Your physical business address, including the country, and an e-mail address or a telephone number that consumers can use to contact you easily?

ABOUT THE SALE:

- What you are selling, with enough details that consumers can make informed buying decisions?
- A list of total costs you'll collect from the customer, and the currency used?
- The existence of other routine costs?
- Any restrictions or limitations on the sale?
- Any warranties or guarantees associated with the sale?
- An estimation of when the buyer should receive the order?
- Details about the availability of convenient and safe payment options?

ABOUT YOUR CONSUMER PROTECTIONS:

- Your return policy, including an explanation of how a consumer can return an item, get a refund or a credit, or make an exchange?

- Where the consumer should call, write, or e-mail with complaints or problems?
- The opportunity for a consumer to keep a record of the transaction?
- Your policies on sending unsolicited e-mail solicitations to consumers, including an opportunity for consumers to decline these offers?
- Information about easy-to-use and affordable dispute-resolution programs you participate in?

DO YOU USE FAIR BUSINESS, ADVERTISING, AND MARKETING PRACTICES?

- Do you provide truthful, accurate, and clear information on your Web site?
- Can you back up the claims you make about your goods and services?
- Are your advertising and marketing materials identifiable to consumers as such?
- Do you disclose who's sponsoring an ad if it's not otherwise clear to consumers?
- Do you respect consumers' choices not to receive e-mail solicitations?
- Do you take special care when advertising to children?

DO YOU USE FAIR INFORMATION PRACTICES THAT INCLUDE:

- A notice to consumers about your information-collection practices, such as what personally identifiable information you collect, how you use it, and whether and with whom you share it?
- Choices about how personally identifiable information is used and whether it is shared with others?
- Procedures to ensure accuracy, including, for example, allowing consumers reasonable access to their information?
- Security measures that are appropriate to the transactions on your Web site?

We now turn to the tools a "New Age" international marketing manager can use to implement all of the previous practices.

New Tools for the New Age International Manager

The "Old Age" international manager relied, first, on "snail mail," then on telegrams, then on the telex, then on the telephone, and now on facsimile machines.

The "New Age" manager has a whole new collection of communication tools. The World Wide Web, invented in the late 1970s and early 1980s, has become an information source to billions of people, grander than any encyclopedia anyone ever imagined. The Internet, on which the World Wide Web runs, offers an unimaginable amount of information at speeds that are almost instantaneous.

This new Information Age has allowed companies, as well as single individuals, to create electronic Web sites. With these Web sites, even the smallest company can give potential customers access to its products or services. Therefore, the Internet and its World Wide Web offers us the globe as a marketplace for our business-to-business ventures.

Now, consider the ubiquitous cell phone. According to the research firm Garnter Inc., it is estimated that global sales of cell phones—which are increasingly able to access the Internet—will reach one billion in the year 2009. Asia remains the fastest-growing region, accounting for one of every four phones sold; this will increase to one in three in 2009.

In addition to the popularity of cell phones there is the advent of e-mail. The first e-mail was sent between two computers in 1972, and since then, the symbol "@" has taken on a whole new meaning. E-mail lets even the most modest user communicate quickly and inexpensively with people in just about every part of the world. Moreover, business forms, advertising artwork, questionnaires, and all kinds of printed forms can be transmitted, bills can be paid, and families can stay in touch whether they are in the farmlands of the Midwest or the battlefields of Iraq.

The next step in this grand evolution is "real-time" moving images of ourselves and our distant contacts appearing on our laptops or on screens in conference rooms. Today, high-speed Internet connections are routinely being used by banks, law firms, corporations, and other businesses to permit face-to-face dialogues. It is called "video conferencing," and the equipment it requires includes encrypted messaging systems, digitized video streaming software, plasma screens, video cameras, microphones, and speakers. In conferencing, two groups assemble in conference rooms thousands of miles apart, their images are cast on large screens, and the meeting begins. Video conferencing can also include person-to-person meetings from hotel rooms back to corporate headquarters or conference rooms; it is easily done on a laptop equipped with a camera, all very inexpensively.

Next on the horizon is three-dimensional imaging. Such holographic imaging is already being used in laboratories and could evolve into capabilities that we've seen only in futuristic TV shows and movies. We remember it on the TV series *Star Trek*, where Captain Kirk would issue that iconic phrase "Beam me up, Scotty," meaning "Send my three-dimensional image to some other location."

Instead of sitting in front of a camera and seeing a one-dimensional image on a flat screen, we will see and converse with one another's high definition 3-D image transported to the chair across the table, just as if that person were sitting there in reality.

In short, the Internet has caused a major revolution in efficient communications. We can now communicate faster, farther, and cheaper than ever before in our history.

But what impact will this have in regard to world travel? What will it mean for the international marketing manager who has spent his or her early career living out of a suitcase? Clearly, businesses are using the technology of Web conferencing more often because of the rising costs of traveling, both domestically and internationally. Personal travel, with the related expenses of meals and accommodations, becomes less attractive when a sales manager can communicate via e-mails and Web-based conferencing. Surely, personal travel for purposes of commerce can be reduced . . . but can it be completely eliminated? No, of course not.

What are some *specific* advantages the Internet brings to international commerce? Here are some answers.

Using the Internet for Routine Communications

Exactly how will the Internet impact tomorrow's international business? Let's begin with the easiest and most obvious benefit that the Internet has brought to e-commerce—daily, routine business communications.

There is absolutely no doubt that the Internet—primarily, e-mail—vastly improves the speed, content, and ease of everyday business tasks such as these:

- Sending simple, routine daily messages at any hour of the day about miscellaneous topics that, in the past, would have been communicated by telephone, fax, or hard-copy mail.

- Communicating day-to-day marketing matters between a source and its customers, such as the placing of orders, sales results for the previous week or month, sales forecasts, information about competitors' actions, price lists, and so on.

- Discovering glitches in shipments and deliveries.

- Resolving problems regarding product performance and quality.

- If communication is between a source and its wholesalers or other types of distributors abroad, the e-mails can specify inventory levels and forecasts for future orders. Similarly, in routine financial reporting between subsidiaries, franchisees, or licensees, information can be relayed about the previous month's or quarter's profit and loss statements, as well as balance sheet data.

- Exchanging ideas about the current marketing plans and modifications for the future.

- Keeping track of personnel data, such as the addition or loss of key employees.

- Answering questions about simple legal matters or other company policies.

- Sending copies of proposed advertising, sales promotion materials, and packaging artwork, along with proposed translations to check for accuracies.
- Coordinating travel schedules for managers in the home office and the overseas branch, agent, or wholesaler.

Businesses are also quickly moving to an "Intranet" with tools like SharePoint that allow colleagues to share documents from the same file without cluttering up servers with huge amounts of e-mail. SharePoint and Lotus Notes are business collaboration tools used especially within a business's own network. An Intranet is a piece of the Internet carved out virtually for a business that no one outside the business can access.

As each year passes, communications are being facilitated by other technological devices such as Internet phone services, total international cell phone access, teleconferencing, BlackBerrys, and other types of mobile, portable, handheld equipment (called personal digital assistants, or PDAs). And there is more:

- Internet phone service (also called VoIP for voice over internet protocol) is currently being used by millions of people for both local and long distance calls via either desktop or laptop computers. It requires only an Internet connection, and there are free telephonelike services available (e.g., Skype) that you can set up yourself. The result is that your laptop or PC acts just like a telephone.
- Cell phones that work anywhere in the world are already readily available and are becoming less expensive. (I had a house guest in my Midwestern home recently who was awakened several times each night by direct cell phone calls from Djibouti, the capital of the former French Somaliland, on the southern entrance to the Red Sea.)
- A trademarked combination of a cell phone and an Internet receiver called BlackBerry began in 1998. Celebrities like Al Gore and Oprah Winfrey helped to publicize it. In 2005, George Stephanopoulos, the former adviser to

President Clinton, wrote a piece in *Time* magazine about it. He said that some users seem to depend on their Black-Berrys almost as much as their wristwatches. It liberates them from their offices but also chains them to anyone who can access them. Stephanopoulos wrote, "Does that also make it easier to avoid the deeper connection that happens face-to-face (when we aren't tempted to steal a glance at the BlackBerry on the table)?"

The new mobile communications networks consist of (1) wireless transmission systems, (2) mobile products (PDAs, cell phones, laptop computers), and (3) applications to run on mobile products.

If all these technological, wizard-type products make your head spin, odds are you will get dizzier and dizzier with each passing year because of the innovations ahead.

Meanwhile, it is necessary to pause on occasion and remember some simple rules for the most basic of all Internet usage, e-mail. These rules might be called "e-etiquette." Here are a few rules, according to *American Salesman* magazine:

- The subject line is critical and should be similar to a book title or a chapter heading.
- While e-mails are termed "instant communication," be patient for responses.
- Don't turn your e-mails into short, rapid dialogues back and forth. Send complete messages, but if you simply want an acknowledgment, say so.
- Remember, there is a great difference between the "Reply" button and the "Reply to All" button. The first is intended as a reply to the original sender; the second will send your message to all the addresses on the original message.
- Avoid forwarding long, amusing stories and lists to a whole host of friends and associates. E-mail nationwide is being cluttered with these often unnecessary messages.

Now we turn to the actual practices of buying and selling over the Internet.

Internet Auctions

In June 2004, the Federal Trade Commission published a very useful and informative guide to Internet auctions. You can obtain a copy by contacting the FTC at www.ftc.gov. Here are some essential things to know about this hot phenomenon, which began in 1995.

Internet auctions offer buyers a "virtual" flea market from which to choose an endless array of merchandise from around the world. They also provide sellers with a worldwide storefront from which to market their goods. One of the most popular and successful of these aimed at the general consumer is, of course, eBay.

Huge corporations such as car companies and aircraft producers, however, use these Internet auctions to issue specifications for a simple, high-volume part and then invite suppliers any place in the world to bid for a contract to provide that part. The prize goes to the lowest bidder. This is often called a "Dutch auction." Auctions such as these have already saved millions of dollars for American manufacturers.

Less grand and more individual online auctions can be risky business when it comes to fraud, deception, and unfair practices in the marketplace. According to the FTC, complaints generally deal with late shipments, no shipment, or shipment of products that aren't the same quality as advertised; bogus online payment or escrow services; and fraudulent dealers who lure bidders from legitimate auction sites with seemingly better deals. Most complaints involve sellers, but in some cases, the buyers are the focus.

Here are some basic rules for both sellers and buyers:

- Internet auctions are online bazaars. Some are business sites that physically control the merchandise for sale and then accept payment for the goods. Others are person-to-person activities where the seller—not the site—has the merchandise.

- These person-to-person sites require the seller to register and obtain a "user account name" or a "screen name" before he or she can place items for bid. Sellers must also agree to pay a fee every time they conduct an auction.

- Many sellers also set a time limit on bidding and, in some cases, a "reserve price," meaning the lowest price they will accept for an item. When the bidding closes at the scheduled time, the highest bidder "wins." If no one bids at or above the reserve price, the auction closes without a "winner."

- Successful bidders usually pay by credit card, debit card, personal check, cashier's check, money order, or cash on delivery. Credit cards may offer buyers the best protection; however, online payment services offered by many banks today are also popular with both buyers and sellers. To complete a transaction, the buyer tells the online payment service to direct appropriate funds to the seller.

- Before bidding, try to become familiar with the auction site. Never assume that the rules of one auction site apply to another. If the site offers a step-by-step tutorial on the bidding process, use it. Find out what protections the auction site offers buyers. Some sites provide free insurance or guarantees for items that are undelivered, nonauthentic, or not what the seller claimed. Try to determine the relative value of an item before you bid. Be skeptical if the price sounds too low to be realistic.

- Check on warranties and who pays for shipping and delivery. Check on the seller's return policy. If you have questions, e-mail or phone the seller.

- When bidding, establish your top price and stick to it. Save all transaction information.

- Before paying, know and understand what form of payment the seller accepts. Protect your privacy. Never provide your Social Security number, driver's license number, credit card number, or bank account information until you have checked out the seller and are certain that you are using an encrypted site.

- Many sellers use online escrow services to handle payments. Check them out with a Better Business Bureau or a state consumer protection agency. To limit your exposure, consider reserving a separate credit card, stored-value card, or bank account to use only for online transactions.

When problems arise, here are some places to turn for help:

- The attorney general's office in your state
- Your county or state consumer protection agency. Check the phone book for listings of county and state government offices.
- The Better Business Bureau
- The Federal Trade Commission. File a complaint online at www.ftc.gov or call toll-free 1-877-FTC-HELP (1-877-382-4357).

Online Learning

Another aspect of the Internet that may interest our venerable international marketing executive is e-learning, or "online learning," as it is often called. Entire university systems have taken up this specialized form of education, with the University of Phoenix in Arizona being one of the prime examples.

Phil Britt in *EContent* magazine wrote that across the country and throughout the world, large firms are using e-learning via the Internet to educate their employees and customers wherever they are. With estimates of growth at 11 percent per year, by 2007 e-learning is estimated to be a $5 billion industry. Within this new form of education, the terms *synchronously* or *asynchronously* are used frequently. The latter refers to the ability of a user to access the so-called classroom at any time of the day or night that he or she wishes, whereas the former term refers to accessing in "real time," meaning only at the original time and place. Britt wrote that in the United States, "An estimated 80% to 90% of all companies and organizations with more than 10,000 or more employees are either currently creating e-learning internally or are planning to do so." Our international marketing executive can use these electronic "classrooms" to train salespeople overseas, to train service personnel for repairs, or simply to educate overseas customers about new products.

Universities routinely offer degree completion programs via e-learning. Just one example is a woman located in Florida who took all of her nursing degree courses via the Internet from the University of Wisconsin campus in Green Bay, Wisconsin. She never actually saw or visited the campus itself until she decided it might be fun to travel there to accept her diploma. Early research that compared e-learning with learning in the actual classroom shows that there is little loss of quality between the two. E-learning programs can also be modified easily and as needed.

Unfortunately, there can be a nefarious side to e-learning around the world in the form of bogus college or university "degrees for sale" houses, primarily located in the Far East. These spam-type senders offer "official" degree diplomas—undergraduate, graduate, medical, legal, and so on—for a modest fee, sometimes under $100. If you haven't received one of these offers yet, you probably will!

Security Checks

The U.S. Federal Trade Commission warns that when consumers open accounts, register to receive information, or purchase products from your business, it's very likely that they entrust their personal information to you as part of the process. If their information is compromised, the consequences can be far-reaching: consumers can be at risk of identity theft, or they can become less willing—or even unwilling—to continue to do business with you.

Paraphrasing from the FTC publication, these days it's just common sense that any business—here or overseas—that collects personal information from consumers also should have a security plan to protect the confidentiality and integrity of the information. Financial institutions are especially required to have a security plan for just that purpose.

Threats to the security of your information are varied, from computer hackers to disgruntled employees, to simple carelessness. While protecting computer systems is an important aspect of information security, it is only part of the process. As an example, the executive education unit of the School of Business at the University of Wisconsin (Madison) begins each and every morning with a complete computerized check for hackers or other illegal forms of access to its data bank.

Consider these points (issued by the FTC) when designing and implementing your information security plan:

- Implement regular risk-assessment programs to identify internal and external risks to the security, confidentiality, and integrity of your customers' personal information.

- Periodically monitor and test the safeguards.

- Adjust your security plan according to the results of the testing.

Although the security planning process is universal, there's no "one size fits all" security plan. Every business faces its own special risks. Safeguards depend on the size and complexity of the business, the nature and scope of the business, and the sensitivity of the consumer information it keeps.

The FTC offers two Web sites to help you tackle the most serious threats:

1. *The 20 Most Critical Internet Security Vulnerabilities* (www .sans.org/top20) was produced by the SANS Institute and the FBI. It describes the twenty most commonly exploited vulnerabilities in Windows and UNIX. Although thousands of security incidents affect these operating systems each year, the majority of successful attacks target one or more of the vulnerabilities on this list. This site also has links to scanning tools and services to help you monitor your own network vulnerabilities at www.sans.org/top20/tools.pdf.

2. *The 10 Most Critical Web Application Security Vulnerabilities* (www.owasp.org) was produced by the Open Web Application Security Projects (OWASP). It describes common vulnerabilities for Web applications and the most effective ways to address them. Attacks on Web applications often

pass undetected through firewalls and other network defense systems, putting at risk the sensitive information that these applications access.

IT experts suggest that companies without highly trained network security staff should outsource to highly rated companies that offer security.

For more information on privacy and information security, access the Gramm-Leach-Bliley Safeguards Rule at www.ftc.gov/privacy. Or, contact the FTC toll-free at 1-877-FTC-HELP (1-877-382-4357). The FTC enters Internet, telemarketing, identity theft, and other fraud-related complaints into Consumer Sentinel, a secure online database available to hundreds of civil and criminal law enforcement agencies in the United States and abroad.

Will the Internet Make the International Marketing Manager Obsolete?

Now that we've surveyed some of the revolutionary and positive effects of e-commerce and the Internet on both domestic and international business, it's time to once again examine the crucial question: what does all this mean for the traditional American executive who is responsible for dealing with clients, customers, and other contacts around the world? Will it mean that he or she will simply sit in an office accessing all of the company's customers via a laptop or a desktop PC? Will it mean tremendous dollar savings in unnecessary travel and accommodations? Will it end that insidious malady known as "jet lag"? In other words, will it mean conducting business *totally* via electronic technology?

To begin to answer this intriguing question, let me regress to the year 1957. That was the year after I joined The Parker Pen Company. I vividly remember it was also the year Parker assigned a talented researcher to do a study on the future of the pen, or "hand-held writing instrument," as it was called. In the 1950s, almost everyone had a fountain pen or a ballpoint pen, the latter having been introduced to the world just ten years earlier. Such a "hand-held writing instrument" was a valuable personal product, regarded as essential as one's wristwatch or eyeglasses. Pens were used by people at home and in offices almost every hour of every day for writing notes, letters, signatures, checks, or other such daily tasks.

It was also about this time, however, that the first plastic credit cards started to appear. Here was an innovation that, on first examination, seemed to completely eliminate the need to write out checks by hand. Our researcher came to the conclusion that in light of this development, "in this new 'checkless society,' the hand-held writing instrument will become obsolete."

So there I was, a junior executive new to a company that appeared to be facing early obsolescence. What a grim future! Fortunately, our futurist was wrong. In fact, totally wrong! Ironically, today we probably have more "hand-held writing instruments" in public use than at any other period in history. We simply cannot get along without them. So, the plastic credit card did not make handwriting obsolete.

Now let's apply that lesson to e-commerce and the Internet. With the sea change in personal communications documented earlier in this chapter, it's agreed that the Internet will have a profound and beneficial effect on many of the duties of an international sales or marketing executive. But will it eliminate the need to personally fly thousands of miles around the world seeking new sales and new distribution outlets?

My answer—and the answer of dozens of my fellow international executives whom I have interviewed in the last ten years—is a resounding "No!"

Let me explain. In chapter 9, I describe the two basic types of business cultures in the world: (1) the "deal-focused" culture, and (2) the "relationship-focused" culture. The former describes the United States, Canada, and much of Central Europe, and refers to our dictums in business stressing that "time is money . . . don't waste time in socializing . . . the deal is the goal, so get the deal signed and move on to the next market." The latter type—"relationship-focused" cultures—refers to the way business is conducted in much of the Far East, the Middle East, Southeast Asia, and all of Latin America. In those regions, the "relationship" is just as important as the "deal." People in these regions rely on building personal rapport between individuals in business and on creating a sense of mutual integrity, honesty, and trust. They view your company as a shadowy entity thousands of miles away, back in the United States. It is you, the person representing your company, who is the key contact.

In international business these two cultural traits often clash. We Americans enter a "relationship-focused" culture with our "deal-focused" dictums that say, "Don't waste time visiting museums, indulging in long lunches or dinners, or generally socializing before getting down to business." Meanwhile, our counterparts in "relationship-focused cultures" want more time to "get to know you." They want to build strong relationships before "getting down to business." In some countries this may take hours—even days or even multiple visits before a deal or a contract is signed.

A veteran American international businessman put it bluntly. Having done business in East Asia for many years, he knew the value of frequent late-night visits to restaurants and nightclubs with his customers, involving long multicourse meals and the imbibing of wines and liquors. He put it this way: "In this new age of e-commerce and the Internet, if my customer in Japan or Hong Kong or Taipei is a computer—a computer that places orders with me automatically—it's hard for me to take that computer out one night and get drunk with it!"

Another executive was even more descriptive. He said, "When a crisis occurs at the other end of our distribution chain, I don't want to travel over there and smash a *computer*. I want that single throat to choke!"

Another example of how new technologies and new developments do not necessarily make the old ways obsolete occurred in the United States after World War II. At that time, the two largest retailers in the United States were Sears, Roebuck & Co. and Montgomery Ward. The two giant companies were fierce rivals, each with hundreds of retail outlets spread across the United States. After WWII, the management of Ward, then headed by Avery Sewell, looked into the future, determined that there would be a recession, and thus restricted its growth of retail stores. General Robert E. Wood, the president of Sears, saw it differently. He determined that the postwar years were a time to expand, to invest in more retail outlets but also to expand into a totally new form of retailing—*catalog sales stores*. It was a partial throwback to Sears's origins in the late nineteenth century when a thick Sears catalog was an icon and mail orders were just as common as retail sales. At that time Sears catalogs could be found in the homes of millions of Americans, many of them located on farms and in other wide-open spaces of the country, where it was difficult to actually visit a retail store.

Wood's new idea was simple: combine the catalog system with small—very small—stores. In that way, customers could walk into a catalog sales store, examine a catalog, deal with a clerk, and possibly even inspect samples of the products, then place orders that would be shipped directly to their homes. These Sears catalog stores quickly spread across the country. They may have helped to give birth to the present-day macrodistribution business, known as the "catalog sales" channel, which has become enormous in worldwide commerce. Wood's catalog stores are just a memory now, but mass distribution of catalogs once again reigns. Today, throughout the United States, both retail stores and the ubiquitous mail order catalogs thrive side by side.

The same may apply to the old way of generating international sales. That old way means packing a suitcase, filling a sales sample case, and boarding international flights for points all across the globe. The new way means e-mails, video conferencing, cell phones, and—eventually, as described earlier—3-D holographic imaging. But the new way still has a fundamental need for the eyeball-to-eyeball, across the desk, personal relationship.

So, to answer the question at hand, I believe that e-commerce and the Internet will greatly improve communication modes and facilitate international commerce, but they will not make the need for person-to-person relationships obsolete.

Time will tell.

Some Guidelines for Selling over the Internet

Before you sell your product or services via e-commerce, the Federal Trade Commission has issued guidelines that have been adopted by twenty-nine countries working together as members of the Organization for Economic Cooperation and Development.

According to the FTC, these guidelines set out principles for voluntary codes of conduct for businesses involved in electronic commerce. The guidelines offer advice to governments in evaluating their consumer-protection laws regarding electronic commerce. They also tell consumers what to expect and what to look for when shopping online.

According to the FTC, "The goal is to build consumer confidence in the global electronic marketplace by working to ensure that consumers are just as safe when shopping online as when shopping offline—no matter where they live or where the company they do business with is based."

Following are nine guidelines, as spelled out in the FTC report titled "Electronic Commerce: Selling Internationally—A Guide for Businesses," dated March 2000.

E-businesses that adhere to the guidelines must:

1. *Use fair business, advertising, and marketing practices.* They (must) provide truthful, accurate, and complete information to consumers and avoid deceptive, misleading, or unfair claims, omissions, or practices. The businesses must also back up all claims, such as claims about how well a product works or how quickly a product will arrive. They must make sure that advertising and marketing are identifiable as such and, when appropriate, identify the ads' sponsors.

2. *Provide accurate, clear, and easily accessible information about the company and the goods or services it offers.* They must disclose the information consumers need to understand whom they are dealing with and what they are buying. They must post the company's name, its physical address, including the country, and an e-mail address or a telephone number that consumers can use if they have questions or problems. They also must provide a clear, complete description of the product or the service being offered.

3. *Disclose full information about the terms, the conditions, and the costs of the transaction.* This means providing consumers with a full itemized list of costs involved in the transaction,

designating the currency required, as well as the terms of delivery or performance and the terms, the conditions, and the method of payment. If appropriate, they must also include information about restrictions, limitations, or conditions of the purchase; instructions for proper use of the product and any safety and health-care warnings; warranties and guarantees; cancellation or refund policies; and whether after-sale service is available. If it's possible to carry out a transaction in more than one language, they must make available all important terms and conditions in each language.

4. *Ensure that consumers know they are making a commitment to buy before closing the deal.* These businesses must take steps to protect consumers who are merely "surfing" the Internet from unknowingly entering into a sales contract. They must give the consumer a chance to change the order before committing to the purchase or to cancel it altogether. They must also allow the consumer to keep a record of the transaction.

5. *Provide an easy-to-use and secure method for online payments.* They should adopt security measures appropriate to the transactions to make sure that personal information is less vulnerable to hackers. (See further on for more details on payments.)

6. *Protect consumer privacy during electronic commerce transactions.* They must disclose their privacy policies or information practice statements prominently on their Web sites, and offer people choices about how their personal information will be used. They must give consumers the opportunity to refuse having their personal information shared with others or used for promotional purposes.

7. *Address consumer complaints and difficulties.* They must have policies and procedures to address consumer problems quickly and fairly and without excessive cost or inconvenience to the consumer. They must also take advantage of alternative dispute-resolution mechanisms.

8. *Adopt fair, effective, and easy-to-understand self-regulatory policies and procedures.* They must extend to electronic commerce the same basic level of protections that cover other forms of commerce. The agreement encourages businesses to work with consumer representatives to develop policies and procedures that give consumers the tools they need to make informed decisions and to resolve complaints.

9. *Help to educate consumers about electronic commerce.* In this way, they are helping to create a consumer-friendly electronic marketplace. These businesses work with governments and consumer representatives to ensure that consumers understand their rights and responsibilities when participating in online commerce.

Years ago, when someone prepared to travel internationally—whether on business or as a tourist—the mantra was "Passport, money, and tickets—that's all you really need to travel almost anyplace in the world."

Today, that basic list still applies but with several amendments: a *valid* passport and visa(s), money (in the form of at least two credit cards, plus a sensible amount of cash or traveler's checks), and tickets. And, of course, don't forget your medications and a few changes of clothes.

But today, wise travelers abroad also consider other essentials: several types of insurance (health and cancellation), reading material that provides background information on your destination(s), and information on how to communicate with your home base (e.g., international phone cards or cell phone services).

You'll find a more complete checklist in the next chapter, "Essential Things to Know When Preparing for Travel Abroad."

7

Essential Things to Know When Preparing for Travel Abroad

Take twice the money and half the clothes.

—An experienced world traveler

Remember how simple it was ten years ago to plan and schedule a trip overseas? Pick up the phone and call a travel agency. No fees, no hassles, lots of support information about routes, costs, visas, and alternate flight schedules.

Since that time, major innovations have evolved: Homeland Security, airlines filing for bankruptcy, booking flights via the Internet, airlines putting the squeeze on travel agencies by reducing or eliminating commissions, diminishing frequent-flyer perks . . . these are just a few. Travel books published just ten years ago contained little or nothing about these modern developments.

Travel agents have rebounded by concentrating on cruises and packaged tours. Of course, they can and will still book airline flights, but they are forced to charge the traveler a flat fee for the service rather than offer the service free because in the past they received commissions from the airlines. In direct competition are the online booking sites such as www.expedia.com, www.travelocity.com, and www.priceline.com, which advertise discounted fares and rates for airlines, hotels, auto rentals, cruises, and so on.

The Internet offers multiple ways to book flights, reserve hotel rooms, research destinations, and get weather forecasts for any major city in the world.

In summary, preparing for your trip abroad has taken on, not one, but several new dimensions.

Here are some suggestions to help you prepare for your trip abroad:

- Let's start with books that are currently available to assist you with overseas travel. Almost any bookstore, but especially bookstores that specialize in travel, will have a huge assortment of helpful books. Also, don't forget to check your local library for the same materials.

- Then there is our old friend the local travel agent, who can do much, if not all, of the work for you. With the airlines and the online booking sites squeezing travel agents out, however, they are increasingly focusing on travel packages, cruises, and the like.

- Finally, there is the lure of the Internet. You'll encounter a mind-boggling array of Web sites to examine. Ironically, one of those—www.travelsense.org—is operated by ASTA (the American Society of Travel Agents) and offers many pages of helpful travel tips. These services are outlined at the end of this chapter.

Essential Things to Do before You Leave

Do your homework on the country—and the culture—you'll be visiting. Your local library, bookstore, and a new genie—your computer and the Internet—will provide you with reams of background information.

- Check your calendar. Not a U.S. calendar but one for your destination country or countries. Learn whether any national holidays are scheduled for your travel dates. It's taboo to try to conduct business in a host's country's holiday period. For instance, in much of Europe, the entire month of August is considered the annual vacation period. In East Asia, the New Year holidays are fifteen-day periods that shift from January through February because they are determined by a lunar calendar. In the Middle East, Ramadan is a most holy period when locals must fast from sunrise to sunset—obviously, not a good time for a visitor to drop in. It varies throughout the year. One international planner lists holidays for every country and religion worldwide and can be purchased from www.go-global.com. The planner also provides all international country codes, metric and U.S. standard conversion tables, airline distances between cities, and more.

- Order an extra supply of business cards. You'll be passing them out like candy to children. Also, make business appointments well in advance. Don't expect to be successful if you wait to set up appointments after you disembark from the airplane.

- School yourself on how you will communicate back and forth with your home office, whether by international cell phone, fax, Internet, or whatever. The fax machine is particularly inexpensive for folks at home to keep in touch with you if you have provided them with fax numbers at the hotel or the business you'll be visiting; however, the charges for sending faxes back to the United States from your hotel overseas can sometimes be significant.

- Plan to keep a daily journal. Take notes on everything. You'll be amazed at how memories fade from one country to the next, and how helpful those little jottings will be on your future visits.

- As suggested earlier in this book, make copies of your passport, driver's license, and all credit cards. Stow them away in a suitcase or another safe place, in the event you lose a wallet or a purse. If you lose your passport, the nearest U.S. embassy or consulate will reissue it if you can produce a photocopy of the original.

- Make certain that your medical insurance follows you abroad. For instance, Medicare does not. (See more on medical insurance later in this chapter.)

- Pack an extra dose of patience because doing business overseas usually takes more time than expected.

- Do you or does a member of your travel group have food allergies? Go to www.foodallergy.org. There you can buy one of two booklets, "Dining Out and Traveling with Food Allergies," or "Traveling with a Food Allergy: Foreign Sources of Information."

- What about wheelchair-accessible accommodations? Go to www.sath.org, run by the Society for Accessible Travel and Hospitality, which offers links to sites of wheelchair-accessible locations.

- A third valuable site for medical emergencies belongs to the U.S. State Department. You will be directed to English-speaking physicians and hospitals around the world via www.travel.state.gov. Or, if you are already in your foreign destination, go to your local embassy or consulate for information on English-speaking health-care sources.

Avoiding That Crazy Malady Called Jet Lag

A story has been told and retold that when John Foster Dulles served as U.S. secretary of state (1953–1959), he paid a visit to Egypt to negotiate American assistance in the building of the Aswan Dam, a huge dam that would be 1.25 miles long and would span the Nile River. Slated to provide an enormous supply of electrical energy, the dam would be of major benefit to the country. According to Dulles's own account, however, he became irritated during the talks and abruptly broke them off. Quickly taking his place was our old Cold War adversary at the time, Russia, which agreed to support the project and thus acquired the friendship and cooperation of the Egyptians for several decades, wielding increased influence in the Middle East. Later, Dulles attributed his poor diplomacy and timing to one thing—jet lag! He claimed it left him disoriented, and he lost an important hydroelectric project and the friendship of a nation all because of lack of sleep.

What is this insidious ailment that can affect our acumen so significantly, and what causes it?

The answer lies in our own natural wake-sleep rhythms, called either *diurnal* or *circadian rhythms*. These terms basically mean being accustomed to staying awake during the daytime hours and then sleeping during the nighttime period. Over the years, our bodies become attuned to this pattern of sleep and wakefulness. We all know that lack of sleep causes agitation, irritability, and weariness. When we board an airliner for an eight, ten, or twelve-hour flight, we rudely interrupt our sleep pattern by passing through numerous time zones. Thus a plane leaving Chicago at 6:00 p.m. for an eight-hour flight to London arrives there at 8:00 a.m. local time . . . but that's only 2:00 a.m. "body time." No wonder our bodies complain and resist.

There is no simple cure for jet lag, and some people suffer more than others. The highly respected travel guru Peter Greenberg claims it never bothers him, but in my own thirty years of international travel I have never found one magical solution. For ten years I traveled to Japan, Hong Kong, and other countries in that part of the world, visiting them as often as four times each year. I tried many methods to combat jet lag, but it always won. The results were always the same: I was sleepy when I should be awake, and awake when I should be sleepy; I had a feeling of numbness for two, even three days and a feeling that my brain was working thirty seconds behind everyone around me. Yawning was frequent; doses of caffeine would snap me out of it temporarily, only to let me return to the numbness all over again. One moment I couldn't wait to lie down, yet when I did find sleep, I'd soon wake up and be unable to return to that blessed state.

What to do? Following is a conventional list of so-called cures. I list them on the chance that one of them will succeed for you.

- Drink lots of water. Consume several glasses before your flight departs, several during the flight, and several after your arrival. This alleviates the dehydration caused by the higher oxygen content in the cabin.

- Don't turn to alcohol to make you sleep. It makes the dehydration worse and is actually a stimulant for many of us.

- Get up and exercise as best you can by walking up and down the cabin aisle.

- Some travelers have found success with melatonin, an over-the-counter hormone that can be taken as a supplement to help reset the body's clock.

- A more direct aid might be sleeping pills. Again, they come in two forms: over-the-counter brands and prescription forms. Use whichever one helps you the best.

- Some travelers start to make the time adjustment several days before departing by eating and sleeping either earlier or later, depending on whether they're flying east or west, so as to set their body clocks in time with their destinations. This technique takes planning and discipline.

- My wife swears that her formula works, but for me it's torture. When she flies, say, from Chicago to London, she knows she won't get a full night's sleep and that she'll arrive there bright and early in the morning. Therefore, on her arrival she forces herself not to succumb to taking a nap but instead toughs it out and stays awake until evening time.

- Some scientific studies claim that exposing the body to light helps to alleviate the jet lag condition. They claim that this is a way of tricking the body into thinking, "Well, it's light out so it must be daytime and I should stay awake."

- I've observed some travelers who board their flight, don a sleep mask and ear plugs, grab a pillow and a blanket, recline the seat, and try to sleep for the entire journey. That may be the only antidote—sleep itself. But I've found it awfully difficult to do when flight attendants are passing

back and forth, the captain is making repeated announce-
ments, and your seatmates are chatting or moving around.
Some observers claim that first-class passengers do this
more frequently than others do because they have more
room to recline and are disturbed less. But, again, I've
found that when you're paying thousands of dollars more
to fly first or business class, it seems counterproductive to
ignore the fine food and drink, the wonderful service, and
the extra amenities.

- Finally, another tactic is to plan your itinerary to allow a day
or two of complete rest and relaxation after you've arrived
at your destination and before embarking on strenuous
sight-seeing or a critical business session.

Travel Insurance

Things can and do go wrong when traveling. And while travel insurance can't keep the rain or cold from dampening your spirits on your
dream vacation or an important business trip, it can save you money
if you have to cancel your trip or you have a medical emergency far
away from home.

Whether for business or pleasure, international travel involves
some risks. Lost luggage, a personal emergency necessitating an early
return, a medical emergency requiring hospitalization, missed connections, lost money invested in nonrefundable tickets—all of these
make travel insurance attractive.

(The following comes from the country's leading travel insurance
provider, Travel Guard International. More information on Travel
Guard can be found on page 146.)

Over the last five or six years, travel insurance providers have
developed a wide variety of niche and customized products for virtually every type of international and domestic travel, including sport
enthusiasts, students studying abroad, business travelers, and leisure
travelers of all ages. Travel insurance falls into two categories: (1) per-
trip packaged policies designed for travelers going on a single trip, and

(2) annual plans that provide coverage for multiple trips throughout the year.

The cost of insurance is usually based on your age and the cost of your trip. As a general rule, you can assume it will cost approximately 5 to 7 percent of your total trip cost. Most plans include insurance that covers trip cancellation, trip interruption, medical evacuation, baggage loss, and travel delay.

The circumstances for reimbursement vary, depending on the insurance company. Some circumstances include the death, injury, or illness of a family member back home, but the definition of "family member" may vary by policy. Other covered reasons for trip cancellation differ slightly, depending on the company, and may include bad weather, an accident en route to the airport, financial default of the travel supplier, a terrorist incident, jury duty, military duty, fire or flood damaging your home, or a strike by airline or cruise line employees.

As with all insurance, read the small print. One key component is whether your policy covers preexisting medical conditions.

Medical Evacuation

While it's uncommon, occasionally business or leisure travelers may have an injury or an illness while traveling that requires medical evacuation. In these days of tsunamis, terrorist acts, and insurrections, however, the cost can be astronomical.

> A physician from Traverse City, Michigan, broke his hip in Sri Lanka. He had paid his insurance company $140 for travel coverage up to $300,000, including evacuation to the nearest quality medical facility. An air ambulance flew him to India, where seats were removed from a British Airways jet to accommodate him. He was flown on a stretcher to London and transferred to a flight to Toronto; then he took an air ambulance to Saginaw, Michigan, and another aircraft to Traverse City.

Some HMOs and PPOs (preferred provider organizations) typically cap their evacuation coverage at about $1,000. Other insurance plans may limit coverage only to circumstances where an injury or an illness threatens the life of the policyholder. One caveat is that you must contact the provider before the actual evacuation, not after. But the cost of an air evacuation from, say, a Caribbean island to a Miami hospital can approach six figures.

Travel Medical Insurance

One of every two travelers heading to a foreign country will experience some sort of health problem, according to Phyllis Kozarsky, a physician who consults at the U.S. Centers for Disease Control and Prevention. Most are relatively minor problems, such as traveler's diarrhea, but heart attacks, motor vehicle accidents, and other more serious conditions are also common.

As stated earlier in this book, many Americans don't realize that their health insurance coverage doesn't necessarily travel with them. Medicare and Medicaid HMOs rarely cover American travelers if they become ill or are injured while traveling outside the United States. Even if your health plans do provide coverage outside the country, you are often subject to higher deductibles and co-insurance payments.

You can find both annual and per-trip travel insurance plans that include emergency medical coverage. Typically, these plans cover doctor, hospital, or dental expenses incurred due to an accident or an illness while traveling. If you plan to travel outside the country for a long period of time—say, several months or years—you may want to consider a travel medical plan from a provider such as Multinational Underwriters (www.mnui.com).

If you decide that you don't need travel medical coverage, you should consider taking a credit card that has a high credit limit because clinics and hospitals in other countries often require payment immediately and will not wait for reimbursement through an insurer.

What Your Credit Card Covers

Your credit card may offer some travel protection or assistance services, but these rarely include actual trip cancellation benefits or emergency or medical evacuation costs. Usually, your credit card coverage will be limited to flight accident insurance (if you die in a plane crash, your beneficiary receives the policy proceeds), rental car insurance, or limited baggage insurance. Be sure to read your card's terms and conditions, or call your credit card provider's toll-free line for guidance.

For more information, visit www.travelguard.com. Travel Guard International is the industry's leading travel insurance provider, covering more than 8 million travelers worldwide each year. Based in Stevens Point, Wisconsin, Travel Guard makes its products available through a network of ten thousand travel agencies and from its Web site. In addition to providing the full range of travel insurance plans, Travel Guard offers twenty-four-hour "911" travel emergency service, emergency medical assistance, last-minute or emergency travel and flight changes, lost luggage tracking, pre-trip travel advice, and more.

Preparing a Carry-on Survival Kit

Here is a suggested list of "survival" items to include in your carry-on luggage. The objective is to be able to cope for several days in the event your checked luggage is misrouted or (alas!) lost. Keep in mind the ever-changing antiterrorism rules on U.S. airlines regarding liquids in carry-on luggage.

- Passport, traveler's checks, and airline ticket
- Valuables, such as jewelry
- Reading material
- Motion-sickness and pain medicine, as well as sleeping aids
- All prescription medicines packed in their original bottles
- A small penlight, a ballpoint pen, and perhaps an extra pair of eyeglasses or sunglasses
- A small tube or plastic bottle of sunscreen
- Adhesive bandages
- An eye mask, ear plugs, and an inflatable neck pillow
- Antacid, plus diarrhea remedies
- An all-purpose antibiotic salve or cream
- A toothbrush and toothpaste

- Deodorant
- Shaving gear
- Some foil-wrapped moist towelettes packs
- A folding or collapsible umbrella
- A small travel alarm clock

Finally, an experienced traveler also packs a bathing suit, a change of underwear, and even one extra change of clothes. Women include their complete makeup kits within their carry-on luggage, plus necessary feminine products.

More Tips to Help You Prepare for Your Trip

- Some countries, especially in remote destinations or southerly climes, require immunizations in advance, maybe even as long as six weeks in advance. The Centers for Disease Control can be accessed at www.cdc.gov, and it lists which shots are required or recommended for various countries.

- On a fitness program? You cannot always be certain that fitness gyms will be available at your hotel. One veteran traveler suggested that the best single form of exercise can be performed in your own hotel room if you pack a simple jump rope. Jumping rope is aerobic and uses all of the major muscle groups.

- Packing for a trip can be a special challenge. Make liberal use of medium-size plastic storage bags and larger bags from your dry cleaners for suits, sport coats, and dresses. They help to reduce wrinkles. In a pinch, you can steam out those wrinkles by hanging the garment in the shower and turning on the hot water until steam rises.

- What's the single most important safety factor when you're aboard an aircraft of any kind? Buckling your seat belt. Ranking closely behind this are paying attention to the safety instructions given by flight attendants before each flight, and noting where the nearest emergency exit is located.

- It's helpful to know that the concierge at your hotel can be your very best friend. From arranging theater tickets to simply advising you on the rules for tipping in that locale, most concierges are storehouses of knowledge.

Incidentally, the term *concierge* dates back to the Roman Empire when slaves stood guard at the doors of inns and dwellings. In the Middle Ages, the concierge was the guard of the castle.

- One of the scariest words for travelers is *diarrhea*. Here are some ways you can prevent it:

    Don't eat shellfish or seafood unless it has been boiled for a minimum of eight minutes.

    Stay away from raw salads and fruit.

    Avoid fruit that you can't peel yourself.

    Avoid food that's been stored and reheated.

    And, of course, there is the water. Follow these guidelines:

    - Always drink water that's been bottled and sealed.
    - Never drink from public faucets or fountains, and don't use water from these sources to brush your teeth.
    - Avoid drinks with ice cubes—even if the water is safe, the cubes could be made from contaminated water.

And here is the "first commandment" of staying healthy: wash your hands at every possible occasion.

Bathrooms of the World

The locale for our necessary bodily functions is provided around the world in many different forms. Here is a sample of possible surprises you might encounter behind that universal door.

- In the United Kingdom, the letters "WC" on a door signify "Water Closet," the British term for "bathroom."

- In many countries, you won't even find a door. Along the autobahns of Germany, for example, you will probably spot a car or a truck stopped along the side of the road with the driver or the occupants standing facing the bushes in that all-too-familiar posture.

- In France and other European countries, be prepared to find women bathroom attendants in the men's lavatories. In some buildings you may even find unisex outer bathrooms (for washing the hands) with toilets and little roomettes for use by both sexes.

- In many European hotels and resorts, you will find a small, extra basin that is set low to the floor in the bathroom. This is called a "bidet" and is used for bathing one's private parts. It's also an excellent washbasin for underwear and socks.

- In Japan, there is a growing trend to spread all the electronic gadgets around the bathroom. Their controls are located on an electronic panel, unfortunately with Japanese characters explaining each button's purpose. One button flushes the toilet, another sends warm air up out of the toilet to dry your bottom, another may play music, and yet another button causes water to shoot upward as if in a bidet.

- In more exotic locales (such as Japan and the Middle East), you might be directed to the door supposedly leading to the toilet, but when you enter, you find what appears to be an empty room. Then your eyes will be drawn to a hole in the cement or ceramic floor, fronted by two foot imprints etched into the surface. Your brain quickly solves the riddle and says, "That's where you place your feet in order to squat over the innocent-looking hole." A certain competitiveness rises up, and you think, Well, if they can hit that hole, so can I. Then a second puzzle appears: no toilet tissue. Instead, there is a water spigot and, perhaps, a small vessel such as a metal pitcher. Once again, logic rises to the occasion, along with a recollection: "In the Middle East, one eats only with the right hand because the left hand is reserved for bodily hygiene." That's when you put all three elements—water, pitcher, left hand—into a logical equation that provides your solution.

- Finally, when inquiring about the location of a bathroom, use the word *toilet* instead of one of the euphemisms we Americans enjoy so much, such as *restroom, washroom, john,* and so on. Also, avoid using such confusing phrases as "making a pit stop," U.S. military terminology (*latrine* and *head*), and the "boy's" or "girl's" room. (One American visitor to Peru told her host she wanted to "wash her hands" so the gentleman led her toward the toilet where they met some workmen scrubbing and painting. The host said, "Oh, don't leave, men. My guest just wants to wash her hands.")

Summary—Preparing for Your Trip Abroad

The American Society of Travel Agents (ASTA) has a Web site that provides a gold mine of information on tips for traveling abroad. You can access it at www.travelsense.org and link into "Travel Tips." Here, courtesy of ASTA, is the site's table of contents:

- Adoption Travel
- Accessible Travel
- Documents and Papers
- Hotel Tips
- Tools for Travelers
- Holiday Travel
- Women Traveling Alone
- Planning a Honeymoon
- National Parks

- Buying Travel Online
- Avoiding Travel Scams
- Why Use a Travel Agent?
  Benefits
  Travel Agent Q&A
  Cruise Line Executive on Travel Agents

Before You Leave

- Packing Tips
- Traveling with Children
- Traveling with Pets
- Traveling with Grandchildren
- Student Travel
- Travel Alerts
- Tips on Buying Travel Insurance

Transportation

- Airport Security
- Guide to Charter Flights
- Car Rental Tips
- Cruising Tips
- Driving Tips

While You're There

- Tipping
- Health & Safety
- Eating Healthy
- Eco-Tourism

Coming Home

- Clearing U.S. Customs
- Food, Plant & Animal Import Guidelines

- Flying during an Airline Strike
- Health & Safety

In the next chapter are sketches of eleven of the most popular tourist and business destinations around the world. Entire books have been written about each one. I hope that these condensed descriptions will stimulate and encourage you to search your library, surf the Internet, and generally do more homework on any potential destination(s). After over forty years of international travel, I can personally attest that your journey will be richer and more thoroughly enjoyed if you do this so that when you land—in whatever country it may be—you at least have a nodding acquaintance with the people, their history, and their culture.

8

Some Essential Things to Know about Eleven Popular Destinations

In an attempt to describe some characteristics of eleven important cultures, I will now indulge in a dangerous inclination we all share: making generalizations and resorting to stereotypes.

One example of a generalization is that "Americans are generally considered to be friendly." We know, however, that not *all* Americans are friendly. According to the *American Heritage Dictionary*, a stereotype is "a conventional, formulaic, and usually oversimplified conception, opinion, or belief." V. Lynn Tyler of the David Kennedy Center for International Studies at Brigham Young University in Provo, Utah, once advised me, "Yes, stereotypes are problematic . . . but the only thing worse is ignorance."

So I begin this chapter with a proviso: I will try to describe general characteristics and behavior of eleven popular international cultures (Canada, Mexico, Japan, China, Germany, France, Italy, Brazil, Russia, India, and the United Kingdom), but as you read about them, bear in mind that there will always be exceptions.

Canada

A wonderfully revealing book titled *The Great Canadian Trivia Book* was written by Mark Kearney and Randy Ray, two award-winning Canadian journalists. They subtitle their book *A Collection of Compelling Curiosities from Alouette to Zed*. It is filled with scores of obscure but intriguing facts about our closest neighbor. For example, did you know that as recently as 1920, Canada had a plan to invade the United States? Or that Canada is the second largest country in the world, after Russia, and is larger than China, the United States, Brazil, and Australia? Or that Canada almost got called Ursalia?

The first and perhaps most important characteristic of the relationship between Americans and Canadians is captured in the following incisive observation: Americans are benevolently ignorant about Canada . . . while Canadians are malevolently well informed about the United States.

Let's put that claim to a test.

If you are an American, can you name five or more famous historic Canadian figures? When I ask that question at seminars in the United States, I am usually met with embarrassed silence. Someone might venture, "Wayne Gretzky?" or "Michael J. Fox?" On the other hand, a very large number of Canadians can name long lists of famous Americans from our history books.

Then, in the same seminar, I will follow with another type of question: "What is the *one* characteristic you would use to describe Canadians?" After a pause, the answer is usually, "Oh, that's simple. They're just like us."

The truth is that our friendly neighbors to the north are fiercely proud of their own individual heritage and are chagrined when airily classified by Americans as "just like us." And that may be precisely why Americans are accused of being "benevolently ignorant" about Canadians.

There is yet another helpful observation that may apply to all of the countries described in this chapter. How many times have you read about opinion polls taken in various parts of the world where the question is asked, "What do you think about America and Americans?" The answer is often "We like individual Americans, but we don't particularly like the American government and its policies." This explanation might soothe our individual egos a bit when we hear that someone "doesn't like America."

Here are some helpful—maybe even essential—things to know about the people who live north of us along the longest, least-guarded border in the Western Hemisphere. (With thanks to the *Canada e-Book* published on the Canadian national Web site.)

- Early in this decade, enormous quantities of oil have been found embedded in the sands of Alberta—enough, according to a report on CBS's *60 Minutes* program, to satisfy the oil needs of the United States for decades but difficult to extract.

- In 2002, most of Canada's population of 31.4 million lived within 125 miles (200 kilometers) of the United States. In fact, the inhabitants of Canada's three biggest cities— Toronto, Montreal, and Vancouver—can drive to the U.S. border in less than two hours.

- Though U.S. citizens used to travel freely across the border, post–September 11 regulations now require a passport for reentering the United States.

- In 2002, the majority of Canadians—six out of every ten— lived in the two provinces of Ontario and Quebec, home to fifteen of the largest urban areas in the country.

- The three prairie provinces (Alberta, Saskatchewan, and Manitoba) are known for their agricultural production, but the populations there have moved into urban areas. For example, in 2002, a full 42 percent of Saskatchewan's population lived in the cities of Regina and Saskatoon. Edmonton and Calgary were home to 63 percent of all Albertans, and 60 percent of Manitobans lived in the province's lone metropolitan area, Winnipeg. The province of British Columbia, on the coast of the Pacific Ocean, is Canada's third-most-populous province.

- In contrast, the polar region, consisting of the Yukon, the Northwest Territories, and the most recently formed territory, Nunavut, is relatively empty. It consists of 41 percent of the Canadian landmass but only 0.3 percent of the population.

- The remaining provinces of Canada are labeled the Province of Quebec and the Atlantic Provinces (i.e., all the land and the islands bordering the Atlantic Ocean).

(Pop quiz: Without looking back, name the provinces in Canada. Many Canadians could probably name a large number of the individual states in the United States.)

Here are more facts about Canada:

- Most American schoolchildren know that Christopher Columbus is credited with discovering America in 1492, and many are aware that perhaps a thousand years ago, the Viking explorer Leif Ericson very likely landed in what is now Canada. But, according to *The Great Canadian Trivia Book*, Chinese historians indicate that it is possible that a Buddhist monk named Hui-Shen may have discovered Canada in 499. "These historical works describe a country called Fusang that bears a resemblance to the west coast of North America. Although some historians claim the description best fits Mexico, others believe it is closer to British Columbia."

- The first census to take place after Confederation was conducted in 1871, when it was determined that Canada's population was about 3.7 million. At that time, most Canadians lived and worked on family farms, and the country was young, with more than one-third of the population under the age of fifteen. Today, with 36 million people, the majority live in cities. The birth rate has declined, and now less than one-fifth of the population is under fifteen years old. Each year, approximately 200,000 new Canadians arrive from around the world.

- With such a large influx of new arrivals, it is natural that Canada would be a country of many tongues. Even when the first French-speaking and English-speaking settlers arrived, the "First Nations" people (the preferred Canadian term for Indians or Inuit) spoke no less than twelve Aboriginal language families. In 2001, some 59 percent of Canadians claimed English as their first language, 23 percent claimed French, and 18 percent listed a nonofficial tongue. Of the latter, Chinese was the next most popular, followed by Italian and German. In that same year, 3.8 million Canadians regularly spoke at least two languages at home. Therefore, about 18 percent of the population can speak and understand both official languages—English and French—and most, if not all, government employees are bilingual. Many Americans are aware that the cities of Montreal and Quebec have French-speaking majorities.

- Principal religions in Canada include Roman Catholic, Anglican, Baptist, and other Protestant churches.

- Favorite sports are hockey, speed and figure skating, football (Canadian style), baseball, soccer, rugby, curling, skiing, tennis, swimming, golf, lacrosse, field hockey, track and field, and gymnastics.

- Some of the many Canadian-born people who enjoy celebrity status in the United States are Rich Little, Wayne Gretzky, Robert MacNeil, Mary Pickford, Lorne Greene, Paul Anka, William Shatner, Saul Bellow, John Kenneth Galbraith, the former senator Sam Hayakawa, Alan Thicke, Michael J. Fox, and Jim Carrey.

But perhaps the highest level of celebrity has come to Canada via two Montreal men who have turned the Las Vegas entertainment scene upside down with their revolutionary circus cum ballet Cirque du Soleil. Guy Laliberté, president, and Gilles Ste-Croix, vice president of creation and artistic director, have ten different versions of their unique, exotic extravaganza performing around the United States, with four separate shows in Las Vegas pulling in as much as $1 million per night in ticket sales. The Cirque hits have helped to tip the scales in Las Vegas to the point where entertainment offerings bring in more dollars than gaming revenues do. All the Cirque productions feature bizarre but artistic costuming, makeup, and music, plus the use of a totally new, contrived language. The success of Cirque du Soleil was featured twice on CBS's *60 Minutes* in 2005. Reporter Lesley Stahl described the Cirque phenomenon as "a sea change for Las Vegas that hasn't stopped." Coming up next are a Cirque show featuring the spirit of the Beatles and a production for the Disneyland theme park in Japan.

Some cultural characteristics of Canadians (and here remember our caution about stereotypes) are:

- Canadians are generally friendly and open to one another. They are especially proud of their heritage, which is even more diverse than that of the United States. But they like to emphasize that they are not just U.S.-type people living in Canada. Many Canadians see Americans as more aggressive and materialistic than themselves.

- Gestures and body language—both positive and negative— are similar on both sides of the border.

- Canadians are often described as "more conservative" and "more self-deprecating" than people in the United States are.

- Eating habits in Canada tend to be a bit more formal than in the United States, with many people eating in the continental style—that is, with the fork constantly in the left hand and the knife remaining in the right.

- Canadians celebrate four national holidays that are different from those we celebrate in the United States:

  1. Victoria Day (third Monday in May)

  2. Canada Day (July 1)

  3. Thanksgiving (second Monday in October)

  4. Boxing Day (December 26)—As in the United Kingdom, this day is devoted to visiting friends and relatives and comes from the old British tradition of giving small boxed gifts to service employees or the poor.

- Canada is known for its universal national health insurance, which covers doctor fees and most hospital costs for all Canadians.

- The metric system is used for all weights and measures in Canada.

- The English language used in Canada is distinctive because of the utterance "Eh?" that is often heard at the end of a sentence. And, by the way, Americans sometimes call the beautiful, graceful geese that migrate southward out of Canada "Canadian geese." Wrong. Geese don't have a nationality. They are more properly called "Canada geese."

To conclude on the note that we began, for people who like trivia, *The Canuck Book*, by Ian Walker and Keith Bellows, claims to contain a bevy of "Canada's biggest, best, longest, least, oddest, oldest, and most ridiculous." One entry in the book records that "The World's most audacious *streaker* is Montreal's Michel Leduc. It seems he trotted out among 500 dancing Catholic schoolgirls during the closing ceremonies of the 1976 Olympics (in Canada) and was seen by a television audience of some two billion people."

For an informative and entertaining book on both Canada and our other neighbor, Mexico, I recommend *Put Your Best Foot Forward: Mexico/Canada*, by Mary Murray Bosrock. This wonderful handbook was written to help us negotiate new trade opportunities as the result of the North American Free Trade Agreement (NAFTA), which began on January 1, 1994, and is being phased in over fifteen years. As of the year 2008, goods and services should flow smoothly across all of North America. In her book, Ms. Bosrock quotes John G. Mott, who, at one time, served as partner in charge of International Tax and Business Advisory Services for the Americas at the firm Arthur Andersen. Mr. Mott advises that "While NAFTA promises an era of free trade, the term *free* is a misnomer. In reality, a preferential system of trade is unfolding." It should also be noted that Ms. Bosrock is the author of three other books, dealing with Asia, Russia, and Europe, in her Put Your Best Foot Forward series. We owe her a debt of gratitude for aiding in our understanding and appreciation of cross-cultural communication.

Mexico

On my very first trip to Mexico, I very nearly got arrested. Here's what happened.

Years before the NAFTA agreement went into effect, some engineers in my company learned that I was heading for Mexico City and they asked me whether I would carry a package to their counterparts in our Mexican factory. I assured them that I would, and soon afterward a wrapped package was delivered to my desk with a letter taped to it. I later learned that the package contained certain machine tool parts required for the manufacturing operation in Mexico City.

On my arrival at the airport in Mexico City, I went through customs and the examiner stopped me, looked suspiciously at the brown paper–wrapped package, and asked in halting English, "Wot iss inside?" I said, "Some things from our factory in the United States." The customs agent looked at the envelope, opened it, and read it. With a disapproving look in my direction, he then called over two of his colleagues and they, too, studied the letter. They went into a huddle, arguing back and forth rather vigorously. Finally, frowning at me, they all suddenly burst into laughter, wrapped the package back up, and said, "Go! Go! Go!"

When I arrived at our Mexican offices I told the manager there what had happened. He said, "Let me see the letter." After reading it, he also burst into laughter, then explained, "The items in this package normally require a separate permit for entry into our country. You were carrying illegal items. Your friends back at the home facility were trying to pull a fast one on you. But even worse, your friends back home wrote across the top of the letter 'Watch out for the *mordida!*'"

"So?" I replied. "What's *mordida*?"

"In English it means 'little bites,'" he explained, "but in Spanish it means 'bribe'!"

He continued, "I suspect the customs agents were, at first, startled to see illegal parts being openly sneaked into Mexico . . . but then, realizing your naiveté, they decided your pals at home were playing a joke on you and so they let you pass through."

So, with that as an introduction, here are some essential things to keep in mind when visiting Mexico:

- As with Canada, Americans are regarded as friendly and important to the economic well-being of the country, but the U.S. government is often viewed as a "big brother," and we could probably add, "a big *overbearing* brother." One nineteenth-century president of Mexico is often quoted as saying, "Poor Mexico. So far from God, and so close to the United States."

- It's probably not a good idea to bring up the subject of Iraq in Mexico. Many Mexicans think that the United States went to Iraq because of economic and oil issues.

- Mexico City is situated at an altitude higher than a mile and a half, so be wary of doing strenuous exercise when you visit there.

- No visa is required to visit Mexico, and U.S. citizens can stay for up to three months. Proof of citizenship and a photo ID are necessary, however, and a passport is now required when returning to the United States.

- Mexico is about three times the size of Texas. Varied temperatures are found within the country, from hot and dry in the north to very humid in the south, where tropical jungles flourish. Mexico City is located on a high and cool plateau between two mountain ranges.

- A source of great pride among Mexicans is their heritage from ancient Indian civilizations, which built large cities with engineering feats that rival those of the ancient Europeans and Egyptians. In 1521, the Spanish conquered the Aztecs and, in turn, three centuries later, in 1821, were overthrown by Mexican independence forces. From 1846 to 1848, Mexico fought against the United States, and a turbulent period followed until the 1920s and 1930s.

- As for historic national identity, the Spanish conquered the Indians, and most Mexicans of today are a fusion of the two. The result is called *mestizo*, meaning literally "mixed." According to Professor Paula Heusinkveld, a scholar on Mexico since 1965, today that blend is more complete than in any other place in Latin America.

- Spanish is the official language in Mexico, and while written Spanish is basically the same throughout the rest of Central and South America, from country to country one finds many slight variations in pronunciation, spelling, and the meanings of certain words. So, a word of caution: By all means practice your Spanish—it will be appreciated—but don't be surprised if you stumble on one of these anomalies and eyebrows are raised. For example, in Mexico you might *coger un taxi*, meaning "to get a taxi," but in Argentina to *coger un taxi* means, basically, you "fornicate a taxi."

For many decades my former employer, The Parker Pen Company, produced bottles of liquid ink with the brand name SuperQuink. Its redeeming feature was that it dried in an instant. Therefore, an advertising slogan was developed that said, "Dries fast with wet ink." The copy in English continued, 'To avoid embarrassment [meaning "to avoid messy writing'] use Parker SuperQuink." The ad campaign proved to be very successful in the United States so it was decided to extend it into Mexico. Consequently, thousands of metal signs were produced with the slogan translated directly into Spanish: *Para evitar embarazo* [to avoid embarrassment] *compra Parker SuperQuink* [buy Parker SuperQuink]. Unfortunately, no one in the U.S. offices realized that in Mexico the phrase *para evitar embarazo* was actually a colloquial expression for "to avoid pregnancy." So on signs all across the country, Parker was saying, "To avoid pregnancy, buy Parker SuperQuink." An apocryphal story afterward that was encouraged by the Parker marketing people explained, "Actually, our ink sales increased after that episode."

- And that leads us to another essential: when providing advertising copy for the Mexican market, or when writing important documents that need to be translated into Spanish, be sure to rely on an expert translation firm or a person intimately acquainted with Mexican Spanish.

- The population of Mexico is around 105 million, with 20 million people living in the area around Mexico City, making Mexico the largest Spanish-speaking country in the world. Mexico City is competing for the rank of the largest city in the world.

- The Mexican government is a federal democratic republic consisting of thirty-one provincial states and the federal district of Mexico City. Therefore, the official title of the country is "United States of Mexico," which in Spanish is Estados Unidos de Mexico.

- Meeting and greeting in Mexico is only slightly different than in the United States, with these variations: men usually bow the head slightly when shaking hands, and good male friends might perform the *abrazo*, meaning the "embrace." A hug is usually accompanied by a slight pat on the back with the left hand. Women who are good friends often greet one another with a very light kiss on the other woman's right cheek. A man should probably avoid shaking hands with a woman unless she extends her hand first.

- Just as in European countries like Germany, Austria, Switzerland, and elsewhere, don't jump to the use of first names until invited to do so. Titles such as "Doctor," "Professor," and other honorary designations are valued in Mexico and should be respected. As in other Latin countries, Mexicans often have three names: the first name is the Christian given name, the second is the father's family name, and the third is the mother's maiden name. So, a person named Pedro Gonzales Lopez tells you that his first name is his given name, the second name is his father's family name, and "Lopez" tells you that he comes from his mother's family branch, which was the Lopez branch. In addressing this person, however, the proper usage would simply be "Señor Gonzales." Finally, if this person's last two names are hyphenated—Gonzales-Lopez—then it would be proper to use both when addressing him.

- If you are from the United States, refer to yourself as a North American (*uno Norteamericano* if you are a man, and *una Norteamericana* if you are a woman). Remember that Mexico is just as much a part of the American continent as the United States is. The word *gringo* is not necessarily a bad word. It is slang but is derogatory only in its use and context.

- Body language and gestures have some important differences, compared to those in the United States. Generally, two Mexicans will stand closer to each other than two Americans would. And there may be more casual body contact—a prolonged handshake, a touch of the elbow, and so on—but certainly not between men and women. Two gestures that are often considered slightly rude are (1) putting your hands inside your pocket, or (2) standing with your hands on your hips. Conservative dress styles (darker colors, for example) are the safest choices. And blue jeans are considered too casual for business wear. Never wear shorts or halter tops when visiting churches.

- Punctuality is an important difference. Americans abide by deadlines, commitments, and schedules. Mexicans dislike living their lives in measured segments. Time is regarded as more flexible and fluid in Mexico. Being, say, thirty to forty-five minutes late for an appointment or an engagement is not viewed as being impolite. And so it is with business discussions. Americans are taught that "time is money" so "let's get down to business." Mexicans believe that it is more important to proceed slowly, to get to know one another and build a mutual relationship. The same applies to the hours for dining. Lunch is served between 1:00 and 4:00 p.m., and the same is true with dinner, which usually does not begin until 8:00 p.m.

Bill was in Mexico City for his very first visit. On his first evening there, he left his hotel room at about 6:00 p.m. and went down to the lobby. His Spanish-oriented companion asked, "Where are you going?" Bill replied, "I'm going for dinner." Whereupon his colleague advised, "Good luck. Most restaurants around here don't even open until seven or eight o'clock."

- On elevators, the sign for the ground floor is "PB," meaning *planta baja*. Therefore, the first floor is what we would consider the second floor.

- If you wish to attend a bull fight, check with the concierge at your hotel for the best choices.

- Before eating a meal, it is polite to say *"Buen provecho"* (bwen-pro-VEH-choh), which means, roughly, "Good eating," or more literally, "May it benefit you."

- In the marketplace, Americans tend to dislike haggling. Mexicans enjoy and expect it.

- Americans tend to be informal and not conscious of rank or status. Mexicans (especially in business) lean more toward formality and are conscious of education, family, and social status. There, proper etiquette is a sign of proper breeding.

- If you are invited to a dinner at a private home, it would be appropriate but not necessary to bring flowers. Avoid yellow marigolds because they are associated with funerals and cemeteries. Red flowers are used for casting spells.

- When a girl celebrates her fifteenth birthday, it is considered a very important event in her life, signifying she has reached maturity. This is called *quinceanera*, and many Mexican families celebrate this with large parties either at home or in restaurants.

- There will very likely be more American women in business than there are Mexican women; however, American businesswomen will be welcome and respected, especially if they have professional skills and are competent.

- Be patient in business negotiations. In business relations, your first visit and first contacts may be considered the beginning of a relationship, and it is unusual to expect to finalize agreements at that time. If you are totally new to Mexico, consider working through a contact—the commercial attaché at the U.S. embassy, a bank affiliated with your U.S. bank, or a law firm recommended by your U.S. lawyers. Your state may even have an office in Mexico for the purpose of generating trade.

- Mexicans are generally very gracious in their hospitality and will go to special lengths to host you.

One example of this hospitality possibly going too far occurred to Calvin, whose automobile company had a factory located in Monterrey, Mexico. Calvin and some of his engineering colleagues checked into their hotel and soon learned that nights can get very cold. So they told the hotel manager that they would like some extra blankets sent to their room. The next evening, while dining in the hotel restaurant, several suggestively dressed ladies appeared at their table, saying "The manager sent us to make certain you don't get cold tonight." Wisely, the Americans declined.

This has been a short course on Mexican culture and society. Hopefully, these capsules of information will convince you to do even more research.

Mexico has an abundance of attributes: beautiful and diverse scenery, luxurious hotels for tourists, a fascinating history with wonderful museums and historic sites, and people who are warm and extremely hospitable.

But it should be mentioned that both Mexico and the United States have had their share of national malfeasances. In the United States, it has been the disclosures of corporate greed and book-fixing. In Mexico, it is drug wars, killings, and executions, especially along the U.S.-Mexican border. From time to time, the U.S. government has had to issue "travel advisories" warning tourists and other visitors to avoid seedy districts and stay off the streets at night. Naturally, this has had a chilling effect on tourism in Mexico. The view from Mexico is that, in actual fact, it is the United States that is the source of demand for illegal drugs.

The other sensitive issue is illegal immigration. On the northern side of the border, there is a dichotomy between the need to attract migrant workers, especially in agriculture, and opposition to illegal aliens who take away jobs from U.S. citizens and give birth to their children in the United States in order to gain citizenship.

Neither of these large and serious issues will be solved easily or soon, but it behooves the visitor and the host alike to realize that we must work together to alleviate these complex problems.

Japan

Quick! What words or phrases would you use to describe the Japanese? At various cross-cultural training exercises I have held for Americans, here are some of the typical answers I hear:

Polite

Formal

Quiet

Inscrutable

Gracious

Courteous

Those stereotypes are sometimes true. But there is more—much more—to know about dealing with the Japanese. Here are a few essential "Do's & Taboos."

- In chapter 1, we've already learned about the "bow" at the moment of greeting. When bowing, keep your arms straight and extend your hands down the sides of your legs. This applies to both men and women. Also, be prepared for both the bow and having a hand extended outward to you, Western-style. But don't grip the hand too tightly. In general, the Japanese have been conscientious about learning Western ways.

Several of my books have been translated into Japanese. When I explained to the Japanese publishers that they probably would want to edit and rewrite many sections of my books because they related topics from the American viewpoint, the reply I received was, in effect, "That's exactly what we wish to know. We want to know how Americans view protocol and etiquette from their own eyes."

- Don't expect much direct eye contact. It is considered slightly rude or impolite to keep prolonged eye contact.

- The worst social offense you can commit is to embarrass a Japanese person. Yet oddly—for us—the Japanese will smile as a way of hiding embarrassment. Be aware that when you laugh, a wide-open mouth is considered to be impolite. You've probably seen photos and movies of Japanese—especially Japanese women—covering their mouths when laughing or giggling.

- Bodily contact—even casual touching or back-slapping—should be avoided.

- Saying "no" is very difficult for the Japanese. They view it as something that disrupts the harmony of the situation, and harmony is extremely important in Japanese society. In fact, when you speak, the Japanese may nod their heads and say, "Yes," or *hai* (pronounced "hi"). But they are not saying, "Yes, I agree." They are saying, "Yes, I hear you . . . but I don't necessarily agree." Robert Moran, a good friend and a respected academic, has written a book with one chapter on this topic cleverly titled "In Japan, Don't Take Yes for an Answer." The reason is that the Japanese use very indirect wording to indicate "no." Such phrases as "That might be very difficult" or "Ahhh . . . that is very interesting" is about as far as they might go.

- Gift giving is very prevalent in Japan. It is not considered a bribe or an obligation but more a means of building a respectful relationship. You might be on the receiving end of a very luxurious gift—an electronic device, a painting, even a watch. Therefore, be prepared to carry along some gifts to hand out in return. But be aware of status in Japan. In other words, the more stature a person has, the more valuable the gift should be. Also, avoid gifts with any suggestion of advertising imprinted or engraved on them. To prevent any scintilla of embarrassment, you might indicate that your gift is not a gift but a "memento" of your visit, or you could say that the gift is intended not for just one person but for the entire organization.

- In your daily communication, be aware that Americans are considered very "low-context" communicators—meaning, we don't like to leave anything to the imagination; we like details and explicit language. American lawyers are considered "low context" because they like to spell everything out, even though it may involve complicated, arcane phrasing. The Japanese, on the other hand, are considered "high-context" communicators. That means, "It goes without saying." It is akin to twins who seem to have a hidden or unspoken form of communication between them. They each understand in a few words what the other one is trying to say.

- Blowing one's nose in public should be avoided, if at all possible. The Japanese will seek out the nearest restroom to perform this bodily act, washing their hands when finished.

- Western men should not open doors or hold chairs for Japanese women. In fact, among the older generation of Japanese, men will precede spouses or female employees when walking.

- To understand the Japanese ethos, it is helpful to read up on the history of that remarkable country. Until the 1500s, Japan had sealed itself off from the outside world. The Portuguese were the first to penetrate that self-imposed isolation via trade and trading ships. This is evident in the Portuguese word for "thank you," *obrigato*, and the similar-sounding word for "thank you" in Japanese, *arigato*.

- An anomaly is that while the Japanese avoid bodily contact, you will observe trains and subways with people packed shoulder to shoulder. Anthropologists explain that crowded trains are something the Japanese must endure, so they regard their bodies as little islands of personal space.

- In business, the safest route is to dress conservatively. Avoid wild colors or styling.

- In business discussions, be prepared for periods of silence. Americans find this disconcerting. We tend to want to fill in conversational gaps. But among the Japanese, it is very common to have long pauses during discourse.

- In Japanese businesses, hierarchy and levels of status are especially important. The higher the stature, the more respect is deserved. This even applies to seating around a conference table or in a dining room. And very often, the person who seems apart from the conversation is the highest ranking one present. Therefore, it is advisable to have a Japanese national accompany you to help you recognize who's who.

- Business decisions are made by group consensus. Each business decision must be "signed off" on by many different sets and levels of managers. Agreement means "harmony," and as explained earlier, harmony is highly prized in Japan.

- Final decisions in business seem, to Americans, to take agonizingly long to achieve. The first reason is the practice of "group consensus." The second reason is that it takes a long time to build trusting relationships.

One of my publishers traveled to Japan and worked with the Japanese very successfully over the years. Finally, at one point, after eleven years of doing mutual business, the head of the Japanese company said, "Now I feel like we have become real friends."

- Japanese audiences may react differently to speeches than American audiences do. Here are just two examples.

The governor of my state traveled to Japan, and one of his duties was to address a large audience of Japanese businessmen. At the conclusion, he complained to his international trade adviser, "That was a disaster! I looked out at that audience and no one was listening. Many of them had their eyes closed. Others were nodding off." His adviser explained, "No, no, Governor. When the Japanese close their eyes and nod, it means that they are concentrating heavily on what is being said. When the Japanese learn English, they often learn the written form first. Spoken English therefore is a bit more difficult to comprehend."

A second anecdote involved an American businessman who spoke to a Japanese audience using an interpreter. In this case, he was instructed to say a few words or sentences in English and then wait for the interpreter to translate. In typical American fashion, the American began by telling a joke. We learned later that this is what the Japanese interpreter actually said:

"American is beginning his speech with joke."

"This is customary in America."

"Frankly, you won't understand joke so I won't repeat it."

"He thinks I'm telling you joke now."

"I will tell you when he is finished. Polite thing to do is laugh."

"Now!"

With that cue, the audience erupted in laughter. After the speech, the American went up to the interpreter, shook his hand, and said, "Thank you! I've told that joke many times, but this was the best reaction I've ever received!"

For Americans, doing business or even visiting as a tourist in Japan is something of a challenge because its culture is so remarkably different from our own. Thus, it is worth doing your homework. I can recommend the following five books for more insight into this wonderful but—for Americans—somewhat mysterious land.

Japanese Etiquette & Ethics in Business (Fifth Edition), by Boye DeMente

Hidden Differences: Doing Business with the Japanese, by Edward T. Hall and Mildred Reed Hall

With Respect to the Japanese: A Guide for Americans, by John C. Condon

The Economist Business Traveller's Guides: Japan

Put Your Best Foot Forward Asia: A Fearless Guide to International Communication and Behavior, by Mary Murray Bosrock

China

Each year, more startling facts come out of China. For example, China's economy is currently growing four times faster than that of the United States.

I recently received an e-mail containing dozens of fascinating and little-known facts about China. Among them was this statement: "If the population of China walked past you, in a single file, the line would never end because of the rate of reproduction."

No source was listed, so I checked Google and learned that the population of China in 2005 was estimated to be 1.3 billion. Included on the Web page about China was a population scorecard, like an adding machine screen, showing how often a new birth occurred in China, and, indeed, there was a new birth in China almost every second. That seemed to verify the previously quoted astounding statement.

About the same time, I read a report from the National Intelligence Council, quoted in part by the Knight Ridder newspapers, stating that in the year 2020 both China and India are expected to be the major players in the global economy. According to the same report, the United States will continue to be the most important country across all dimensions of power—economically, technologically, politically, and militarily. Yet India, China, and perhaps other countries such as Brazil and Indonesia will have vastly increased global power.

If all of these forecasts about China are true, it behooves us to take a close look at this burgeoning giant.

I first visited China on business in 1976 with a mixed group of businessmen from the Midwest. Shortly before this, President Richard Nixon had made his historic visit to China and reached agreement with China's president, Mao Zedong, to open the doors to Western interests. The first of the visiting groups to arrive were specialists—chemists, engineers, scientists, and the like. Our group was reputed to be the first one from mixed businesses. We had top officials from the John Deere Corporation, Ingersoll-Rand, International Harvester, several Chicago banks, a prestigious law firm, and the Arthur Andersen public accounting firm.

Apparently, visitors like us were new to Chinese officialdom. We sensed they were having trouble determining how to handle us. At that time, the Chinese government was divided into various national industries, and it seemed that to make any inroads into China, we would have to consult with the national industry appropriate to our category whether it be agricultural machinery, banking, or consumer goods, which is where I was designated.

The first conclusion our group reached was that the Chinese were simply not interested in mechanizing their agricultural sector. The John Deere and International Harvester representatives were virtually ignored. The reason was simple. Mechanizing the agriculture of China would put hundreds of millions of Chinese laborers out of work.

Much to my amazement, I was told I had a special appointment to confer with the officials in charge of consumer goods. The reason quickly became apparent. I represented The Parker Pen Company, and China was Valhalla for the pen business. That was because everyone—and I mean everyone—had to carry a pen. The Chinese language consists of pictographs, or ideographs, which means "pictures." There is no alphabet, as we know it, in the Chinese language. And at that time there were virtually no typewriters in China. Everyone wrote with pen and paper. Today, computer programs have been designed to enter the Chinese ideographs using the Romanized alphabet, or pinyin, and transfer them to paper.

Within ten years, Parker was selling our pens in the duty-free stores that accepted U.S. dollars or foreign exchange currency (FEC) only and were therefore a useful source to collect needed dollars to buy essential products from the United States. Today, some Parker pens are actually made in China and exported back to the United States.

The purpose of telling you about Parker Pen is that it helps to dramatize the amazing changes that have occurred in China in the last twenty-five years. The Chinese market has opened up to the West to the point where Americans now flock to China in search of new commercial relationships.

In June 2005, *Time* magazine documented what it termed the *new revolution* that has occurred in China in just the last ten to twenty years. Here are some statistics:

- In 1985, there was just one skyscraper in Shanghai. Today there are three hundred.
- Cell phone ownership has risen from zero in 1996 to more than 300 million today.
- Car ownership has jumped from 10 million in 1996 to more than 30 million today.
- It is estimated that by 2025, China will double the amount of oil it consumes each year.
- Total exports from China have risen from $200 billion in 1999 to almost $600 billion in 2005.
- Each year China graduates six times as many engineers as the United States does.
- There are more Chinese studying English than there are people in the United States who speak American English.

Doing Business in China

Richard R. Gesteland and George F. Seyk have written a wonderfully informative book titled *Marketing across Cultures in Asia*. In the opening pages they explain that there are three key concepts to understanding how Asians conduct business:

1. The importance of relationships.
2. The importance of hierarchies.
3. The use of time.

Relationships mean just that. People in a relationship-type culture prefer to do business with individuals they know—family, friends, or someone who is well-known to them. That's why they may take long periods of time to do business with strangers, particularly foreign strangers. One way to cope with this is to employ the help of a local third-party "go between."

The next key word in Gesteland and Seyk's tutorial is *hierarchy*. Business in much of Asia is built on strata of management. That is, one level of management rests on top of many lower levels, and decisions must rise to the top with total consensus at each level before proceeding onward. The concept of hierarchy can be demonstrated in other practical ways. Among the Japanese, it is said that on the golf course the person among the foursome with the highest status, or rank, tees off first, and then down through the other three players. Age is another indicator of status, with more respect resting with the older members of a unit.

As for the *time* factor, we can turn to the famous anthropologist Edward T. Hall. He gave us the terms *monochronic* and *polychronic*. The former are great respecters of punctuality; the latter are the opposite and dislike schedules and deadlines. Examples of monochronic societies are Germany, Switzerland, the Netherlands, Canada, and the United States, which tend to respect and to practice punctuality. At the other end of the spectrum would be societies in Latin America, much of the Middle East, and South and Southeast Asia.

Now that we've started listing tips and traits, let's continue with a few rather important do's and don'ts.

- According to forecasts of global trends published by the National Intelligence Council in 2005, a group of senior intelligence analysts predicts that the world economy is expected to be about 80 percent larger in the year 2020 than it was in 2000, with the average per capita income roughly 50 percent higher.

- Furthermore, U.S. intelligence reports predict that China and India will be major economic forces by the year 2020. At that time, China's gross domestic product, the total value of goods and services, will be greater than that of any Western country except the United States.

- China's exports to the United States will exceed and become more important than exports from Canada, traditionally our largest trading partner.

- Confucius has had a profound influence in China. He stressed obedience and respect for authority. "China has had a very strict code of behavior in effect for two thousand years. Carefully prescribed forms of behavior cover virtually every aspect of conduct. The higher one is on the social scale, the more meticulous and demanding the rules of behavior." (From *Business China*, by Peggy Kenna and Sondra Lacy.)

- In 2004, China's economy grew at its fastest pace in eight years, increasing at an annual rate of 9.5 percent. A dozen years ago, China didn't even import oil. Today it is the second-largest oil market. In 2004, China's oil demand jumped 17 percent.

- China is also a fascinating destination for tourism. Americans can now take nonstop direct flights from Chicago to Shanghai by flying over the North Pole. Once in Shanghai, the commercial capital of the country, they are confronted with a forestlike jumble of huge cranes and metal scaffolding integral to the process of constructing a totally new landscape of high-rise buildings. In the 1920s and 1930s, when Shanghai was a colonial city, it was considered the "Paris of the East," and its opulent decadence drew travelers from around the world.

- Farther to the west is Beijing, the seat of government and also the location of the Forbidden City, the home to emperors and empresses over the centuries. Within an hour's drive or more is one of the greatest single structures ever built by man—the Great Wall of China—and one of the few man-made structures that can be seen by astronauts in outer space. Farther west still is Xian, where emperors built armies of terra-cotta statues, each with different and distinctive facial features, and then buried them.

- In the south is the bustling industrial area of Guangzhou, formerly Canton, as well as one of the world's most beautiful ports and most exotic cities, Hong Kong.

- Numerous dialects are spoken across China. The written language in China is standard and understood by all, but Mandarin Chinese is the only dialect that is spoken across the country. Cantonese, which is prevalent in Hong Kong, is the second most widely spoken dialect. China has fifty-five ethnic minorities, however, with the Han ethnic group being the largest. Yet even among the Han there are purportedly fifteen hundred different dialects. Villages separated by just a few miles may speak entirely different dialects. "No one can clearly answer the question how many dialects there are in China," said Zhang Hongming, a professor of Chinese linguistics at the University of Wisconsin, in a *New York Times* article. The Wu dialect is widely spoken in Shanghai, but it shares only about a 31 percent similarity with Mandarin, or roughly the same as English and French, according to Professor Zhang.

- The official name of the country is "The People's Republic of China." It is considered an atheist nation with small numbers of minorities practicing Islam, Buddhism, Taoism, and Christianity. The country has ninety-five cities with populations exceeding one million.

- Once again, according to the Harris, Moran, and Moran book *Managing Cultural Differences*, "China is a hierarchical society, which often makes it difficult to practice Western management theories of empowerment and delegation. The Chinese rank among the toughest negotiators in the world, but they are reputable and honorable." Also,

"Seating arrangements during formal meetings are a critical issue. Guests are seated according to their business or social status. Personal information that Westerners consider private, like salary, is discussed in China since in most state-owned companies it is common knowledge what individuals earn."

- In China, the family name is always mentioned first. For example, Deng Hsiaoping should be addressed as Mr. Deng.

- When doing business in China, it is important not to focus on one individual but on the group of individuals working for a particular goal. Similarly, in conversations, an individual who repeatedly uses the word *I* is thought to be centering everything on him- or herself.

- The Chinese are not a touchy-feely society. They avoid open displays of affection, and when they converse, spatial boundaries between people are wider in China than in the United States.

- Modern communications are used freely in China, but the Chinese believe that important business should be conducted face-to-face.

Finally, it is important to remember that there are three important national holidays in China:

1. National (Independence) Day—October 1–7
2. International Labor Day Holiday—May 1–7
3. Chinese New Year—A fourteen-day period based on the lunar calendar that occurs sometime during January and February.

Germany

In geographic size, Germany is a little smaller than Montana, yet it is a major player in world politics and economics. Since the reunification of West and East Germany, its combined economy leads the other European Union countries that share the euro as a common currency.

There are four distinct zones in Germany: lowlands in the north; the central uplands, which include various small mountain ranges; then come the wide valley and gorge created by the Rhine River; and in the south, the forested mountains and plateaus that lead into the Swiss Alps.

Some Things to Know about the German Language

- There are three genders for German nouns: masculine, feminine, and neuter.

- Compound nouns abound in German. This may be why there seem to be excessively long words that appear untranslatable.

- A major problem for Germans learning English is our inconsistent spelling. "Spelling in English requires a good memory," says Peter Hoyng, a German graduate student studying in United States. In German, if you can pronounce the word, you can usually spell it.

- Studying English is compulsory in most German schools, and because there is also a sixty-year history of military presence of American and British soldiers, many adult Germans are able to speak at least some English.

- In Europe, German is the most frequently spoken language (after Russian), with some 85 million people considering it their mother tongue. German is also spoken throughout Austria and in major parts of Switzerland.

- Americans who have studied "school German" in the United States should understand that because of regional dialects in Germany, some misunderstandings may arise.

- Whereas a French menu may read and sound like poetry, when it comes to food German is regarded by many people as a most unattractive-sounding language. The travel writer Bill Bryson observed that if you want whipped cream in your coffee, you order it *mit Schlag*. Bryson then asked,

"Now, does that sound to you like a frothy and delicious
pick-me-up, or does it sound like the sort of thing smokers
bring up first thing in the morning?" Other foods that
Bryson said sound unappetizing include *Knoblauchbrot*,
Schweinskotelett Ihrer wahl, and *Portion Schlagobers*.

In all your communications with Germans, remember that good
manners are both expected and respected throughout Germany.
Edward T. Hall, the famed anthropologist, observed that "language is
a direct reflection of culture and German is no exception. Just as the
verb comes at the end of a German sentence, it takes a while for
Germans to get to the point." He advises Americans to be patient and
wait for Germans to make their point. Also, Americans should follow
suit and repeat key issues at the end of their presentations.

Hall believes Germans respect honesty and directness. He advises
Americans to use examples when giving a presentation. Turning the
tables, Germans believe that Americans tend to exaggerate and often
resort to puffery. As a general rule, Germans avoid overstatement.

For a penetrating examination of the German and French cultures
in comparison to our own, read *Understanding Cultural Differences:
Germans, French, and Americans*, by Edward T. Hall and Mildred Reed
Hall.

Other Essentials to Know

- The climate in Germany is similar to that of the lower
  Midwestern states in the United States—generally temper-
  ate and mild, with warm summers and wet winters.

- Germany shares borders with nine other European
  countries.

- Exporters to Germany should realize that Germany is a
  decentralized collection of states and regions as diverse as
  those in the United States.

- For tourists, Germany has a rich assortment of attractions,
  from the Black Forest in the southwest, to the Baltic Sea
  ports and resorts in the north. In the central region, the
  Rhine River offers picturesque river cruises past centuries-
  old castles. Also in this region, running roughly parallel to

the Rhine, is the so-called Romantic Highway, with each village, town, and city offering picture-postcard settings along the auto route.

- Germany's population is nearing 85 million residents, with the great majority living in urban areas. In recent years, Germany has been the destination for millions of immigrant laborers seeking work, which, while benefiting manufacturing, has created conflicts within the society. About 70 percent of the German population is Christian, divided almost equally between the Protestant (mainly Lutheran) and Roman Catholic faiths.

Here are some other characteristics of German culture:

- Germans are generally considered to be industrious, thrifty, and orderly. They appreciate punctuality, privacy, and skill.
- The full month of August is the traditional month when most German residents take vacations, so it is a difficult time to expect to conduct business.
- Germans dress fashionably, especially in public, while summer wear often consists of shorts and sandals.
- The handshake is the universal form of greeting, and only very close friends will embrace. A man should wait for a woman to extend her hand.
- Titles are much more important in Germany than in the United States; therefore, it is important to learn and use titles such as Doctor, Professor, and so on. As for using first names, it is best to wait to be invited to address a person by his or her first name. Instead, use other titles such as *Herr* (Mr.), *Frau* (Mrs.), or, if she is under eighteen, *Fraulein* (Miss). When you meet adult businesswomen, use the term *Frau* whether or not the woman is married.
- Inappropriate gestures include the following: chewing gum or cleaning your fingernails in public, talking with your hands in your pockets, and placing your foot on the furniture. Crossing your fingers does not signal "Good luck"

because Germans "squeeze the thumb" to indicate that. "Squeezing the thumb" is done by making a fist with the thumb folded inside the other fingers.

- While being hosted in Germany, it is appropriate to bring flowers—but always an odd number of flowers, and avoid roses since they symbolize a love relationship. Other types of gifts are usually wrapped.

- Germans eat in the continental style—that is, with the fork constantly remaining in the left hand, the knife in the right. Both hands should also be kept above the table, resting lightly at the wrists. Germans do not customarily favor drinks with ice, as they consider cold drinks to be unhealthy.

- Germans seem especially fond of fast, expensive automobiles, and on expressways (called autobahns), the faster cars are respected and deferred to when passing. The most popular sports are hiking, skiing, swimming (sometimes nude at certain hours in some hotels), cycling, tennis, and soccer (football).

- Germans take great pride in education, and, as one might expect, there is 99 percent literacy in their country. Nearly every occupation and skill has a special school for training.

- Medical care is provided free or at minimal cost to all citizens.

- According to *New York Times* correspondent Thomas L. Friedman, the age of globalization began the day the Berlin Wall was torn down.

- "Codetermination" among labor and management is a heavy influence in the structure of business there. This means that workers have direct input into the management of any firm with more than five employees. Therefore, German unions are very strong and provide workers with many more rights than do unions in the United States.

- Germany is known for providing long vacation periods to all workers. They are customarily taken in July, August, and

December, and little work is done during regional festivals such as Oktoberfest or Carnival prior to Lent.

- Germans enjoy spirited discussions, with religion, politics, and nuclear power discussed freely. But speaking of personal subjects or one's private life is constrained to good friends only.

- Germans are generally not physically expressive. People in the north of Germany are considered restrained, unemotional, and even stoic. Contrasting with them are the Bavarians in the south, who are more demonstrative and socially outgoing.

- Happily for Americans, English is the main foreign language taught in German schools, and most businesspeople are comfortable using it.

France

To begin this section, it is probably most appropriate to point out that the word *etiquette* is of French origin.

Two important areas of etiquette in France are (1) the use of the French language, and (2) gestures and body language. So here we go.

Using French

Don Ryan is a successful Midwestern businessman who purchased and renovated a small retirement/vacation home north of Marseille in France. He has studied French for several years but still quickly apologizes for his faulty grammar and pronunciation. Accordingly, when he once entered a French drugstore, he approached the druggist and began, *"Je regrette, mais je ne parle pas Français"* ("I am sorry, but I do not speak French"). The very Gallic druggist dipped his head, looked over his spectacles, sighed, and replied in perfect English, "That's quite all right. No one is perfect."

That single piece of dialogue illustrates the attitude of the French toward their language. In one word, pride. But we might warn that in some sectors, it is almost a militant pride.

Gilles Bousquet is the dean of international studies at the University of Wisconsin in Madison and is from Aix-en-Provence in southern France. "Americans who go to France and try to use their instant phrase books will probably be cut off most of the time by the French," he advised. "The French would [prefer to] talk to Americans in English—even if their English is not good—rather than hear their own language destroyed. The French are not at all tolerant of attempts. Only if one's French has been learned formally should he or she attempt to use it extensively while in France."

Other Francophiles advise that this is especially true in Paris and its environs. In the countryside, however, people tend to be more tolerant and understanding when visitors try to speak their language.

The first tip to remember, then, is to understand that above all other cultures, the French are probably the most nationalistic when it comes to language. The second tip is that if you attempt a few French words and phrases, be prepared to be corrected, even put down. Don't be dismayed. Many French people are flattered that you will at least try to speak their language. This is especially true of young people and some businesspeople who are struggling to learn American English. In a few lucky cases, such a mutual struggle creates a bond.

Above all, French is a beautiful language, and in their spirited conversations the French enjoy sincere debate, tests of logic, and witticisms. As one Francophile said, "Like the French opera, even a French menu can be an expression of poetry."

Gestures and Body Language

The mode of handshaking in France is usually as follows: a light, quick, single handshake, which is done with great frequency (arrivals, departures, each and every day). A strong pumping handshake is considered uncultured. In general, the person of higher rank or status extends his or her hand first. Also, when entering a room, greet and shake hands with each person in the room. A French woman offers her hand first, except when the man she is greeting has a higher social or professional status. Don't quickly jump to using first names; wait to be invited to do so.

Close friends, family members, and young people often kiss on either cheek, but it is really just "touching" cheeks or "kissing the air."

Depending on the region of France, it may be one, two, three, or four kisses on alternating cheeks.

French body language and behavior are very restrained in professional settings. They gesture infrequently, but you can still read a great deal about them from their facial expressions. In social situations, the French gesture easily.

Some gesture taboos that should be avoided are as follows:

- Resting your feet on tables or chairs.
- Using toothpicks, nail clippers, or combs in public.
- Conversing with your hands in your pockets.
- Chewing gum in public.
- Slapping your open palm over a closed fist (a rude gesture).
- Yawning, stretching, sniffling, or scratching in public.
- Holding loud conversations in public.
- Snapping the fingers of both hands.

The French may refrain from smiling at strangers in public since extensive smiling often suggests dim-wittedness to them.

Some unique gestures in France are:

- Forming a circle with your thumb and forefinger and placing your hand over your nose, then twisting. This signals that "someone nearby is drunk."

- The "O.K." sign (thumb and forefinger forming a circle) in some parts of France signifies "zero" or "worthless." (I once took a hotel room in the south of France and when the concierge asked, "How is your room, sir?" I responded with the "O.K." gesture. Miffed, he said, "Well, if you don't like it, just say so.")

- Playing an imaginary flute is a way to signal that someone is talking on and on and becoming tiresome. It also implies that you are not sure that the person is telling a true story. This is a rude gesture in a formal setting.

- Hand kissing is identified with the courtly French but is not used much anymore.

When dining, the French use the continental style, with the fork constantly held in the left hand. Also, rest your wrists lightly on the table and do not put your hands in your lap. Bread or rolls are broken, eaten with the fingers, and placed next to your dinner plate, usually directly on the tablecloth. At very formal meals, fruit is peeled with the knife and eaten with a fork. Cheese is served often, but cut a slice from the side, not from the tip of the wedge. The French are sometimes uncomfortable picking up a sandwich, French fries, and other such foods with the fingers. Wine is almost always served when dining, along with mineral water. Finally, when approaching the dining table, allow your host to indicate where you should sit.

Other Essentials to Know

Here are some valuable facts and tips paraphrased from the wonderful book *Managing Cultural Differences* (sixth edition), by Philip R. Harris, Robert T. Moran, and Sarah V. Moran.

- France is twice the size of Colorado and is the largest country in Western Europe, with a population exceeding 60 million and literacy reaching 98 percent.

- The French sense of time is casual, except for lunch. Lateness may be permissible for people of status but not for subordinates. They enjoy their two-hour lunches, their seven official holidays, and four or five weeks of vacations, usually in August.

- In business circles, gender diversity is less than in the United States.

- Some specific traits from the Harris/Moran/Moran book are:

    1. The French enjoy leisure and socialization.

    2. French society is stratified with sharply defined competing classes.

3. The French are very status conscious, and social status depends on one's social origins.

4. French people are friendly, humorous, and sardonic.

5. Personal honor and integrity are valued in France.

Dress is more formal and conservative than in the United States but it is always fashionable. At the beach, you may change into a bathing suit by holding a towel around yourself and undressing underneath it. On public beaches of the Atlantic and the Mediterranean, as well as at swimming pools, be prepared for topless or even nude bathers.

Italy

As for Italy, in *Managing Cultural Differences*, the authors quote from Xan Smiley's "A Survey of Italy," which appeared in the July 7, 2001, issue of the *Economist*:

> The first thing to say about Italy is that, however grubby its politics or flaky its economics, it is still for most of its inhabitants and visitors, one of the most delightful countries in the world. Its combination of man-made and natural beauty, cultural heritage and clement climate is second to none. Its people are blessed with charm, humor and the ability to enjoy, [and] let others enjoy, life."

With a population of 58 million, Italy enjoys a high per-capita income and is one of the United States' most important trade partners. In 2004, the United States was Italy's fourth-largest foreign supplier and the largest supplier outside the European Union. Yet Italy is only slightly larger than the state of Arizona.

There are twenty regions in Italy and three distinct geographic areas: the south, with Naples as its metropolitan center; the central midsection, with Rome as its focal point; and the north, with the industrialized region of Milan. In addition, Italy boasts one of the most unique cities in the world, Venice, which is literally sitting on water. The islands of Sardinia and Sicily are also part of Italy. Uniquely, Italy houses two independent nations: San Marino, on the coast of the Adriatic Sea, which has been independent since the fourth century; and Vatican City, situated within the city of Rome, which is the home of the Catholic Church.

One could argue that much of Western civilization originated on the Italian peninsula. Italy's history dates back several thousand years to the Etruscan age, between the eighth and second centuries B.C. The Etruscans, in turn, influenced the Roman Empire, which later borrowed from the Greek culture.

More recently, from 1922 to 1943, Benito Mussolini brought fascism to the country and allied himself with Germany's Adolf Hitler in World War II. In 1943, with the invasion by U.S. military forces, the fascists were overthrown and Italy supported the Allies.

The official language is Italian, although from city to city the dialects differ. The most common second language is English.

Tourism is a major industry, and, for many Americans, Italy is a "must-visit" destination. As a result, Italians have become uncommonly tolerant of outsiders. They believe that hospitality is an ancient Mediterranean tradition, an outgrowth of international trade connections. They welcome visitors because many of their own kin, relatives, and descendants have immigrated to other locales around the world.

Pasta and wine are the staples of Italian cuisine. There are more than two thousand different names for a bewildering variety of pasta shapes, and at least four thousand brands of wine, more than anywhere else in the world.

Italy has been called "the Garden of Eden of Gestures," mainly because all Italians are extremely expressive, not only in their spoken language but also in gestures and body language. There is actually a special dictionary of gestures in Italy, so take care because some of them may not mean what you intend.

Here are some specific common gestures you should know:

- Italians are known for being among the most demonstrative of all nationalities.
- Italians shake hands when meeting and departing.

- Italians are known for engaging in more physical contact than other Europeans do: cheek kissing among good acquaintances, embraces between men who are good friends, a lingering handshake with the other hand over your hand or at the elbow, and so on. You might also observe two male Italian friends walking along arm in arm. And Italy is one of the few remaining places in the world where a man may kiss the hand of a woman in greeting.

- When visiting churches, women should not wear shorts or sleeveless or skimpy tops or blouses.

- Italians may stand very close to you when conversing and may even poke your shoulder to demonstrate a point.

- In crowded public places, there are often no clearly visible queues.

- At the dining table, the host and the hostess will usually sit at opposite ends of the table, with the male guest of honor seated at the right of the hostess and the female guest at the right of the host.

- Your host should pour the wine, and many Italians consider it unfeminine for a woman to pour wine.

- Although Italians drink wine every day with their meals, they seldom over-imbibe. In fact, they drink wine for its taste more than for its effects.

- Refrain from eating until your hostess begins to eat.

- A knife and fork placed above your plate are used for dessert.

- It's best to cover your mouth when yawning.

- Shrugging the shoulders signals "I don't know" or "I don't care."

Specific hand gestures in Italy include the following seven:

1. The chin flick. This involves brushing the fingernails of one hand under the chin and continuing in an outward motion. In Northern Italy, it means, "Get lost. You are annoying me."

In Southern Italy, it is negative but not insulting. It can mean, "There is nothing," or "no," or "I cannot."

2. The "hook 'em horns" gesture—the palm and the fist pointed outward with the forefinger and the little finger extended upward—is called the *cornuto*, which means the "horns of a bull" and signals "your female mate has been unfaithful."

3. The "cheek screw" is done by pressing the extended forefinger into the cheek with a twisting motion, as if creating a dimple, and this connotes "I see a pretty girl."

4. The "hand purse." Hold your hand outward, palm up, with your thumb touching the curled fingers. Among Italians, this is a common gesture used for punctuating and emphasizing speech.

5. The "eyelid pull" is done by pulling a corner of one eye down with the index finger, and it conveys "alertness."

6. The "forearm jerk" is a well-known insulting gesture in many parts of the world, but especially in Italy. It's a full-arm gesture, the fist upraised with the other hand slapped downward into the elbow joint. It represents a phallic symbol and means "Up yours!"

7. The "finger" refers to a clenched fist, the palm facing inward, with the middle finger raised upward stiffly. And that, too, is a phallic symbol and is terribly rude.

Some general, often used gestures are these:

- When waving good-bye, hold the palm up with the fingers wagging up and down.

- Tapping the hand to the forehead, like a salute, means "You're crazy."

- Kissing the fingertips indicates that something is beautiful, whether it is food, art, or a woman.

- The "thumbnail bite" is done by placing the fingernail of the thumb under the front teeth and flicking it outward. It is an insulting gesture purportedly seen in versions of Shakespeare's *Romeo and Juliet* when one member of the feuding families aimed it at the other family member, causing great animosity between them.

- Rubbing the thumb rapidly against the fingers indicates "money."

- In some areas of Southern Italy, nodding the head back may indicate "no."

In business relations, Italians are very proud of their heritage and appreciate it when visitors show respect. As in many other countries, few women are in decision-making positions. In certain family companies, however, a woman may be in the driver's seat. These women are sophisticated, well-to-do, polished in their social and professional skills, and often very powerful.

In business negotiations, Italians can become loud and emotional during stressful periods. When conversing, they may gesticulate wildly and appear volatile, but this is also a sign that they are simply having an enjoyable conversation. Wit and humor are valued and socializing after business affairs is important. Developing mutual respect is also crucial, and trust must be earned.

It is imperative to make business appointments well in advance, but Italians also consider time to be fluid so they have a relaxed attitude about punctuality. Detailed agreements and contracts with numerous rules are not popular, and Italians like to haggle over prices.

Be conscious about using proper titles. Suitable attire is key in style-conscious Italy. Business cards are essential with details in both languages, Italian and English. Gift giving is fairly common among business associates.

Here are more traits that are common among Italians:

- As in much of Europe, a gift of red roses sends a signal of secret "romance." Why? Consider the Latin term *sub rosa* (meaning "secret") and the fact that in Catholic churches many of the confessional booths have roses carved above the door signifying confidentiality. Flowers should be conveyed in odd numbers and never give chrysanthemums because they are considered flowers of the dead.

- The number "13" has mixed messages. It is unlucky to have 13 at a dinner table, and Friday the 13th is considered unlucky. But in Naples, for example, where superstitions abound, 13 is considered lucky and the number 17 is considered unlucky.

- Other popular superstitions with negative connotations: a black cat crossing your path, sleeping in a bed with its foot facing the door, putting a hat on the bed, breaking a mirror, spilling salt or oil or pouring wine backward (with your hand held under the bottle), placing a loaf or bread roll upside down.

- In restaurants, check the bill to see if a gratuity has already been added. This is common in many European countries.

- The midday meal is usually the main meal of the day and may last as long as two hours.

- Butter is not common for bread or rolls and olive oil is used instead, and wine and bottled water will usually be present for the midday and evening meals.

- Public toilets may be a bit scarce, but almost every bar has one, and in Italy a bar is often nearby.

- Soccer (football) is the most popular sport in Italy. Bicycling, horse racing, skiing, tennis, boxing, fencing, swimming, and track and field are also favorites.

- Opera is a fashionable cultural pastime, and visits to the beach are enjoyed by all.

In summary, you'll find that Italians often multitask, are punctual in the north but not as much in the south, are high-context communicators, are warm and friendly, respect hierarchy, are competitive, do not like to take risks, and are often unpredictable but love routine.

Remember *la dolce vita* . . . so enjoy!

Brazil

In the 1980s, when I was assigned to manage all of Parker Pen's operations in Latin America, I was told that Brazil was the largest and most
prosperous country on that continent. There was, however, also a popular but very cynical saying about Brazil that went like this: "Brazil is
the land of the future . . . and it always will be."

Blessed with abundant natural resources, a large and diverse
population, and a fun-loving culture, in those years Brazil was
stricken with rampant hyperinflation, something rarely encountered in the history of the United States. What is hyperinflation?
That's when inflation runs amok. Most populations in the world
become seriously troubled if the rate of inflation reaches double digits. Hyperinflation means the inflation rate could be in *triple* digits
and even higher. In fact, at one point during 1987 to 1997, the rate
of inflation was 2,000 percent! Part of the reason for this runaway
devaluation of Brazil's currency was that for fifty years the government was run by the military.

What were the consequences of such out-of-control inflation?
Rents could double every ten weeks. Credit cards charged 25 percent
a month in interest. The cost of food and clothing went up 40 percent. It meant there were few, if any, piggy banks in Brazil. Why save
money in a bank? Each day and each week that money became less
valuable, perhaps by as much as 50 percent a month! According to
Leslie Evans of the Latin American Center at UCLA International,
"During those ten years [1987–1997], 40 percent of the GNP was
eaten up by inflation, and everyone got rid of cash as fast as possible, because it lost value sitting in your pocket. No one saved money.
And the majority of people were reduced to buying only the essentials of life, which devastated whole industries that produce all kinds
of optional goods and services." There had been only eight cases of
hyperinflation in the history of mankind, half of these after World
War II.

In the mid-1990s, Brazil started to work itself out of the inflation
spiral. The name of its currency was changed four times. The government tried price freezes and currency changes, but these did not work,

according to Leslie Evans. Reform after reform followed. Finally, by 1997, price increase rates dropped to reach standard international levels, and hyperinflation was over.

Today, the mantra "Brazil is the country of the future" has miraculously come true, and the reason is *ethanol*. According to a *60 Minutes* segment in the summer of 2006, Brazil has managed to turn one of its largest agricultural products—sugarcane—into ethanol gas; consequently, unlike most of the rest of the world, Brazil is no longer dependent on the world supplies and price of oil for the production of gasoline. A bright future, indeed.

Still, Brazil's problems are not totally solved. Even with its vast natural resources, a large labor pool, and economic power ranking it the regional leader, it is plagued with highly unequal income distribution among its population. A 1995 World Bank study reported that Brazil had the most unequal wealth distribution in the world. The Amazon Basin is suffering from deforestation, and in the largest cities—São Paulo and Rio de Janeiro—air and water pollution reign.

It is truly a land of contrasts. From the rich, opulent beaches of Rio de Janeiro, one can view on nearby hillsides the shantytowns occupied by the very poor. The population is also a contrast of colors—from the darkest to the whitest skin and every shade in between.

Here are some basic facts about Brazil today.

- The population is estimated at about 176 million. It is the fifth-largest country in the world. The Amazon River is the world's longest river.

- Brazilians today are descendants of the Portuguese, Germans, Italians, Spanish, and Polish.

- Whites represent 53.7 percent of the population; mulattos (mixed white and black) 38.5 percent, blacks 6.2 percent; and small numbers of Japanese, Arabs, and Africans make up the rest.

- Roman Catholics are in the majority, with 73.6 percent of the population, and Protestants represent 15.4 percent.

- Portuguese is the official language.

- Eighty-six percent of the population over age fifteen can read and write.
- The official name of Brazil is the "Federative Republic of Brazil." And the Portuguese spelling of Brazil is Brasil.
- The country is divided into twenty-six states and one federal district, the capital of Brasilia.
- The currency is called the *real* (pronounced ree-AHL).
- One of the most fascinating cities in Brazil is Manaus, deep in the Amazon River basin. Because of its remoteness from other trading centers, it is designated a free port and therefore offers many consumer products normally prohibited from being imported. Manaus has had a fascinating history since the beginning of the twentieth century, when it was a major producer of rubber for vehicles, especially in World War I.

A special mention should be made of football (soccer). It is a national addiction. And the "king" of Brazil, therefore, is Pele—a legendary player in the 1990s and earlier who is regarded worldwide as the most talented soccer player in history. In his twenty-two-year career, he played 1,363 games and scored 1,282 goals. His teams played in and won fifty-three titles, including three World Cups.

Another quality that prevails in Brazil is love of family—and "family" casts a wide circle on both sides of a marriage. Relatives often live with one another, party with one another, and support one another. This has engendered a special loyalty among family members, where, by the way, the man dominates. Speaking of family, Brazilians are particularly proud of their children and appreciate your attention to them.

Brazilians consider themselves "special" among all the Latin cultures on the continent.

Here are some do's & taboos to remember when you visit Brazil:

- A handshake is the traditional greeting between both men and women, especially in a business setting.

- Cheek kissing is also common among friends. How does a man know when a woman expects an "air kiss" on the cheek? When she shakes hands, the man may notice a slight tug toward the woman.

- When arriving and leaving, it is customary to greet and bid farewell to each and every person present, unless, of course, it is a large group.

- And here's another contrast: In much of the rest of Latin America, *titles* are important . . . but not so in Brazil. In fact, one may quickly jump to a first-name basis in Brazil.

- Brazilians usually understand Spanish, but they do not consider themselves Hispanics; therefore, it is best to communicate, whenever possible, in Portuguese.

- Brazilian men love good jokes and love to laugh, but you should avoid ethnic jokes and try not to mention Argentina, a country that has long been considered a historic rival. Also, don't discuss politics, religion, and other controversial subjects.

- The Brazilian version of our Mardi Gras is called *Carnaval*, a five-day celebration that always precedes Ash Wednesday, the beginning of Lent. It is an impossible time to conduct business.

- Punctuality is not necessarily a virtue in Brazil. But patience is.

- Brazilians like to conduct business through personal connections. An individual in this role may be referred to as a *despechante*. In Portuguese, that means someone is considered an "expediter."

- To make a toast, the proper word is *Saude*, which simply means "Health."

- Business entertaining is common, and quality is appreciated. Similarly, you might want to pack a small selection of gifts, but avoid anything black or purple, since these are considered "funereal" colors.

- Brazilians are expressive in body language, and touching is more common in Brazil than in the United States. When conversing one-on-one, be prepared to find the other person standing very close to you. One hand gesture to avoid is the "O.K." sign (the forefinger and the thumb forming a circle) since it refers to a part of female anatomy.

- Don't chew gum in public. It is considered rude.

- Try to avoid looking like a tourist. Don't wear shorts or athletic shoes (sandals may be better), and, if possible, don't carry a camera. This may be an invitation to pilferage or worse. Fabrics made of natural fibers are probably best, because the climate is generally warm.

- Brazilians enjoy their food, and in the south one popular dish is a *churrasco*, which we would consider a barbecue, but the Brazilian version features a variety of meats and therefore is more elaborate. Be prepared for frequent servings of small cups of very strong coffee. Fruit is often served as a separate course after lunches and dinners. Table manners dictate that the fruit should be peeled and eaten with a knife and fork.

- Brazilians often eat in the so-called continental style—that is, with the fork held constantly in the left hand. Don't eat anything with your bare hands.

Whether you visit Brazil as a tourist or on business, it is a very popular destination. New businesses are welcomed, and tourists are appreciated. For either type of visitor, two favorite purchases are semiprecious stones and well-made leather goods. Cuisine and wines are usually of high quality and great variety. For a rare vacation tour, consider a cruise from Manaus down the Amazon River. One warning: the beaches of Rio are world famous, but so is pilferage, usually at the hands of groups of young children who roam the beaches. Vehicular traffic—as in most highly populated cities and countries—is fast and heavy, so it's definitely better to favor taxis rather than to experiment on your own.

All in all, it appears that Brazil has succeeded in truly becoming "the land of the future."

Russia

In one of Woody Allen's better stand-up comedy routines, he boasted how he had recently taken a speed-reading course. He claimed that as a result, he had read the entire volume of *War and Peace* in one hour.

"Wanna know what it's about?" Allen asked.

"It's about Russia."

It would take the average visitor more than a simple speed-reading course to become acquainted with a country that is 1.8 times larger than the United States and that has a history stretching back many centuries.

But perhaps the year that transformed Russia into the economic power it is today is the year 1989. Ronald Reagan triggered the turn-around with his famous words "Mr. Gorbachev . . . tear down this wall!" Sometime thereafter, the Berlin Wall did come down, and it effectively signaled the end of the Cold War.

In his book *The Lexus and the Olive Tree*, the author Thomas L. Friedman argues that when the Cold War ended, it was succeeded by the age and concept of "globalization." Friedman described globaliza-tion as meaning "a new, very greased, interconnected [global eco-nomic] system. We are [now] all one river." He followed the success of that book with another best-seller, *The World Is Flat*. That book describes globalization in more detail.

Russia has a landmass that stretches through eleven time zones. On the eastern side Russia is located in Europe, while its larger west-ern part is in Asia. More characteristics of modern-day Russia are supplied by the *CIA World Fact Book*, found on the Internet under "Russia":

> [Russia is] the largest country in the world in terms of area, but unfavorably located in relation to major sea lanes of the world. Despite its size, much of the country lacks proper soils and climates, either too cool or too dry for agriculture. Environ-mental problems are enormous: air pollution from heavy industry, emissions of coal-fired electric plants, and trans-

portation in major cities; deforestation, soil erosion; scattered areas of sometimes intense radioactive contamination; groundwater contamination from toxic waste; urban solid waste management; abandoned stocks of obsolete pesticides.

In spite of this, the *CIA Fact Book* reports that in 2005 Russia ended its seventh straight year of growth, averaging 6.4 percent annually since its financial crisis of 1998. "But a weakness still exists," the CIA claimed. "President Putin has made little progress in building the rule of law, the bedrock of a modern market economy."

What about doing business in Russia? Three scholars, Terri Morrison, Wayne A. Conaway, and George A. Borden, Ph.D., have compiled a wonderful book titled *Kiss, Bow, or Shake Hands*, with the subtitle "How to Do Business in Sixty Countries." And here's the first key tip for doing business in Russia: "Western business people have learned how important restraint is when negotiating with the Japanese; never lose your temper when dealing with Japanese. The Russians are the exact opposite. Russian negotiations almost always involve temper tantrums, dire threats, and walkouts. Loss of temper during negotiations is expected by the Russians. Only in one crucial area are the Russians and the Japanese alike: they both have tremendous patience. Both cultures prize endurance, which often puts impatient North Americans at a disadvantage."

Here are some tips regarding daily interactions with Russians:

- Russians respect the "queue" (a line) almost as much as the English do. Long lines are a common occurrence, so be respectful and polite and never "jump the queue," as the English would say . . . meaning, never butt in front of people ahead of you.

- Americans are known for smiling a great deal, even on public sidewalks. But in places like France and Russia, smiling in public places suggests that a person might be simpleminded. In smaller private gatherings, Russians may be more friendly and open and may smile more often. Also, in private gatherings Russians are not afraid to show emotions.

- Most of us have seen pictures of the common Russian greeting among men—the Russian "bear hug," perhaps accompanied by cheek kissing. And here, three quick pecks on alternate cheeks are common. When two people are not close friends, however, the handshake—a good, firm handshake along with direct eye contact—is the customary greeting.

- A peculiar taboo in Russia takes place in the seating areas of public places, like a theater. In the United States, we face the screen or the stage and sidle in past others who are seated or who perhaps will stand to give us more space. Not so in Russia. That is considered impolite. Why? Well, consider that you are placing your derriere virtually in their face. In Russia, when entering an aisle, always turn and face the people who are seated.

- The "O.K." sign, ubiquitous in most places in the world (except in Brazil and Nigeria), is ambiguous in Russia. As an import from the West, it is accepted as the signal for "all right," "good," and "fine." But in some parts of Russia it could be considered a vulgar gesture, signaling "a---hole."

- A unique rule of body language applies when departing a Russian home. It is considered bad form to shake hands across the threshold. When you visit a Russian home, it is appropriate to bring small gifts: high-quality writing instruments, pictures or books about your home community, CDs of pop music, good soap, and small items of clothing are appreciated.

- For businesswomen visiting Russia, it is probably a good idea to retain a trustworthy Russian man or woman to act as guide, interpreter, driver, and general aide. In Moscow, people who are available for these duties can be found through the International Women's Club, the American Women's Organization, and the British Women's Club.

- Avoid the black market, especially to exchange currency at more attractive rates than the official exchange rate.

Bartering is common. Street crime has increased so take extra precautions regarding robbery, abduction, and extortion.

- The thumbs-up gesture is positive and shows approval. Shaking the raised fist shows disagreement and anger, which is the same interpretation as in many other countries around the world.

- As in much of Europe, Russians usually eat in the continental style—that is, with the fork remaining in the left hand.

- Want to count with your fingers? Start with the pinkie— yes, the little finger. Begin from left to right, bending the little finger into the palm, then the same with the ring, middle, and index fingers, and finally the thumb.

- Hailing a waiter is simple. Just nod your head in his direction or raise your hand and finger.

- When you make a toast in Russian, the proper word is *"Na zdorovie,"* pronounced Nah ZDROH-vee-eh.

- In Russia, English is spoken extensively. It is widely taught in Russian schools, and it is said there are more teachers of English in Russia than there are people in the United States who speak Russian (excluding those native Russians who have emigrated to the United States).

- In Russia, observe the "three P's" of behavior, as suggested for most other countries around the world. These are patience, politeness, and perseverance.

As in many Latin countries, people in Russia often have three names. The first name is the Christian or given name (in the United States, we simply say "the first name"); then comes the father's Christian name; and, finally, the family name or surname. These treble names also come in masculine or feminine form. For example, a man would be called *Ivan* (his given name) *Petrovich* (taken from his father's first name, *Peter*) *Suslov* (his last, or family, name). A woman whose first name was Natasha, however, would feminize those names in this manner: *Natasha Petrovna Suslova*. When you come to know a Russian very well, you can address him or her by using the first two names. Therefore, using the previous example, you would address the man as *Ivan Petrovich*. Also, don't be surprised if couples have different surnames, meaning family names. Women in Russia do not automatically take their husband's name and often prefer to retain their own.

When greeting one another, men and women will very likely shake hands. This is usually done each and every time they meet. Among good friends it is common to kiss the cheeks (three times, alternating cheeks) and often this is a real kiss, not just the "air kiss" given in other countries. This cheek-kissing greeting is done both woman to woman and man to man.

You may also observe that when in public, good friends (whether men or women) may walk arm in arm and even hand in hand, between sexes and bisexually. This merely signifies good friendship and does not necessarily have any sexual connotation.

It's very possible a Russian acquaintance will ask you, "What is life really like in the United States?" This is more than idle curiosity; Russians are genuinely interested. It's also good to be prepared for more disturbing questions such as, "Does everyone in the United States carry a gun?"

When visiting private homes or attending official dinners, it is very common to exchange toasts and give short speeches. Course after course will be washed down with vodka, with toasts in between that may evolve into "duels" to see who can drink the most. Dinner conversation is very popular and may last for long periods of time.

For tourists visiting Russia, Lenin's Tomb in the Red Square of Moscow seems to be the highest-priority destination. Lenin was the first premier of Soviet Russia and is considered the man who, according to Russian tourist publications, "changed the world." He died on January 21, 1924, and three days later, his body was preserved and ready for viewing in a temporary wooden house. Lenin's current resting place is in a granite structure that one might equate in importance with the great pyramids and tombs of the Middle East. Other popular tourist destinations are the Kirov Ballet performances, where the likes of Balanchine, Nureyev, and Baryshnikov once performed, and the cities of St. Petersburg and Murmansk.

In the late 1980s and early 1990s, Thomas Loftus, a prominent Wisconsin politician, was named the U.S. ambassador to Norway. During his tour, he visited Murmansk, Russia's largest saltwater port in the far north. The Russian submarine fleet is based there, many of the subs rusting away because of disuse. Learning that some of these ships still had nuclear-powered engines, Loftus inquired of the commanding Russian officer whether it was possible that any radiation could be leaking from the idle ships. The officer smiled mischievously and said, "No, not likely. But let's put it this way. You probably won't have to buy a new battery for your watch."

Earlier, I mentioned that complete shelves of books have been written about each country. That is particularly true of Russia. So if you are planning a visit to this fascinating, ancient country, head for your nearest library and dig in.

India

The June 26, 2006, issue of *Time* magazine featured India as its cover story, titled "Why the World's Biggest Democracy Is the Next Great Economic Superpower—and What It Means for America." *Time* said that if Asia is considered a tiger and the Chinese power is a dragon, then India is an elephant.

Therefore, it is important for citizens from all nations to know certain fundamental facts about this burgeoning country.

According to *Time*, there are "10 ways India is changing the world," as culled from the following sources: the World Bank; the UN; McKinsey & Co.; and a PriceWaterhouseCoopers report.

1. In 2005, India's gross domestic product (GDP) exceeded $800 billion and is growing at the second-fastest rate in the world—an average of 8 percent in each of the last three years.

2. Revenues of $36 billion came from India's Internet-technology industry.

3. The stock market in India has created twenty-three billionaires, ten of whom reached this milestone in 2006.

4. Each year about 50 million Indians travel on airlines, and the sales of motorcycles and passenger cars have doubled.

5. Where is the largest film industry? Not in the United States. The India film industry, known as "Bollywood," produces close to a thousand movies each year.

6. American tourists are flocking to India—618,000 in 2005.

7. Indians are immigrating to the United States, and about 2 million people of Indian descent live in the United States.

8. More than any other country, India has an estimated 5.7 million people living with HIV.

9. As of July 2006, India's total estimated population was 1,095,351,995. That makes it the second-most-populous nation in the world, and it is projected to be the most populous by 2015. Life expectancy is 64 years for men and 65.5 for women.

10. Finally, most of us know the names of three prominent cities in India as Bombay, Calcutta, and Madras. Within the last few years, Indians have reverted back to the original names of those cities. Bombay has become Mumbai, Calcutta is now Kolkata, and Madras is Chennai, changing what millions of Indians have been taught over many generations.

India is roughly one-third the size of the United States; half of the country is under cultivation and one-fourth is forested. Three basic seasons occur in India: a hot summer (March to May), the rainy season (June to September), and a cool winter (October to February). Variations to this pattern will be found according to region and elevation.

When you visit India, make your plans according to these seasons. The June to September period is the monsoon season. Many tourists visit in October, which is generally not too hot or too cool. In the so-called winter (mid-December and January), in the northern cities the nights can be astonishingly cold but are comfortably warm in the south.

According to the *CIA Fact Book*, India is one of the most ancient countries in the world. The Indus Valley civilization dates back at least five thousand years. Aryan tribes from the northwest infiltrated onto Indian lands about 1500 B.C. and merged with earlier Dravidian inhabitants to create the classical Indian culture. Arab, Turk, and Afghan Muslims ruled for ten of those centuries, followed by Portuguese and Dutch traders. By the nineteenth century, the English controlled India, but in 1947, under Mahatma Gandhi, independence from Great Britain was achieved. In 2007, India celebrated its sixtieth anniversary as an independent democracy.

India has six countries for neighbors: Bangladesh, Bhutan, Myanmar (previously called Burma), China, Nepal, and Pakistan. India is bordered on the west by the Arabian Sea, and the Bay of Bengal is situated between Myanmar (Burma) and Pakistan.

As for religions, 80.5 percent of the population are Hindus, with Muslims ranked at 13.4 percent, Christians at 2.3 percent, Sikhs at 1.9 percent, and the rest as "others" or "unspecified."

Hindi is the national language and the primary tongue of 30 percent of the people, but English enjoys associate status and is considered the most important language for national, political, and commercial communication. There are fourteen other official languages and some three hundred dialects.

Returning to India's position as the "next great economic power," the *Time* article's author, Michael Elliott, asserted, "Fueled by high-octane growth, the world's largest democracy is becoming a global power [and] why the world will never be the same."

The impact of India and its people is all around us. Just observe college campuses in the United States. One of the largest ethnic groups will be Indians. India is also probably turning out the greatest number of computer specialists in the world. And in the field of medicine, conventional wisdom states that some of the best and the brightest Indian students come to the United States for their education, but only a small number return to their home countries. And when we say "all around us," that includes telephone service companies created by U.S. firms but which are staffed by Indians who are located in India.

As for gestures and body language, here are some important forms taken from my book *Gestures: The Do's and Taboos of Body*

Language Around the World, Revised and Expanded Edition. Lists like these offer generic information, so this material may also be found in other reference books on India:

- Greetings in India take the form of the palms of the hands being pressed together in a praying position, held about chest height, and accompanied by a slight bow forward. This is called the *namaste* (pronounced nah-mas-TEH). It can also be used when saying good-bye and is common in countries such as Thailand and Indonesia. Westerners can use this gesture for greetings or farewells, and it will be appreciated because it shows a knowledge of Indian customs.

- Men do not normally touch women in either formal or informal situations. A Western woman should not initiate a handshake with a man. Most Indian women will shake hands with foreign women but not with men.

- When walking the streets, try not to stare, especially at the impoverished; that is considered humiliating for them.

- Ask permission first (1) when taking photographs of people, and (2) before smoking cigarettes, pipes, or cigars.

- Whistling in public is considered impolite.

- If an Indian smiles and jerks his head backward, it could signal "yes." In the south of India, when a person moves his head quickly back and forth, it can mean "Yes, I understand what you are saying."

- Don't pat youngsters on their heads. The head is considered a sacred part of the body.

- As in the Middle East, where the feet and soles of the shoes are considered the lowest and dirtiest part of the body, don't show the soles of your shoes to other people.

- A unique gesture in India is to grasp one's earlobes. It expresses remorse or honesty, as a servant might do when scolded.

- Hosts will often serve you, and to refuse could be an insult. Use the *namaste* to respectfully signal that you have had enough food.

Remember that today, many Indians have been educated in the United States so they are aware of American ways and may actually perform some of the previous gestures that are considered incorrect in India.

When conducting business in India, remember that patience will serve you well. Plan to be kept waiting, and don't be offended if your business host takes phone calls, signs documents, or receives an impromptu visitor. Also, finding the right partner or go-between is often wise. Connections are important in Indian business circles. Another area for caution is when using the English language because Indians have probably learned British English, with its many variations from American English.

When doing business, you need to consider hierarchy, status, power, and caste. Hindus belong to whatever caste they are born into, and they cannot move up the caste ladder by becoming millionaires or attaining Ph.D.s.

In business, Indians are strongly relationship focused. This means that it is important to take time to build rapport, friendship, loyalty, and respect before you consummate a big business deal.

Finally, the most significant recent trend in India is probably the bridge that has been built back to India by Indians who have emigrated to the United States. As *USA Today* reported in June 2006, Indians "are seeing the benefits of an open economy and consumerism. . . . Many thousands of Indian immigrants with strong ties to the U.S. and India are storming back to their ancestral home-land to cultivate business and cut deals." As one Indian observed, "[B]rick by brick, we are building an 8,000-mile bridge between the U.S. and India."

If you intend to walk across that bridge, I hope this short segment will motivate you to visit your local library or bookstores, surf the Internet, and generally do as much homework as you can in advance. You'll be glad you did.

The United Kingdom

I've saved the best for last. It's best for me because my family and I lived in England for almost four years—four years that were among the most interesting and enjoyable of my entire career. Since that experience, England has been my all-time favorite destination.

First, a comment on terminology. England, Wales, Scotland, and Northern Ireland make up the United Kingdom. "Great Britain" applies only to England, Wales, and Scotland. The "British Isles" consist of Great Britain, Ireland, the Isle of Man, and the Channel Islands in the English Channel. England itself is 50,000 square miles, approximately the size of New York state. Remember that people living in Great Britain are called British, and only the people living in England are called English. Scots live in Scotland, and the Welsh live in Wales.

Anyone who grew up during World War II probably carries a romantic, even heroic, memory of the British people, with their struggle and near annihilation by the Nazis in the early 1940s. Led by Winston Churchill, whom many consider to be the greatest historic figure of the twentieth century, the British faced one of the strongest tests of courage in history. Outnumbered and outgunned, Churchill—who even had the features of a bulldog—stubbornly stood steadfast and rallied his nation. This was especially significant when Adolf Hitler made the strategic mistake of stopping at the English Channel, delayed his invasion of Great Britain, and instead turned his attention to the Russians on his eastern front.

Even today, in the countryside of that "green and pleasant land," as Churchill labeled it, one can still see, albeit faintly, ruins of pillboxes and antiaircraft gun emplacements dug into the earth from that desperate time.

Visitors find a sense of history around every street corner or on the curving, hedge-lined country roads, called "lanes" by locals. England is, in my opinion, one of the few countries where most, if not all, of the famous national landmarks are genuinely impressive and not hokey re-creations. One can rattle off the list: in London one would seek out the Houses of Parliament, Number 10 Downing Street, the Admiralty where Churchill directed the war effort, the Tower of London, St. Paul's Cathedral, Buckingham Palace, the British Museum, Hampton

Court, the London Eye (a huge Ferris wheel on the River Thames in central London), Trafalgar Square, . . . and on and on. Each is deserving of a certain reverence and great respect.

To the south of London are the ports of Southampton and Plymouth, where, three centuries ago, past relatives of many who may read this book embarked on dangerous voyages across the Atlantic to the new land in the west. Approximately a hundred miles to the west of London one also finds Stonehenge. To this day, historians are not certain why and how this ring of huge stones was built at roughly the same time the Great Pyramids were being constructed in Egypt. Not far from London and to the south is Chartwell, the country home of Churchill before and during the war. This idyllic manor is maintained just as it was in the 1930s and 1940s, even to the extent that current newspapers are replaced daily on the same tables that held them sixty and seventy years ago. To the north of London is Stratford-on-Avon (about a two-and-a-half-hour drive), the home of William Shakespeare, plus Manchester, Edinburgh, Glasgow (all three roughly six to eight hours from London by car), and many more famous landmarks.

This barely begins to cover the long list of historic sites, each with its own story worthy of major volumes.

As for historic figures, one could start with Julius Caesar's first exploratory forces, which reached Britain in 55 B.C. The Romans did not invade until A.D. 43, staying until A.D. 426. (Today, jokesters like to tell of discovering coins from that time, clearly marked with the year "B.C.")

The year 1066 was, by all accounts, a watershed year, when William the Conqueror invaded and began a whole new era of political and social change. Monarchs with such familiar names as Henry VIII, Elizabeth I, and Queen Victoria followed.

The British Empire was created by a combination of courageous explorers and naval sea power marked by the defeat of the Spanish Armada in 1588. British influence spread westward to what is now Canada and the United States, beyond to Australia, southward to South and Central Africa, and eastward to India. In those centuries, the British Empire was arguably the greatest power on earth. It was not until World War I that expansion of the empire halted, and a period of shrinkage set in.

Overall, there is only one word to describe the history of Great Britain, and that word is *rich*.

Today the population reaches 60 million and the official language is, of course, English. Beware, though! For many American business-people, the English accent can be mesmerizing. It is said that Americans should never allow the English to make sales presentations verbally, because the sound of British English is so charming that we become bewitched. "Get it in writing," we are admonished.

Another characteristic of the British, especially in business circles, is the preference for conservatism, moderation, and emotional reserve. One claim I frequently heard among wags about the British penchant for conservatism was this: "When the world comes to an end, it will come to England thirty years later."

In addition, the British disapprove of the American habit of con-stantly speaking about "the biggest," "the best," "the greatest," and "the grandest." To the contrary, the average British person avoids statements of extremes and showings of emotion or excessive enthu-siasm. The British also seem to prefer self-deprecation and wryness in their humor. When I lived and worked there, it was said, "You know an Englishman likes you when he will insult you—mildly and good-humoredly—to your face." This prompted me to tell two local col-leagues at a luncheon one day, "Excuse me. I must visit the WC [meaning "water closet" or simply bathroom]. Don't say anything rude about me until I return."

Class-consciousness is still alive in Great Britain but is on the decline. Today, the younger generations, who often lead the world in fashion, music, and the arts, have been quick to break with traditions that span the past centuries.

Politeness, etiquette, and protocol are all respected. For example, among the older generation, one does not quickly jump to first names or "pry" into another person's business occupation. Yet the British are almost universally polite and respectful to visitors.

While living in England, I commuted by train into London from a lovely town called Reigate each day. I had grown accustomed to the friendly inquisitiveness of my hosts, who seemed to enjoy receiving assurances that we Americans were enjoying our stay in England. Uncharacteristically, some English people even struck up conversations with strangers like me who obviously appeared to be American. One of these occasions occurred on my daily train trip aboard the unique British rail system where, quite often, the bench seats face each other. As I sat quietly reading my newspaper, I noticed a properly dressed British gentleman looking over the top edge of his paper. I could see a growing curiosity in his eyes. Not wanting to face even gentle questioning—such as, "I say, sorry to bother you, but you are American. Correct?" And if I would acknowledge "Yes," he might continue, "I have some relatives in a place called Topeka. Do you live near there?"

So, somewhat rudely, I just kept raising my own newspaper to avoid eye contact until we reached Victoria Station, where I quickly exited our compartment. To my surprise, I could hear the same gentleman walking behind me—even quickening his step as if to catch up with me. And indeed he did. Finally, he tapped my shoulder lightly and said, "Pahdon me." After a pause while I anticipated some remote question about the United States, he continued, "But I'm sorry to say I noticed that your fly is open." And then he walked away. What I had misinterpreted as bothersome curiosity was really consternation over whether he should reveal an embarrassing mishap on my part. I realized then that I had much to learn about British demeanor.

Doing Business in England

Remember these helpful tips on your business trips to England:

- Don't wait until the last minute to make business appointments—that is, by flying to London and using the telephone in your hotel room to arrange meetings. The custom there is to book appointments well in advance.

- An alternative to making connections there is to be introduced by third parties.

- During your conversations, it's best not to get too personal.

- Take along a book on the differences between British and American terminology. (See chapter 4 for examples of some of these.)

- Be aware of the growing population of immigrants who have flocked to Great Britain seeking employment in recent years.

- Punctuality is respected, but, as in any large metropolitan city where delays due to traffic are common, it is understood if one arrives slightly late for an appointment.

- British social life revolves around that unique institution "the local"—translation: "the pub." Business lunches may be taken at a nearby pub but also at a good-quality restaurant or a private club.

- Bear in mind that in Great Britain, as in many European countries, the first floor of any multifloor building is called "the ground floor," and what we would call the "second floor" is then referred to as "the first floor." This may seem trivial, but if you are meeting someone on the "second" floor, a misunderstanding could have unfortunate results.

- When talking about sports, what the British call "football," we call "soccer." Other very popular sports are rugby, cricket, and tennis.

- Almost everyone is aware that in Great Britain, autos are driven on the lefthand side of the road, and the driver's seat and the steering wheel are on the right side of the car. The British have a great penchant for automobiles, and a person's rank in business is very often displayed by the make of his or her auto. In other words, the higher someone ranks in his or her company, the finer and more expensive car the person drives.

- As for royalty and the royal family, the queen is still highly respected among the populace, but the institution of royalty seems to be waning.

- During the business day, two refreshment breaks are usually taken: coffee or tea in midmorning and tea in the afternoon. As for spirits, scotch whisky is probably the most popular, along with gin and tonic, and British beer is favored in pubs. But, contrary to myth, beer in England is not served warm. It is more likely to be chilled. "Lager" beer is a light golden color with perhaps more carbonation, while the British beers are darker in color and referred to as "bitter" because they have a slightly stronger "bite." All types of wine are known and valued.

- The British eat in the so-called continental style—that is, with the fork remaining steadily in the left hand. A napkin is called a *serviette*, and proper dining manners are respected and expected.

- To glimpse and understand the seamier side of British life, buy one of the tabloid newspapers. They tend to print more spectacular, racier, and more gossipy stories than, say, the *Times* does.

- The English have the fewest public holidays in Europe. These include New Year's Day, Good Friday and Easter Monday, May Day (May 1), spring and summer bank holidays, Christmas, and Boxing Day (December 26). The latter is named for the tradition of giving small boxed gifts to the postman, servants, gardeners, and so on, but it is also a day for visiting friends and relatives.

- When invited to someone's home, it is appropriate to bring a small gift, such as flowers or a box of candy.

- In England, the "queue" is almost sacred. One never "jumps the queue," meaning to step ahead of someone while waiting in line.

Gestures and Body Language
- Summon waiters at a restaurant by raising your hand. To signal that you would like the check (called "the bill" there), make a motion with both hands as if you were signing your name on a piece of paper.

- Loud conversations and any form of boisterousness in public places should be avoided.

- Avoid staring at people in public. Privacy is highly valued and respected.

- In Wales, when addressing a group, speakers should avoid rubbing their noses, standing with their hands in their pockets, or shuffling their feet.

- If you smoke, it is the custom to first ask whether you may light up and also to offer cigarettes to others in your conversational group. In almost all public places, smoking is banned.

- When drinking socially in British pubs, after paying for a drink, pick up your change. To leave it on the bar could imply that you are leaving it as a tip.

- Other common practices: when yawning, cover your mouth; use handkerchiefs discreetly; remove your hat when entering a building; men should cross their legs at the knees, rather than placing one ankle across the other knee; women cross their legs at the knees or ankles.

- To repeat, politeness and good manners are expected and appreciated.

I will conclude with the wonderful, all-purpose, and familiar word that's used when toasting anywhere in the United Kingdom . . . "Cheers!"

9

Essential Things to Know about Taking Your Show on the Road: Exporting

In the future there will be two kinds of companies,
those that go global and those that go bankrupt.

—C. Michael Armstrong, CEO, AT&T

Companies that export grow faster and profit more. During the last fifty years, that claim has been proved to be true over and over again.

If you are an owner or an employee of a company that is not presently active in selling your product or service overseas, this chapter will lay out, first, the reasons why exporting is an exciting business and, second, how to get started.

Reasons to Export

Here are some essential reasons why exporting can dramatically expand your business horizons:

- The U.S. Department of Commerce estimates that thousands and thousands of small and medium-size American companies are capable of exporting but are not doing so. The reason? They are frightened by such things as "How will I get paid? I don't want to be paid in funny money like pesos or yen or even euros," or "I don't know anything about export shipping and documentation," and finally, "I don't speak a foreign language." As you will learn, all these objections can be quickly and easily overcome.

- Help is readily at hand. The U.S. Department of Commerce operates Export Assistance Centers with 107 offices across the country that offer a selection of services, advice, and counseling—much of it free of charge. In addition, there are 150 international offices in 84 countries. The same may be true within your state government.

- Both the federal and the state governments *want* you to export. No one *opposes* exporting. Labor unions favor exports. Unions know that when a company expands its operations via exporting, this adds more workers to an already successful existing workforce.

- In one sense, exporting is very similar to selling within the United States; it's just that with exporting, you must ship your product over longer distances. The matters of payments, shipping, insurance, and so on are easily handled. Your local bank very likely has an international department that can assist you with payments. The most common form of payment is a "letter of credit." Ask about that. As for shipping, documents, and insurance, these services can be obtained through a broker in your area who specializes in these tasks. Check the Internet or look in the Yellow Pages under "shipping brokers" or "freight forwarders."

The Values of Exporting

The values of exporting are many:

- Exports mean jobs. Exports account for about 12 million jobs in the United States. That's one of every five factory jobs. Exports also mean higher wages. Workers in jobs supported by exports receive wages that are 13 to 18 percent higher than the national average. And in high-tech industry jobs, wages are even higher.

- Small and medium-size companies account for 97 percent of all U.S. exporting firms, but that represents only 30 percent of the value of U.S. exports of goods. This means that just 3 percent of the companies in the United States account for 70 percent of the total value of those exports. Thus, there is tremendous growth potential among small and medium-size companies.

- Exports are on the rise. U.S. exports grew from $57 billion in 1970 to $1.01 trillion in 2003—an increase of nearly 10 percent each year.

- Just about any type of company can offer its product overseas. In my home state of Wisconsin—located about as far away from the two oceans as possible—there are companies shipping a remarkable array of products to overseas markets: beer and honey to Germany; ginseng to East Asia; Christmas trees to Mexico; marine engines to Vietnam; bows and arrows to Japan; and even wooden chopsticks to Hong Kong (Wisconsin has extensive forests). One company—Sta-Rite in Delavan, Wisconsin—makes swimming pool filters containing a special fine grain of sand and is selling them to Saudi Arabia. Thus, we are selling sand to Saudi Arabia! Ohio also ships large quantities of sand to the Middle East because of the sand's high silicone content, which is necessary for the manufacture of glass.

- Exports create incremental sales. These are sales over and above whatever revenues you may receive from within the U.S. market.

- Exports take up unused capacity in your factories.

- Exports can smooth out seasonal fluctuations that you may face within the U.S. market.

- We have two highly attractive export markets as our closest neighbors. Canada and Mexico are possibly closer to your home base than many major U.S. cities are. The single province of Ontario buys more U.S. products than many major countries do. And the North American Free Trade Agreement (NAFTA) has substantially reduced or eliminated duty and tariff barriers to those countries.

- Once you enter the global marketplace, you quickly learn more about your competitors and new advances in your product or service.

Tom Peters, in his bestselling book *In Search of Excellence*, says that "any company that is not doing at least ten percent of its business in exporting is missing the boat."

The First Lesson

The most important lesson to learn when embarking on a search for export sales is that there are two basic types of business cultures in the world. They are deal-focused business cultures and relationship-focused cultures.

We in the United States, along with Canada and much of Central Europe, are considered "deal-focused" cultures. This means the deal is the essence of doing business overseas. We are taught that "time is money" and that we should concentrate on the final objective, which is "the deal." We are taught to avoid wasting time socializing with our hosts in that country or visiting their museums or national historic sites. Instead, we should focus on the target—"the deal"—and move on to the next country.

Where friction often arises is that many other regions of the world, notably Asia, South America, and the Middle East, tend to be "relationship-focused" markets. This means that the relationship between two humans is just as important as the deal. People wishing to do business together must first have rapport, a feeling of trust and understanding, in order to conduct business successfully. In these parts of the world, considerable time might be spent socializing and getting to know one another before even discussing "the deal." Michael P. Wynne, a veteran international business consultant from Naperville, Illinois, puts it this way: "All business is based on relationships, and relationships are built on respect."

Thus, the first lesson in international business is to recognize these two conflicting attitudes and act accordingly. In much of the world, the number-one complaint about American businesspeople is that we are impatient. So, prepare yourself before taking the next step.

Where to Start

This is simple. Run, don't walk, to your nearest U.S. Department of Commerce Export Assistance Center. The folks there are paid to help you! Also, your state's Department of Commerce or Development very likely has trade specialists near you and possibly trade offices located overseas, waiting to help companies from your state. A listing of state offices can be found in the "Directory" section on page 263.

At the U.S. Commerce Department's Export Assistance Center, international trade specialists work as a team to obtain the information you need to succeed. They will assist you in the following areas:

- Determining the best markets for your company. Start with two or three markets, and receive help with customized market research in those markets.
- Evaluating international competitors
- Legal and other regulatory issues
- Settling disputes
- Playing an advocacy role in obtaining contract bids
- Cultural and business protocol
- Finding potential distributors for your product or service

All this is done through one-on-one counseling. In addition there are Web sites, trade shows, trade missions, and dozens of other ways to introduce you to exporting.

Here is what the Export Assistance Center calls the "Exporting Basics Life Cycle":

1. *Prepare to export.* Is your company ready for exporting? Entering foreign markets requires common sense, support from management, and a clear export strategy. A comprehensive "Basic Guide to Exporting" is found on the U.S. Department of Commerce's Web site (www.doc.gov), and it can prepare you for various approaches to exporting.

2. *Research new markets.* Which markets hold the most promise for your products? Who are the major customers and competitors in the market? Use market research reports that are customized to focus your efforts on the most promising markets.

3. *Find and develop trade contacts.* Identify potential buyers, agents, distributors, or joint-venture partners for your product or service. Become familiar with the various partner matching and trade leads offered by the federal government.

4. *Promote your company.* A variety of cost-effective services are available to help you test markets and your exposure overseas.

5. *Conduct actual trade transactions.* Specialists will help you through the web of international transactions. Learn the basics about packing, labeling, documentation, and shipping, or find the freight forwarders in your area who can handle those functions for you.

6. *Finance and insurance.* Will you need to secure additional working capital to manufacture your exports? Will you want to offer finance terms to your customers? The Export Assistance Center staff will tell you about the types of financing tools and government services available to help you conduct your export business and reduce risk.

7. *Follow up on transactions.* Export operations only begin with the sale. Learn how to follow up on transactions and cultivate relationships with your customers.

The Commercial News USA is a magazine-style publication issued six times each year (http://www.export.gov/cnusa) that has timely articles on international trade.

Finding International Partners and Trade Leads

Here are eight specific ways Export Assistance Centers can lead you to your customers:

1. *The U.S. Department of Agriculture.* The USDA offers a variety of trade leads, partner matching, and marketing-assistance programs designed specifically for agricultural and commodity producers.

2. *"BuyUSA."* BuyUSA is an online matching and trade lead service. It connects exporters with international buyers, agents, distributors, and joint-venture partners . . . all online. It can increase your export sales by posting your corporate profile and help you search for business partners and trade leads.

3. *International partner search.* Whether through joint-venture partners, licensees, agents, distributors, or other partners, the U.S. Department of Commerce uses its strong network of foreign contacts to interview potential partners and provide you with a list of up to five prequalified partners.

4. *Gold Key matching service.* This service provides prescreened appointments that are arranged before you go overseas. The U.S. Commercial Service has more than 150 offices in 85 countries. Friends of mine who are new to exporting rave about this particular service.

5. *International trade opportunities through the World Bank and multilateral development banks.* Billions of dollars' worth of international projects are funded every year through these banks. Learn what projects are upcoming in your industry and region of interest.

6. *Online matching with buyers in Japan.* This service is sponsored by the Japanese government's External Trade Organization (JETRO), with offices scattered around the United States. This online service can match your company with interested buyers in Japan.

7. *International company profiles.* Before you do business with a prospective agent, distributor, or partner, this international company profile will give you the background information you need to evaluate the company. This helps to prevent costly mistakes by providing you with quick, low-cost credit checks or due-diligence reports on international companies.

8. *The Platinum Key service.* This service offers comprehensive, customized ways to achieve your business goals through long-term (typically, six months to one year) sustained support.

In addition, here are six more ways the U.S. Department of Commerce can help you meet potential new customers:

1. *U.S. pavilions at certified trade fairs.* You can exhibit at U.S. pavilions certified by the U.S. Commercial Service and increase your chances of finding new customers and contacts. These pavilions offer one-on-one business matching, business counseling from trade specialists, and special exhibit services designed to help U.S. exporters maximize returns through new international sales.

2. *Trade fair certification.* Exhibiting yourself and your products at a trade show abroad can lead to export opportunities. This program was created to help companies make important exhibiting decisions and free you of the concerns you may have about exhibiting outside the United States.

3. *International buyer program.* This program recruits more than 125,000 foreign buyers and distributors to thirty-two top U.S. trade shows per year. U.S. Commercial Service trade specialists arrange meetings for U.S. exporters and

international delegates and provide counseling at the show's International Business Center.

4. *Catalog events.* Promote your company in international markets without traveling. Catalog exhibitions showcase your product literature, videos, and samples to buyers and distributors in promising export markets around the world. U.S. commercial trade specialists translate your company profile into the local language, collect leads, and help you to follow up with interested contacts.

5. *Video services.* This service offers a variety of video aids that allow you to hold business meetings, attend market briefings, meet potential business partners, and more, right from your nearest Export Assistance Center.

6. *Trade missions.* Trade missions save you time and money by allowing you to meet face-to-face with prescreened distributors, sales representatives, or partners in other countries.

If you are exporting agricultural products, the Foreign Agricultural Service is part of the U.S. Department of Agriculture, and it provides a vast array of trade information, much of it available from its homepage at www.fas.usda.gov. Trade and market data are contained on this site, as well as exporter-assistance programs, listings of trade events, and publications dealing with international trade.

By this time, your head might be dizzy with all the services that are available from the U.S. government, the Department of Commerce, and the Department of Agriculture. You may be wondering, "Why does the U.S. government do this?" The answer is simple: for more than twenty years, we in America have been buying more products from overseas than we have sold to those markets. The result is called the "trade deficit," and this also means that our dollars are being sent overseas to pay for those imported products.

Everything mentioned thus far is explained in more detail in a publication called *A Basic Guide to Exporting,* published by the U.S. Department of Commerce. This publication is available through Unz and Company at 1-800-631-3098.

Below is contact information to help you navigate the exportation process.

- The Web site for the Export Assistance Offices is www .export.gov, or call 1-800-USA-TRADE.

- To locate local offices in your area, access www.buyusa.gov/ "state".

- For information on individual countries, access www .buyusa.gov/"country".

If you receive "hits" on your Web site from unknown buyers, ask for the "International Company Profile Service" from the U.S. Department of Commerce Export Assistance Office.

Types of Distribution

Two basic types of distribution are available to you: indirect and direct. With indirect distribution, you find a middleman located in the United States, and that intermediary develops and handles your sales to overseas customers. With direct distribution, you sell either directly to your end customers overseas or to them through wholesalers or distributors in each market.

Indirect Distribution

Indirect distribution can take several forms:

- *Export jobbers, wholesalers, or brokers* are independent firms in the United States that find overseas customers for your product. You have the least amount of control but also the least risk since it is usually a sale on U.S. soil.

- *Commission house or manufacturer's representative.* These firms usually seek out overseas customers for your product or service and take a commission on the sale. Most often, these firms deal with engineered industrial products or highly technical products and involve negotiated sales contracts, installation engineering, and after-sales service.

- *Export management companies* (EMCs) are rarer than in the past but are usually located within the United States; they find customers for your product or service in overseas markets. They will probably handle other noncompeting lines and may even be specialists in your type of product. They usually operate on commission, may or may not take title to the goods being sold, help with financing and shipping, assist in general marketing chores, and most often require an exclusive contract covering specific territories and an agreed-upon period of time.

- *Export trading companies* are also rare, compared to a decade ago, and operate much like EMCs but are usually larger, have firm distribution channels or even subsidiary selling companies overseas, normally buy the product from you and resell to markets or customers they have cultivated overseas, and so on.

Direct Distribution

Direct distribution takes longer to establish and more management time to administer, but these drawbacks are offset by shorter and more efficient pathways and more control over how your product is resold. In this category, it is important to know the difference between a *distributor* and an *agent*. Very simply, an agent is empowered to make obligations on your behalf, whereas a distributor merely buys and sells your product on an arm's length basis.

Here are some direct distribution alternatives:

- Many U.S. companies sell directly to foreign end users or via retailers or wholesalers to end users in the distant market. This is known as direct sales to end users.

- You can also achieve direct distribution by establishing your own sales office in a foreign country whose potential appeals to you. This, of course, involves investing capital in offices and personnel.

- Working with commission sales representatives is another common form of establishing sales overseas. This means appointing certain individuals or sales companies that generate orders, send the orders to you, and in turn receive sales commissions. Sometimes called indent dealers, they are also responsible for ensuring that payments are made by customers.

- A common and very effective way to establish distribution in a foreign land is by appointing exclusive distributors. This was the form chosen by my firm, The Parker Pen Company, which at one time had more than a hundred exclusive distributors, usually one for each distinct market, which most often was a specific country. In this form, you the seller agree not to knowingly sell to other customers in that market. In return, direct distributors are usually required to retain sales personnel, to keep inventories of your product, to supervise advertising and sales promotion, and to provide after-sales service. You, the seller, are expected to provide the exclusive distributor with a preferential price to allow the distributor to compete effectively against others who may try to buy your product in the United States and import it to their markets.

With this form of distribution, the distributor agreement contract becomes vitally important. Consult with your legal advisers about this. Many will suggest a typically long, involved, multi-page document spelling out every possible contingency. We at The Parker Pen Company successfully conducted business with our exclusive distributors on the basis of a simple, single-page letter of agreement that laid out the basic expectations of each party, as described previously. An exclusive distributor has a special incentive to promote and sell your product because of this arms-linked relationship. This distributor considers himself or herself to be your official, sole representative in that particular market. The exclusive distributor takes all responsibilities for importing your product (meaning documentation, shipping, insurance, duties, and tariffs), providing you with purchasing forecasts, hiring sales personnel to sell your product, and providing after sales service. In the case of Parker, this quasi-franchise generated great pride and loyalty to the brand and in many cases continued through generation after generation within the distributorship.

One strong cautionary word about distributor agreements. If and when you may decide to cancel or sever relations with your exclusive distributor, be certain to research—in advance—the local laws for such an action. Overseas governments often impose indemnifications, or penalties, for unjustly canceling distributor agreements. The most famous one, because it is so onerous, is "Law 75" in Puerto Rico. This particular law mandates extremely heavy payments by the source company to reimburse the local distributor for cancellation. The justification for these indemnifications is that over the years many U.S. companies established sales in given countries through appointed distributors, and once the sales streams were established, the U.S. firms said, "Thank you," and installed their own sales forces.

- Licensing, assembling, and local manufacturing are considered major steps forward, in comparison to simply finding direct outlets, wholesalers, or distributors.

  Licensing is defined by the U.S. Department of Commerce as "a contractual arrangement in which the licensor's patents, trademarks, service marks, copyrights, or know-how may be sold or otherwise made available to a licensee for compensation negotiated in advance between the parties." The compensation is usually in the form of royalties. Licensing is more often used when your product is complex or of a large size, and it is difficult to simply export the finished product overseas.

- Investing in joint ventures or establishing wholly owned subsidiaries sit at the top of the ladder of sophistication in creating distribution in an overseas market. The advantages are more control and more direct profits, but the disadvantage is more risk when investing capital in a foreign land.

Patents, Trademarks, and Product Liability

These three separate areas of the law are important for the neophyte exporter to be aware of. In these areas, your first "port of call" will be to confer with your company's legal advisers. Many U.S. law firms do not have experience in international law; however, they may refer you to firms that do. And those firms may have affiliation agreements with law firms located within markets overseas.

Before you sell a single product overseas, it is essential to visit a patent attorney who is familiar with international patents and trademarks. This protects your intellectual property rights from improper and illegal copies of your products or from usage of your brand names and your registered copyrights. The U.S. Department of Commerce specialist in your area can refer you to these patent attorneys. As a general rule, applications for protection must be filed, country by country, and renewed after certain periods of time. Many famous trademarks—Levis jeans, Rolex watches, Johnson Wax products, and, yes, Parker pens—are and have been illegally reproduced in certain foreign markets. Without registered patents and trademarks in those countries, you are helpless to retaliate.

As for product liability, this varies from country to country. The United States is probably the most conscientious in this area of the law, while other countries around the world vary from strong to weak. Again, it is best to obtain legal advice for the country or countries where you hope to sell your product.

A final word about counterfeiting. Once your product has gained sales strength and recognition around the world, it's entirely possible that you will have to deal with counterfeiting.

These are often bold, outright imitations of your product. Your only recourse is to have strong patent/trademark registration and immediately seek local government help in retaliating against the offenders. In the case of Parker pens, we had such severe problems with counterfeit versions of our products, that we had to issue detailed illustrations to our overseas distributors to help them distinguish counterfeit products from the genuine ones.

Pricing Your Product for Export

As you venture into the glamorous and sometime mystifying arena of international sales, you'll find that pricing your product becomes more of an art than it is mere arithmetic. Your customers will be savvy in the complexities of foreign exchange, delaying payments, arguing for lower prices, and general negotiations.

Sometimes these "negotiations" can be amusing:

Barb and Paul were visiting Acapulco, Mexico, shopping among the many small shops loaded with curios and souvenirs. They knew it was the custom here to haggle over the price. Barb was almost fluent in Spanish, so she acted as interpreter for Paul when he saw a carving that he wanted to buy. "Ask him how much," Paul said. The peddler said, "Five hundred pesos." Paul told Barb, "I think that's too much. Offer him half of that." Barb did, and the peddler protested and countered with, "Four hundred pesos." Paul directed, "Go to three hundred." And at this point the haggling bounced back and forth, faster and faster. Suddenly, Barb said excitedly, "Wait a moment. You've actually passed one another! You are now offering him *more* than the price he's offering you!"

Another story comes from Lebanon, the home of the ancient Phoenicians, long considered among the world's first international traders. They sailed the Mediterranean Sea centuries ago, buying and selling goods around its perimeter.

On one of my first trips to Lebanon, I asked our Parker distributor to school me in the ways of negotiations, since his ancestors were among the first and the best international traders. Here's the story he told me:

A worldwide commission was established to locate the first human to land on Mars. The commission naturally started with an American astronaut, asking how much he would require to do the job. He considered the task, muttering,

"Very, very dangerous." And then replied, "One hundred million dollars."

So, the commission members decided to try a Russian cosmonaut, who also considered the dangers versus the reward, and replied, "I would need two hundred million dollars." "Why *two* hundred million?" the commission representative asked. "Simple," the Russian replied. "One hundred million for me and one hundred million for the state—because that's the way we work it here."

Finally, the commission decided to turn to a Lebanese since, after all, he was a descendant of the first great adventurers and explorers. The Lebanese gentleman considered the assignment long and hard and finally declared, "For that task, I would require *three* hundred million dollars." Somewhat aghast, the commission representative asked, "But why three hundred million dollars?" "The answer is simple," replied the Lebanese with a knowing smile. "One hundred million for you . . . one hundred million for me . . . and one hundred million for the American to make the trip!"

As you learned in chapter 6 on e-commerce and its impact on international business, in the matter of pricing your product, there is a new age—an age of transparency—in determining your price lists. Once your prices appear on the World Wide Web, unless they are encrypted, everyone from Hong Kong to Helsinki will have access to them. It will be very difficult to have different pricing for favored customers. To learn more about this new age, refer to chapter 6.

Classifying Your Product or Service

Early in the game, you should learn how your product or service is classified. This is especially important while you gather statistical information for your market research. First, products are categorized broadly into groups and then broken down in detailed classifications. Knowing which classification your product is assigned will help you to glean helpful information such as what similar products are being exported from the United States and into which specific markets, what quantities are being shipped, and how much the revenues generated off these shipments will be. There are many different classification systems. Here are the four main ones:

1. Harmonized System and the Schedule B
2. Standard International Trade Classification (SITC) system
3. Standard Industrial Classification (SIC) system, which is being replaced by
4. North American Industry Classification System (NAICS)

You can learn where your product or service falls within these systems by seeking help from the U.S. Department of Commerce Export Assistance personnel in your state or region.

What Trade Barriers Might You Encounter?

The most common barriers are tariffs or duties, usually expressed as a percentage of the value of the product being imported. "Nontariff" barriers may also exist, such as import quotas or restrictions on your type of product.

Another hurdle might be something called "ISO standards." This stands for "International Standards Organization" for quality, manufacturing, and service requirements; certification; and monitoring worldwide. Originally advocated by the European Union, now about a hundred nations have adopted these ISO standards. In brief, "ISO 9000" refers to quality-management requirements in business-to-business dealings, and "ISO 14000" is primarily concerned with environmental management. These ISO standards are usually very specific to the company's operations to ensure continued improvement and customer satisfaction. Consultants are available to assist a company in applying for them.

Naturally, communication may be a barrier if your potential customer does not speak English. Fortunately, language interpreters can be found and hired in almost any foreign country. (Refer to chapter 4 on the use of English around the world for tips on how to work effectively through interpreters.)

Advertising and Sales Promotion

Here, the first questions you must answer are "What type of advertising and sales-promotion services do you presently employ?" And then, "Are those agencies capable of providing advertising and sales-promotion services in overseas markets?"

The answers to the second question will fall into one of three possible categories: (1) The agencies have no experience in serving international markets, (2) They have no direct experience but do have "affiliation agreements" with advertising and sales-promotion agencies in certain markets, or (3) they have their own branch offices located overseas.

Now the question becomes "Do I want one large, centralized agency here in the United States that has branch offices or affiliated agencies to create and distribute all of my advertising and sales-promotion materials, or do I want to have my distributors in each market advise me on which they believe is the best service agency to use?" These two theories are labeled "centralized" or "decentralized," and there are solid arguments for either practice.

Large U.S. corporations usually prefer the centralized approach. They argue that they can, through one large U.S.-based central headquarters, spread their message at minimum expense by creating and booking mutually agreed-upon advertising in a host of different markets. This way, savings on artwork and production costs can result, and one basic message will appear in diverse markets.

The decentralized approach argues, "Each market is different so we will let the best local advertising experts translate our messages into the local culture. Furthermore, just because a large centralized agency in the United States has strong capabilities here or in a few overseas markets, it does not mean that all of its branch offices have the same levels of expertise."

In my own experience with The Parker Pen Company, we tried both systems. Yet we also operated on the basis of exclusive distributors in every market, which meant that each distributor was our marketing voice and hands in selling our product in that country. My own bias was to favor the decentralized system. We concluded that the local exclusive distributor knew something about advertising and sales promotion in that country and had a stake in the success of each. We also required our distributors to contribute funds toward advertising.

Here is an example of the decentralized system working in Venezuela:

> For markets that could not afford local advertising agencies, we produced artwork and copy from the home office and sent it to our distributors for their consideration. Basic marketing messages used by Parker were that our product carried great "prestige and sentiment" and our product was particularly suited to "gift giving." Therefore, our artwork showed a man presenting a Parker pen set to a woman, with a Rolls-Royce auto in the background.
>
> During a visit to Venezuela, we were puzzled by the poor sales and asked the distributor to arrange a meeting with its advertising agency. People at the agency finally confessed that they did not think our artwork was appropriate. When we asked, "Why?" they simply explained, "There are few, if any, Rolls-Royce autos in Venezuela." So then we asked, "Well, how would you convey the message of prestige, gift giving, and sentiment in new advertising?" They retreated to their drawing boards and came back with a proposal to hire the country's leading film heartthrob to be pictured handing a Parker pen set to a beautiful woman. Sales increased markedly soon afterward.

One maxim we learned when dealing with international advertising and promotion agencies was expressed by the J. Walter Thompson advertising agency when it said, "Our advertising should convert the raison d'etre (reason for being) into the 'reason for buying.'" In other words, it is essential to determine what—in the local culture—is the reason for success or maximum appeal in that market. Then the job of the advertising agency is to convert that into the local vernacular.

> At Parker Pen, one of our exclusive distributors proved this to us. There was a period in the Netherlands when we could not tap the youth market. Our products seemed to identify with

an older generation. Our distributor came up with what at first sounded like a crazy idea. "Professional basketball," he argued, "is taking off like a rocket here in the Netherlands. Young people here love it. I recommend that Parker sponsor one of the teams." We were dubious because more than half of our advertising/promotional budget would be required, but the distributor kept arguing and finally we gave in. Sure enough, in less than a year, our products were being sold vigorously across the counter to the younger generation. Moral: Listen to your local representatives.

You, as the basic exporter and supplier, should always hold final veto power over all advertising matters. But it is important to respect and defer to local judgment regarding the final message, the best medium, and the best price. Your primary responsibility is to make certain your distributor understands your basic marketing philosophy— why your product has been successful. Then you will ask that this be translated and portrayed according to the local culture.

When considering the appointment of an advertising agency in any given market, according to Kenneth Lamm, the senior vice president of Cramer-Krasselt Advertising, you should get answers to the following ten questions:

1. What government regulations apply when advertising in your country?
2. What cultural taboos should be avoided, such things as religious symbols, the use of foreign words, partial nudity, the use of children, and so on?
3. What claims can be made about competitive products?
4. What about including product prices in advertising—is this recommended or not?
5. What types of promotions are permitted? Such things as sweepstakes, free giveaways, special price offers, free samples, free trials, free premiums, and coupons for price reductions.

6. What symbols are important? Examples: in the United States, all of the following suggest "good luck"—a four-leaf clover, the number 7, and a rabbit's foot. Whereas bad luck symbols are the number 13, black cats, and the number 666 (representing the devil).

7. What colors are good and bad in your country?

8. If crowd scenes are used in your advertising, is it important to show diversity in ages, gender, and races?

9. Is humor used in advertising in your country?

10. What other sensitive areas should we avoid to ensure that our advertising is not only acceptable but effective?

After-Sales Service

Whether your product is a machine tool or a consumer product, one bane around the world is the need to get it repaired. If in the United States your luggage, watch, or eyeglasses suddenly need repair, you have a reasonably good chance of getting them fixed. But what happens if you are in Singapore or Stuttgart? A repair or maintenance program that is available in a foreign market, properly managed and run, can not only be a source of marginal profit to your distributor but can literally turn a nonuser into a loyal repeat customer.

Your representatives in each market should understand and appreciate this fact and should be willing to invest in training, keeping inventories of spare parts, and spending the time it takes to manage both. Furthermore, it is useful to have a liberal and speedy repair-parts supply system. Depending on your product and your policies, replacement parts may be supplied at cost or on a cost-plus basis. After-sales service and repair departments can be structured to be profitable or unprofitable or to operate on a break-even basis. That decision will depend on competitive factors in the market. In summary, a wise distributor will establish a smooth and efficient after-sales service facility; the wise exporter will support him at every step.

Agenda for a Typical Visit

Your first venture overseas will probably be to attend a trade fair to examine prospects, observe competition, and possibly meet potential distributors. Soon after that, you should make repeat visits. Here are some tips culled from a dozen well-traveled international trade managers:

- *Set the dates well in advance.* Weeks or months ahead, agree on a mutually convenient time for your visit. Make certain there will be no disruptions, such as national holidays in that country, local political elections, or other supplier firms visiting the customer at that time. Commerce's Gold Key service helps to set appointments and arranges for interpreters.

- *Arrive rested.* Jet lag can be an insidious enemy that can torpedo productive negotiating. If you will be passing through numerous time zones, depart on a Friday or a Saturday to allow yourself at least one day's rest.

- *Spend enough time.* Bear in mind that in many parts of the world, business is conducted at a slower pace than in the United States. In addition to spending ample time with your representative, allow time to visit end customers, service and repair departments, or banking and legal contacts. A visit to the American embassy or consulate and an appointment with the commercial specialist there might expose you to helpful views of trends and conditions in that country. Make these appointments well in advance.

- *First on the agenda.* Your first priority should be dealing with the distributor's immediate concerns. It's highly likely that the distributor will have accumulated a list of problems, some major and some petty, that have been nagging him since your last visit. Review all of these immediately. Clear the air. Then present your own agenda items when his mind is clear, open, and at ease.

- *Review sales results.* You should have data on purchases (note that they are his "purchases" and your "sales"). Any surprises? Any questions? What preliminary conclusions can be drawn? Are any new trends emerging? What should be done to improve (his) sales?

- *Meet with the distributor's sales force and customers.* Take the time to have face-to-face meetings with these key players. You may have to drink quantities of colas and coffee—some with enough caffeine to curl your toenails—but this is an important part of interpersonal relations.

- *Review future marketing plans and forecasts.* Motivating a distributor is selling the future. If a distributor is convinced that there is a good future in handling your product, most of the current problems will evaporate.

- *Other visits.* Visit the advertising agency; take the distributor and his chief aides, possibly with their wives, for dinner, to a show, or to a sporting event. Other helpful places to consider visiting are regulatory agencies, banks, law offices, customs houses, and various government officials.

- *Summarize.* Before leaving for your next destination, sit down with the distributor and summarize what has been concluded. Write those notes in front of him, if necessary, to stress the importance of clear understanding and agreement.

- *Trip reports.* Experienced international executives recommend sitting down and writing a summary report of your visit before you arrive at your next destination. You'll be amazed at how easy it is to confuse one market visit with another.

- *After returning home.* Your first act should probably be to write a simple thank-you letter to the distributor. Also, in the same or a separate letter, once again summarize the major points of discussion and agreement. Finally, begin now to consider when you or someone from your firm will make the next visit to that market.

The Ten Most Common Mistakes
for Potential Exporters

Here, from the U.S. Department of Commerce, are the most common mistakes made by new-to-export companies:

1. Failure to obtain qualified export counseling and to develop a master international marketing plan before you start to export your products

2. Insufficient commitment by top management to overcome the initial difficulties and financial requirements of exporting

3. Insufficient care in selecting foreign distributors

4. Chasing orders from around the world instead of establishing a basis for profitable operations and orderly growth

5. Neglecting export business when the U.S. market booms

6. Failure to treat international distributors on an equal basis with domestic counterparts

7. Unwillingness to modify your products to meet the regulations or cultural preferences of other countries

8. Failure to print service, sales, and warranty messages in locally understood languages

9. In the early stages of your expansion overseas, failure to consider the use of an export management company

10. For complex, highly technical products, failure to consider licensing or joint-venture agreements

10

Two Dozen Quick Essentials for International Business Success

1. International business is not done between businesses. International business is done between people. The person-to-person relationship is more important in many countries than in America. Americans are "deal-focused," while others—principally in East Asia, Latin America, and the Middle East—are "relationship-focused."

2. In all matters involving international business or travel, adopt the "three Ps"—patience, perseverance, and politeness.

3. The role of advertising in international business is to translate your company's raison d'etre into a "reason for buying." The reason for buying among the American public is not necessarily the same outside the United States.

4. In international business, it is presumptuous to export our moral code or to force it upon others—that's called "moral imperialism."

5. Regarding the law and litigation, there is an old Chinese proverb: "It is better to be vexed to death than enter into a lawsuit."

6. Americans and Northern Europeans practice punctuality. In much of the rest of the world, the attitude is "Why live your life in measured segments? Time is a continuous flow."

7. Be careful with your words. Words are like hand grenades—handled carelessly, they will blow up in your face.

8. A gift is not necessarily a bribe. It is a method of building a good relationship. And the best gift of all is a gift of thoughtfulness.

9. *Ethnocentrism* means that we Americans think the axis of the earth runs vertically right down through the United States, and everything revolves around us.

10. Interpreters can make serious mistakes. President Jimmy Carter's Polish interpreter once translated Carter's greeting as "I am here to grasp your secret parts."

11. There is one form of human communication that everyone understands: The smile.

12. More and more American women will be carving out careers in international business. The reason: women make excellent international businesspeople because they are more aware and respectful of cultural differences and less win-win oriented.

13. To avoid sickness while traveling overseas, the best preventative is simply to wash your hands as often as possible. Also, remember that paper currency, when passed from hand to hand, carries many germs.

14. The Bible said it first: treat others—your overseas hosts, clients, customers, agents, and so on—the way you wish to be treated.

15. Humor is enjoyed everywhere, but American humor is usually based on topical issues or a play on words, both of which are difficult to translate into other languages.

16. Sending the wrong American executive to a posting in a foreign country can be one of the costliest mistakes you can make.

17. Two topics to avoid in international conversations are politics and religion.

18. In most of your international dealings, speak as if a wealthy elderly aunt has just asked you how much you think she should leave you in her will.

19. On certain rare occasions, however, it's okay to pound on the table. Just make absolutely certain you are right . . . and don't do it often.

20. It's okay to cancel or terminate an overseas distributor or agent—just be sure that (1) he doesn't owe you money, (2) you first research the legal penalties in that country for terminations (it's called "indemnifications") and, (3) most important, you can replace him with someone better.

21. We are not the "Ugly Americans" (which was the title of a novel in the 1950s), but we are the *uninformed* Americans. Americans are generally considered informal and friendly, but we don't get much practice crossing significantly different cultural boundaries. In Europe and other regions, one can travel five hundred miles and cross into several different cultures.

22. Before visiting any country overseas, do your homework! Learn about the protocol in the countries you visit. The World Wide Web makes it easier than ever to accumulate information on any given country or culture.

23. E-commerce will make a major impact on international business. It will facilitate routine communications, but it

will never replace the eyeball-to-eyeball relationship that is so important in all of Asia, Latin America, Southern Europe, and the Middle East.

24. Finally, practice "chameleon management." This means the ability to adapt to local conditions and practices. It does *not* mean you must discard your basic principles and beliefs.

Epilogue

The rest of the story . . .

—Radio commentator Paul Harvey

In the second chapter, on general protocol, you learned how I stumbled into this business of international protocol, etiquette, behavior, and gestures. You learned why and how my first book, *Do's & Taboos Around the World: A Guide to International Behavior*, was published.

As I explained in that chapter, in 1984–1985 I compiled and edited that first book for my employer, The Parker Pen Company, which published it as a quasi-marketing, public-relations effort. We wanted to tell American businesspeople who needed gifts when they traveled abroad that Parker pens made the perfect gift because, as George S. Parker, the founder, said, "Our pens write in any language."

The following year, 1986, Parker Pen was sold to a group of British investors. I had accumulated thirty years of service with Parker so I was able to take early retirement. My pension, plus a reasonable collection of stock options, made me financially comfortable (I called it a canvas parachute, not a golden one) enough to allow me to move into whatever retirement activity I might choose.

Like most people who retire at a relatively early age—I was fifty-five years old at the time—I assumed I would either go into consulting or have companies knocking at my door asking me to join their boards of directors. Alas, neither one occurred. It was then that I realized I had enjoyed writing the first book and perhaps I should try my hand at a second one.

I chose a subject that I thought I could handle—namely, how to get into exporting. I wrote a proposal and sent it to John Wiley & Sons, the New York publisher that had purchased my first book for retail distribution rights. This is where I now feel sorry for wannabe authors. Every month, editors at national publishing houses receive hundreds of proposals from first-time authors, and most are summarily rejected. Only a very few survive passage through the publisher's sieve. Because I had already had one book published, however, and it was generating sales, I was granted special purview.

My proposal to write a book on the "how to" of exporting was accepted. So, in 1989, my second book was published, *The Do's & Taboos of International Trade: A Small Business Primer*. Soon afterward, *Entrepreneur* magazine called it "the Bible for taking your show on the road."

After this, I decided that since my first book about the behavior one should adopt when traveling abroad had done well, I would now take a reverse viewpoint and write a book on the challenge of hosting international visitors here in the United States. I would describe what international guests found perplexing when visiting the United States. Thus, American hosts could avoid goofs or gaffes while entertaining here. That book, published in 1990, was titled *Do's & Taboos of Hosting International Visitors*. It deals with differences in diets, entertaining, social drinking, conversational taboos, and so on.

In the United States, it seems that certain organizations and program managers think that anyone who writes a reasonably interesting book should also be a reasonably interesting luncheon or after-dinner speaker. As a result, I was now being invited to appear on the speaking circuit.

Stories from the Speaking Circuit

While in high school, I had a teacher named John Davies who excelled in teaching public speaking. Each and every year, one or more of his pupils qualified to become state champions, which would entitle them to compete in the National Forensic League finals. In my senior year of high school, 1949, I chose the category of Original Oratory and managed to win the state title. That qualified me to travel to the national contest held in Longmont, Colorado. I reached the semifinals before I lost and then was demoted to the consolation bracket, which was in radio announcing. In the 1940s and early 1950s, before the advent of national television, radio was still a big, glamorous field. In that contest, we competed by standing behind a curtain as our voices were "broadcast" to an audience seated in an auditorium. Somehow, I managed to take third place.

Filled with self-anointed importance, I returned to my home in Kenosha, Wisconsin, and visited our small local radio station, with the call letters WLIP (named after the owner, William LIPman). I made an appointment with the program manager and announced that I had just taken third place in a national competition and would like an audition. Somewhat reluctantly, he agreed. Immediately after my audition, he notified me there were no openings for neophyte radio announcers. He did ask, however, "Can you type?" Fortunately, I could say yes. He then informed me that they had a summer job open in the station's newsroom. I would work mornings only, five days a week, at fifty cents an hour. My job would be to help the news editor—the sole person in that department—gather and write news stories for the station's hourly news broadcasts.

Although I was considerably disappointed about not using my third-place-in-the-nationals voice on the radio, I was at least near a microphone. Also, my father agreed that even though the pay was meager, it would be good experience before entering the University of Wisconsin as a freshman in the fall. He said that I should accept.

It turned out to be one of the luckiest decisions in my life.

My mentor was a wonderful journalist named Virginia Taylor. She taught me how to "walk the beat," meaning to leave the radio station early each morning; circulate among the police and sheriff's stations, the municipal court, and city hall; and return to the newsroom to write stories about local miscreants and city council agendas for the all-important noon newscast. She taught me invaluable lessons about accuracy and brevity. Just as important, she taught me the differences between writing for the eye (the type of writing you are reading right now) and writing for the ear. Writing for the ear requires (a) shorter sentences, (b) simple syntax, (c) more repetition, and (d) a simple vocabulary. When writing for the eye, the reader can scan up and down and review different portions of the story at will. When writing for the ear, you have only one shot at the audience, so you must convey the content quickly and efficiently.

I was soon allowed to fill in for the regular announcing staff members during their summer vacations, as well as work the weekend shift. My first actual announcing assignment was "The Pet Parade," which dealt with missing pets. WLIP was not, as you can see, a metropolitan-type radio station.

I slowly learned the tricks of radio announcing. As one example, if you "fluff" some words—meaning to mispronounce or scramble words—you should not repeat yourself. If and when you do repeat the error, the listener becomes more aware of your mistake. If, however, you just keep speaking, the listener might momentarily think, "What did he say?" and then, uncertain, just dismiss it.

My biggest mistake occurred one morning when Leo, our veteran announcer, was hosting a phone-in quiz show, and I was reading the commercials between calls. One of our sponsors was a clothing store, and the copy I was supposed to read said, "Be sure to get your smart fighter trunks at Iserman Brothers clothing store." Unfortunately, I fluffed, and out of my mouth came the words "Be sure to get your fart smighter trunks at Iserman Brothers clothing store." Realizing I had made a mistake, I compounded it by blurting out, "Fart smighter trunks? Oh! No! Smart fighter trunks." Leo erupted into uncontrolled laughter, the phones began to ring, and the station manager appeared at the broadcast room window, shaking his finger at me.

In college, I continued my new radio career by working at the University of Wisconsin campus station and then at a downtown commercial station. After graduating, I was drafted into the Army, but once again the coin toss landed in my favor. After basic training in Arkansas, I was transferred to Chicago and assigned to Public Information work. Each day I rode the Illinois Central train into the Loop and did public service programs on radio stations there. I was probably the biggest hypocrite alive because I promoted enlisting in the U.S. Army. One of my duties, however, was to write and announce *The Fifth Army Band* show every Saturday at noon, which was broadcast live for one hour from the WGN studios and on the Mutual Radio network—more than three hundred other stations across the country.

I'll shorten this by saying that after my military service, I spent more than thirty years in business, and during that time, because I was reasonably comfortable speaking before an audience, I volunteered for any speaking situation that came along.

Now, to fast-forward to the 1990s, as my first books appeared on the market, invitations came in asking me to speak. In the last eighteen years, I have spoken to more than four hundred different groups—national corporations, conventions, associations, college campuses, and the like. A handful of speakers' bureaus have listed me on their Web sites and in their catalogs of speakers.

This prompted me to write another book, *Do's & Taboos of Public Speaking: How to Get Those Butterflies Flying in Formation*. Here are some tips on how to get on the professional speaking circuit:

- In the "Book of Lists," where people have ranked their greatest fears, the number-one fear is that of public speaking. I learned from the remarkable John Davies that there are three basic rules for minimizing fear. They are (1) know your subject; don't get up and speak unless you are thoroughly acquainted with your topic; (2) believe in your subject—don't speak about things you don't believe in; and (3) practice, practice, practice. This means what it says—speak in front of a mirror or, better yet, into a video camera, and practice your speech over and over again. That will help you to gain familiarity with and confidence in your words.

- A professional speaker is one who is paid to speak. Therefore, when starting out, accept any and all invitations. For most of them, you won't receive a fee. Speak to every Rotary Club, garden group, Retired Teachers Association, or whatever. During that time, you will sharpen your skills as a platform speaker and will polish your material. Sprinkle your speech liberally with stories. Audiences don't particularly care for preaching or stern lectures. They want to be entertained, and they like to leave with interesting stories they can remember and repeat, especially if the stories are amusing.

- Soon, these groups will hand you checks for $50, $100, or even more. (When I told my eighty-five-year-old father that I was embarking on the professional speaking circuit, he was dubious. "You mean, people are actually going to pay to hear you speak?" he asked. I said, "That's right." After a long pause, he said, "Okay. Give me fifty cents' worth.")

- National speakers' bureaus will not be interested until you have attained fees of $2,000 or more. The reason is simple: bureaus deduct a 25 percent commission from your fee, so you must cross a certain dollar threshold that makes it interesting for them.

- Being a published author helps. People read your books, and if the material is interesting, they will contact you about speaking.

- Appearing on the publicity circuit also helps. (I will describe that in the next section.) The more you appear on TV or the radio or in newspaper columns, the more you are promoted for speaking engagements.

- At this point, it is essential to produce a DVD with short segments showing you in action—either on a speaking platform or on TV—which then becomes your "demo," or audition disc. If clients are paying $2,000 or more, they want to see and hear you in advance. So, start collecting segments from your appearances and have a ten- or twelve-minute arrangement made on a disc. This will become your best marketing tool for future clients.

- One of my speaker bureaus books speakers on cruise ships. This became a special perk for my wife and me. We did nine cruises on various cruise liners, including several for the Cunard line. These are barter arrangements where you give three or four programs over a two-week cruise period, and, in return, you are provided with two first-class passages at no expense to you, except perhaps the cost of airfare for your spouse.

- Here's a tip for negotiating fees. Let's say you have risen to a point where you can command $2,000 per engagement. If the potential client reacts by saying, "Oh, we don't have that much money," a perfectly acceptable response is to ask, "Well, what do you have in your budget?" The client might reply, "All we have is $500 [or $700, or whatever]." Then you must decide whether your time and effort are worth a reduced sum. Incidentally, travel and accommodation expenses are always provided in addition to the basic fee.

Another bonus on the speaking circuit is the interesting people you meet along the way. First, your sponsors are almost always enjoyable personalities from different walks of life—corporate executives, association managers, professors, event-planning managers, and so on. But there may also be more celebrated people doing the program with you. In my travels I have appeared on separate speaking platforms or TV shows with people like Captain James Lovell of *Apollo 13* fame, the former secretary of state Alexander Haig, the Olympic decathlon champion Bruce Jenner, the former Notre Dame football coach Lou Holtz, the former Chicago Bears coach Mike Ditka, the NFL Football Hall of Fame recipient Fran Tarkenton, the former British prime minister John Major, the Broadway and film star Shirley Jones, the singer Nancy Sinatra, the actress Brenda Vaccaro, and the animal expert Jack Hanna of the Columbus Zoo.

Now, I must quickly add that I'm certain none of those luminaries remembers being on the same program with a retired pen salesman from Wisconsin . . . but I sure remember them!

Stories from the Publicity Circuit

Back in the mid-1980s, while I was still at Parker Pen, and in an effort to promote the first book Parker had published, our New York public relations firm decided that I should be the spokesperson to publicize the book. They whisked me out to the East Coast for an immersion course on appearing on television, taught by a wonderful veteran named David Horwitz, who had earlier in his career produced the Walter Cronkite news program for the CBS network.

Horwitz took my training video and edited it down to an audition tape. With that in hand, our PR people managed to get me booked on NBC's *Today* show. Jane Pauley was on vacation on the day of my appearance so I was interviewed by a charming substitute named Ann Garrells. Ann has since had a long and distinguished career as a foreign correspondent for National Public Radio. Thanks to her, my debut on national TV went fairly smoothly, and I was greatly relieved when it was over.

Later that day, the phone rang at my hotel and it was Robert Morton, one of the producers of *The David Letterman Show*. Morton said he had caught my appearance on the *Today* show and had an opening the following evening. Would I be interested in appearing on the Letterman show to talk about gestures around the world? Naturally, I agreed.

The following afternoon at about 5:30 p.m., I was ushered once again into the NBC studios. I had make-up applied and talked with the stage manager, who advised me that I had a six-minute slot on the program, showed me how to enter and where to sit, and warned that I should not get up and leave when we finished because Letterman would move directly from our interview into a commercial. Naturally, I had phoned my wife and three adult children earlier to tell them to watch, so I was extremely nervous.

I was given a seat in the greenroom—television talk for the waiting room. I learned that this term originated in Shakespearean days when actors waited in the "Scene Room" before appearing on stage. While I waited nervously, who should walk in but Connie Chung and her husband, Maury Povich? I learned that they were scheduled to visit with Letterman just before me. Meanwhile, we watched on the greenroom TV monitor as Letterman did some ad lib nonsense, shouting out his window with a megaphone at Bryant Gumbel, the host of the *Today* show, who was seated in a park below. That ended, and Ms. Chung was led onstage for her interview. During her stint, a young coproducer came in and told me, "We're running a few minutes behind because of David's impromptu bit with Bryant . . . so you'll have about four minutes instead of six."

I watched on the monitor as Ms. Chung and Letterman bantered back and forth and then entered into a contest to see which of them could successfully crack three walnuts in the palm of one hand. That seemed to go on and on. The young producer stuck his head into the greenroom and said, "We're really getting tight . . . but don't worry, you'll go on." After a while, Ms. Chung finished, came into the green-room, was embraced and congratulated by her husband, and they both departed.

Then the hammer fell. Two producers told me, "We've run out of time. We won't be able to get you on this show. But we really want you to come back. So we will be in touch with you soon." You can finish this story yourself. I waited weeks and weeks, but there was never a "call back."

So, to this day, Connie Chung owes me one.

In the years that followed, I managed to write other books, for a total of nine, plus two extra editions of the original book and expanded and revised versions of two others.

During that time, I did four book publicity tours and from 1986 to the present have been on the speaking circuit, doing keynoters and luncheon and after-dinner speeches. In addition, with each new book my publisher, John Wiley & Sons, managed to get me appearances on CNN, *The Merv Griffin Show*, the *Regis Philbin Show*, British and Canadian national television, and six separate appearances on ABC's *Good Morning America*.

Here are some anecdotes from those days.

More Anecdotes

As a guest on *Good Morning America*, you travel to New York the day before and go to the hotel designated by the network. On one of these occasions, I was booked at a first-class hotel in downtown

Manhattan. Two young ladies at the reception counter greeted me. I gave them my name, and they entered it into the computer.

"Oh," said one, looking up with a smile. "You're booked in the *Good Morning America* suite. And it also says here that your chauffeur, Pierre, will pick you up here at the hotel at 6:45 a.m. and drive you to the studios." She continued, "And it also says you should just sign for any of your expenses while you are here at the hotel."

Pleasantly surprised, I thanked them and turned away toward the elevators. But as I left, I heard one of the ladies whisper to the other, "Wow! Who was *that*??" The second lady said, "Oh, that was nobody."

After completing another *Good Morning America* appearance, I traveled to Phoenix by way of Chicago. On the flight between those two cities, I had a window seat beside two matronly ladies. I started to edit galley proofs of a new book, and the lady nearest to me said, "Pardon me, but those look like manuscript pages for a book. Is that right?" They explained that they were both retired English teachers from Madison, Wisconsin, and therefore recognized book proofs. I answered, "Yes, they are." "And are you the author?" asked the first lady pleasantly. I nodded yes.

She continued, "Have you written other books?" and I nodded again. "Have you ever appeared on TV?" And I replied, "Yes." "On what shows?" they asked. I explained, "I was on TV in New York just yesterday." Both ladies were now leaning toward me with greater and greater interest. "On what program?" they asked in unison. I replied, "Do you happen to watch *Good Morning America* on ABC?" Excitedly, they responded, "Oh, yes, we watch it every morning." "Well, I appeared on *Good Morning America* just yesterday."

They put their heads together and finally turned to me, saying rather sternly and indignantly, "Well . . . we didn't see you!"

And then they didn't speak to me for the rest of the flight.

I could just imagine them arriving in Phoenix and telling their friends, "One really has to be careful talking to strangers on airplanes. This fellow sitting next to us insisted he was on *Good Morning America* yesterday . . . but we certainly didn't see him."

. . .

On the speaking tour, if you are fortunate, your client may occasionally spring for a limousine to meet you when you arrive at the airport.
Over the years, I've learned that limousine drivers often know the
scoop on all traveling speakers.

I was once booked to speak in San Antonio to two thousand fran-
chisee holders for the Best Western Hotel group at its annual convention. I was the luncheon speaker, and, as it happened, Astronaut Jim
Lovell was the speaker in the morning. This was shortly after the
movie *Apollo 13* was released, so I made certain to attend his program.
He was absolutely fascinating, and, to my mind, he is one of the fore-
most American heroes of our time.

In San Antonio he showed clips from the movie, told us inside
stories about the star of the movie, Tom Hanks, and described in detail
the life-threatening parts of the flight.

Later, after finishing my luncheon program, the limo driver took
me to the airport. At one point, he turned to ask me, "Did you hear
Lovell speak this morning?"

"Yeah," I replied. "He was marvelous."

"I just took him back to the airport," the driver said. "He's written a book. He gave me an autographed copy. And then at the airport
I picked up Fran Tarkenton, the NFL Hall of Fame quarterback for the
Minnesota Vikings. He's the speaker this afternoon. He's written a
book, too, and he gave me a copy."

By this time I could see the driver glancing back at me through the
rearview mirror. I knew that his curiosity was aroused about who I was
and what I was doing there. Finally, he asked, "What were you here
for?" I replied rather weakly, "Well, I was the luncheon speaker."

"Oh?" he asked. "What do you speak about?" I explained that I'd
written a number of books on international business, etiquette, protocol, behavior, gestures, and body language.

There was a rather long pause. "Would you like a copy of one of
my books?" I asked.

Another pause. "No, not really," he said. "I'm really not interested
in that international crap."

Then there are book publicity tours. The way they work is like this:
your publisher hires a firm that has freelance PR hosts in each major

city who know all the media outlets that like to interview authors. So, a tour to eight or ten cities is arranged, covering a two-week period. You, the author, travel each night to a new city and are met the next morning by the local host. Then off you go, doing as many as seven or eight interviews per day — radio, TV, newspaper, magazines, or whatever. It is, needless to say, a flattering but tiring experience.

I noticed that at many TV stations, we were greeted by the program manager who had booked me on the local talk show. Almost invariably, this person greeted me enthusiastically, "We're happy to have you. Thanks for coming. I've read your book and loved it!" For some reason, I doubted that any of them had actually read it, and I was often tempted to reply, "Thanks. What did you think of the ending?" It was actually a trick question because I didn't think they had even opened the cover.

On two occasions, I did appear on Canadian national television on a popular morning talk show with a vivacious and charming hostess named Deenie Moore. At one point in the interview, when we were talking about gestures from around the world, she said, "The gesture I enjoyed the most was this one from Egypt," and she demonstrated by holding her fists side by side, forefingers pointing downward, as she tapped the table repeatedly.

Hesitantly, I said, "I don't recognize that one." Surprised, she looked up and retorted, "You said in your book this means 'I want to go to bed with you!'"

"No, no," I said. "You do it *this* way," and proceeded to hold my fists side by side but with the forefingers *pointed outward* and tapped them gently together. "Ohhhh," she said quickly. "No wonder I didn't have any fun in Egypt!"

As an author, one of the more enjoyable opportunities that is literally at your fingertips is to dedicate a book to someone. I did this in my book on public speaking, and I had the perfect choice. Arthur W. Foster worked for The Parker Pen Company and was, for more than forty years, an absolutely marvelous platform speaker. At quarterly sales meetings, he was always the star, and the company salesmen eagerly awaited each appearance. I learned much from Art, and I incorporated many of those lessons in the book so I was pleased at the idea of dedicating it to him.

I decided not to tell Art but to surprise him and let him discover the tribute himself. When the first galleys of that book appeared, I sent them to Art, who at that time had retired to California. "Read this for me, Art," I said in the accompanying letter, "and tell me if I have correctly recounted everything you've taught me." I mentioned nothing about the surprise dedication.

A week passed. Then another. And finally a third, but no word from Art.

Worried, I finally decided to phone him. "Art? Did you get the galleys?" "Yes," he said. "Well . . . (long pause) . . . what did you think of them?" He replied, "I'm not sure. I haven't gotten past the dedication yet."

Art was so cunning and had such wonderful comedic timing. I realized later that he had purposely left me dangling for those three weeks, while knowing that I would finally phone. He had, I'm sure, devised that punch line much earlier and was merely waiting to deliver it.

Recommended Reading

Book List—International Behavior, Customs, Etiquette

A Beginner's Guide to Crossing Cultures: Making Friends in a Multicultural World, Patty Lane (InterVarsity Press, Downers Grove, IL, 2002)

Brit-Think, Ameri-Think: A Transatlantic Survival Guide, Jane Walmsley (Harrap, Edinburgh, 1992)

Chinese Etiquette (A Matter of Course), Raelene Tan (Landmark Books, Singapore, 1992)

Cross-Cultural Business Behavior: Marketing, Negotiating, Sourcing and Managing across Cultures, Richard R. Gesteland (Copenhagen Business School Press, Frederiksberg, Denmark, 2004)

Cross-Cultural Communication: The Essential Guide to International Business, 3rd ed., John Mattock (Kogan Page, London, 2003)

Cultural Diversity Fieldbook, Simons, Abramms, Hopkins, and Johnson (Peterson's/Pacesetter Books, Princeton, NJ, 1996)

Cultural Intelligence: A Guide to Working with People from Other Cultures, Brooks Peterson (Intercultural Press, Yarmouth, ME, 2004)

Culture's Consequences: Comparing Values, Behaviors, Institutions, and Organizations across Nations, 2nd ed., Geert Hofstede (Sage Publications, Thousand Oaks, CA, 2001)

Culture Shock! China, Kevin Sinclair with Iris Wong Po-yee (Graphic Arts Center Publishing Co., Portland, OR, 1990)

Culture Shock! Korea, Sonja Vegdahl Hur, Ben Seunghwa Hur (Times Books International, Singapore, 1988)

Culture Shock! Singapore and Malaysia, JoAnn Craig (Times Books International, Singapore, 1979)

Culture Shock! Thailand, Robert Cooper and Nanthapa Cooper (Times Books International, Singapore, 1982)

Dealing with the Chinese, Scott D. Seligman (Warner Books, New York, 1989)

The Economist Business Traveller's Guides—a series (South-East Asia, Britain, Arabian Peninsula, and others (Prentice Hall, New York, 1987)

A Fair Go for All: Australian/American Interactions, George Renwick (Intercultural Press, Yarmouth, ME, 1991)

Good Neighbors: Communicating with the Mexicans, John C. Condon (Intercultural Press, Yarmouth, ME, 1985)

Guide to Cross-Cultural Communication, Sana Reynolds and Deborah Valentine (Prentice Hall, New York, 2003)

Kiss, Bow, or Shake Hands, Terri Morrison, Wayne A. Conaway, and George A. Borden (Adams Media, Holbrook, MA, 1994)

Latin American Business Cultures, Robert Crane and Carlos G. Rizowy (Prentice Hall, New York, 2004)

The Lexus and the Olive Tree: Understanding Globalization, Thomas J. Friedman (Farrar, Straus and Giroux, New York, 1999)

Looking at Each Other: Korean and Western Cultures in Contrast, Marion E. Current and Dong-ho Choi (Seoul International Tourist Publishing Co., Seoul, 1983)

Managing Cultural Differences: Global Leadership Strategies for the 21st Century, 6th ed., Philip R. Harris, Robert T. Moran, and Sarah V. Moran (Elsevier, New York, 2004)

Marketing across Cultures in Asia, Richard R. Gesteland and George F. Seyk (Copenhagen Business School Press, Frederiksberg, Denmark, 2002)

The Mexicans: An Inside View of a Changing Society, Paula Heusinkveld (Renaissance Publications, San Jose, CA, 1993)

Mind Your Manners: Managing Business Cultures in Europe, John Mole (Nicholas Brealey Publishing, London, 1995)

Multicultural Manners: Essential Rules of Etiquette for the 21st Century, Norine Dresser (John Wiley & Sons, Hoboken, NJ, 2005)

Passport Books Series, Business Korea, China, Italy, Germany, Mexico— Practical Guides to Understanding Each Business Culture, Peggy Kenna and Sondra Lacy (Passport Books, Lincolnwood, IL, 1994–1995)

Put Your Best Foot Forward Asia, Mary Murray Bosrock (International Education Systems, St. Paul, MN, 1994)

Put Your Best Foot Forward Europe, Mary Murray Bosrock (International Education Systems, St. Paul, MN, 1994)

Put Your Best Foot Forward Mexico Canada, Mary Murray Bosrock (International Education Systems, St. Paul, MN, 1995)

Robert T. Moran's Cultural Guide to Doing Business in Europe, Michael Johnson and Robert T. Moran (Butterworth-Heinemann, Oxfordshire, England, 1992)

"Simple Etiquette" Series (Japan, Thailand, France, Korea, Poland, Italy, China, Germany, Russia, Turkey), various authors (Simple Books Ltd., Sandgate, England, 1988–1992)

The Travelers' Guide to Asian Customs & Manners, Kevin Chambers (Meadowbrook Books, Deephaven, MN, 1988)

The Travelers' Guide to European Customs & Manners, Nancy L. Braganti and Elizabeth Devine (Meadowbrook Books, Deephaven, MN, 1984)

The Travelers' Guide to Latin American Customs & Manners, Elizabeth Devine and Nancy L. Braganti (St. Martin's Press, New York, 1988)

When Business East Meets Business West: The Guide to Practice and Protocol in the Pacific Rim, Christopher Engholm (John Wiley & Sons, New York, 1991)

The World Is Flat: A Brief History of the Twenty-First Century, Thomas J. Friedman (Farrar, Straus and Giroux, New York, 2005).

Books on Japan

Doing Business with Japanese Men: A Woman's Handbook, Christalyn Brannen and Tracey Wilen (Stone Bridge Press, Berkeley, CA, 1993)

Getting Your Yen's Worth: How to Negotiate with Japan, Inc., Robert T. Moran (Gulf Publishing, Houston, 1985)

Hidden Differences: Doing Business with the Japanese, Edward T. Hall and Mildred Reed Hall (Anchor Press/Doubleday, Garden City, NY, 1987)

Japanese Etiquette & Ethics in Business, Boye DeMente (Passport Books, Lincolnwood, IL, 1987)

Japanese Language and Culture for Business and Travel, Kyoko Hijirida and Muneon Yoshikawa (University of Hawaii Press, Honolulu, 1987)

Japan-Think, Ameri-Think: An Irreverent Guide to Understanding the Cultural Differences between Us, Robert J. Collins (Penguin Books, New York, 1992)

The Japan of Today (International Society for Educational Information, Tokyo, 1989)

Simple Etiquette in Japan, Helmut Morsbach (Paul Norbury Publications, Sandgate, England, 1984)

Update Japan, Aaron Hoopes (Intercultural Press, Yarmouth, ME, 1992)

(Note: Similar "Update" books are available for Belgium [1989], France [1989], Germany [1990], Saudi Arabia [1990], and Hong Kong [1992].)

With Respect to the Japanese: A Guide for Americans, John C. Condon (Intercultural Press, Yarmouth, ME, 1984)

Books on Gestures and Body Language

Bodytalk: The Meaning of Human Gestures, Desmond Morris (Crown Trade Paperbacks, New York, 1994)

Manwatching: a Field Guide to Human Behavior, Desmond Morris (Harry N. Abrams, New York, 1977)

The Silent Language, Edward T. Hall (Fawcett Publications, New York, 1961)

MORE RESOURCES

There are dozens and dozens of Web sites available under the heading of either International Business or Cross-Cultural Communications.

- The International Business Center (www.internationalbus inesscenter.org) runs one of the best sites. The not-for-profit organization identifies and maintains a broad range of dynamic resources for use by international businesspeople, international business students, and professors at international business schools throughout the world. Stephen Taylor is Executive Director.

- The Internet Public Library (www.ipl.org) has a section devoted to International Business and describes its subject matter as follows: "Doing business in international markets, and business information specific to geographic regions of the world." It begins by listing twenty-four resources dealing with everything from international economics and lists of foreign embassies on the Web to information on press and culture, education, commerce and trade, tourism and employment.

- Probably one of the leading educational institutions for all things international is called "Thunderbird," which is located in Glendale, AZ, a suburb of Phoenix. Its Web site is www.ThunderbirdGlobal .com. I have lectured there numerous times and hired some of its graduates. There are thousands of Thunderbird graduates scattered around the world and they seem to enjoy helping one another. The unique name, Thunderbird, derives from a World War II U.S. Air Force base originally located on the present site. For many years it was officially known as The American Graduate School of International Management but was recently renamed The Garvin School after one of its benefactors. This is a one-year (trimester) graduate school specializing in three basic aspects of international business: marketing, finance, and government service. It also specializes by geographic regions. Over 30 percent of students are women, and another large contingent are from foreign countries. There is also an executive education component for business professionals already in international business who want to update or improve their skills, particularly in language proficiency.

- In its own words, Hoover's (www.Hoovers.com) provides "access to over 16 million U.S. and international companies; coverage of Canada, UK, continental Europe, and Asia. International news from 3,000 newspaper, press releases, and industry sources. Wireless access and e-mail alerts, and easy-to-use search, list building, and reporting tools."

- For more Web sites dealing with international *education*, turn to www.directoryofonlineschools.com.

- If your interest is in cross-cultural *training*, here are some suggested Web sites:

  www.peoplegoingglobal.com

  www.circlesofexcellence.com

  www.kwintessential.com.uk

  www.culturalsavvy.com

  www.LemonLimeConsulting.com (for expatriate training)

- To join a national association of protocol experts, consider the International Association of Protocol Consultants (IAPC) in McLean, Virginia (www.protocolconsultants.org). IPAC was founded by Washington, D.C., protocol professional Alinda Lewris with the collaboration of famed protocol and etiquette author Letitia Baldrige, at one time protocol advisor to President and Mrs. John Kennedy. Mailing address: P.O. Box 6150, McLean, Virginia, 22106-6105. Phone: 703-759-4272.

- CultureGrams (www.culturegrams.com) is a must-have source of concise reports on 190 different countries as compiled and published by The David M. Kennedy Center for International Studies at Brigham Young University. Each report offers excellent tips on a country's climate, history, population, language, religion, personal appearance, greetings, gestures, visiting, eating, family lifestyle, diet, recreation, holidays, and on and on. Data for each of these countries was compiled by young missionaries of The Church of Jesus Christ of Latter-Day Saints who travel the world, into the homes of inhabitants, spreading the word of the Mormon Church.

Directory of State International Development Organizations

The State International Development Organization consists of thirty-four state-sponsored offices whose purpose is to encourage and assist companies of all sizes to become involved in exporting. Here is a listing of the states that have them.

United States

Alabama
401 Adams Avenue, 6th Floor
Montgomery, AL 36130
Fax: 334-353-1330

Alaska
Division of International Trade and Market Development
550 West 7th Avenue, Suite 1000
Anchorage, AK 99501
Fax: 907-269-7461

Arkansas
Arkansas Department of Economic Development
One Capitol Mall
Little Rock, AR 72201
Fax: 501-682-7394

Arizona

1700 West Washington, Suite 220
Phoenix, AZ 85007
Fax: 602-771-1204

California

(Note: the California Trade and Commerce Agency ceased operations in
December 2003.)

Colorado

1625 Broadway, Suite #1700
Denver, CO 80202
Fax: 303-892-3820

Connecticut

Connecticut Department of Economic & Community Development
505 Hudson Street
Hartford, CT 06106
Fax: 860-270-8070

Delaware

Delaware Economic Development Office
820 N. French Street, 10th Floor
Wilmington, DE 19801
Fax: 302-577-8499

Florida

Enterprise Florida
2801 Ponce de Leon Boulevard, Suite 700
Coral Gables, FL 33134
Fax: 305-569-2686

Georgia

75 Fifth Street, NW, Suite 1200
Atlanta, GA 30308
Fax: 404-962-4121

Hawaii

Hawaii Department of Business, Economic Development & Tourism

250 South Hotel Street, 5th Floor
Honolulu, HI 96813
Fax: 808-586-2589

Idaho

700 W. State Street
P.O. Box 83720
Boise, ID 83720-0093

Illinois

Office of Trade & Investment
100 W. Randolph, Suite 3-400
Chicago, IL 60601
Fax: 312-814-6581

Indiana

Department of Commerce
1 N. Capitol Avenue, Suite 700
Indianapolis, IN 46204
Fax: 317-233-1680

Iowa

Iowa Department of Economic Development
200 East Grand Avenue
Des Moines, IA 50309
Fax: 515-242-4918

Kansas

1000 S.W. Jackson Street, Suite 100
Topeka, KS 66612-1354
Fax: 785-296-5263

Kentucky

Kentucky Cabinet for Economic Development
2300 Capitol Plaza Tower
500 Mero Street
Frankfort, KY 40601
Fax: 502-564-3256

Louisiana

Louisiana Department of Economic Development
P.O. Box 94185
Baton Rouge, LA 70804
Fax: 225-342-5349

Maine

Maine International Trade Center
511 Congress Street, Suite #100
Portland, ME 04101
Fax: 207-541-7420

Maryland

217 East Redwood Street
Baltimore, MD 21202

Massachusetts

Massachusetts Office of International Trade & Investment
10 Park Plaza, Suite 4510
Boston, MA 02116
Fax: 617-227-3488

Michigan

300 North Washington Square
Lansing, MI 48913
Fax: 517-241-3689

Minnesota

1st National Bank Building
332 Minnesota Street, Suite E200
St. Paul, MN 55101-1351
Fax: 651-296-3555

Mississippi

P.O. Box 849
Jackson, MS 39205
Fax: 601-359-3605

Missouri
301 W. High
P.O. Box 118
Jefferson City, MO 65102
Fax: 573-526-1567

Montana
International Trade & Relations Bureau, Business Resources Division
P.O. Box 200505
Helena, MT 59620-0505
Fax: 406-841-2728

Nebraska
Office of International Trade
301 Centennial Mall South
P.O. Box 94666
Lincoln, NE 68509
Fax: 402-471-3365

Nevada
Global Trade & Investment Department
108 East Proctor Street
Carson City, NV 89701
Fax: 775-687-4450

New Hampshire
International Trade Resource Center
17 New Hampshire Avenue
Portsmouth, NH 03801
Fax: 603-334-6110

New Jersey
N.J. Commerce & Economic Growth Commission
20 West State Street,
P.O. Box 820
Trenton, NJ 08625-0820
Fax: 609-292-5509

New Mexico
1155 South Telshor, Suite 203
Las Cruces, NM 88011
Fax: 505-521-4211

New York
International Division, Empire State Development
633 Third Avenue, 33rd Floor
New York, NY 10017-6706
Fax: 212-803-2399

North Carolina
4320 Mail Service Center
Raleigh, NC 27699-4320
Fax: 919-733-0110

North Dakota
N.D. Department of Commerce
51 Broadway, Suite 505
Fargo, ND 58102

Ohio
Ohio Department of Development
77 South High Street
Columbus, OH 43266
Fax: 614-463-1540

Oklahoma
Global Business Services
700 N. Greenwood, Suite 1400
Tulsa, OK 74106
Fax: 918-594-8413

Oregon
121 S.W. Salmon, Suite 205
Portland, OR 997204
Fax: 503-222-5050

Pennsylvania

Commonwealth Keystone Building
400 North Street, 4th Floor
Harrisburg, PA 17102
Fax: 717-787-6825

Rhode Island

One West Exchange Street
Providence, RI 02903
Fax: 401-273-8270

South Carolina

1201 Main Street, Suite 1600
Columbia, SC 29201
Fax: 803-737-3104

South Dakota

1200 South Jay Street
Aberdeen, SD 57401
Fax: 605-626-3004

Tennessee

312 8th Avenue N.
Nashville, TN 37243
Fax: 615-741-5829

Texas

Office of International Business
Office of the Governor, Economic Development & Tourism
P.O. Box 12428
221 E. 11th Street
Austin, TX 78701
Fax: 512-936-0445

Utah

State of Utah International Business Office
324 South State Street, Suite 500
Salt Lake City, UT 84111
Fax: 801-538-8889

Virginia

Division of International Trade
901 East Byrd Street, West Tower
Richmond, VA 23219
Fax: 804-371-8860

Washington

International Trade Division
2001 6th Avenue, Suite 2600
Seattle, WA 98121
Fax: 206-956-3151

West Virginia

International Division
1900 Kanawha Boulevard E.
Charleston, WV 25305-0311
Fax: 304-558-1957

Wisconsin

International Division
201 West Washington Avenue
Madison, WI 53703
Fax: 608-266-5551

Wyoming

214 W. 15th Street
Cheyenne, WY 82002
Fax: 307-237-3283

Other Jurisdictions

Puerto Rico

Puerto Rico Economic Development Administration
State Trade Office
P.O. Box 362350
San Juan, PR 00918
Fax: 787-754-9645, 787-764-1415

Virgin Islands

116 King Street, Frederiksted
St. Croix, U.S. Virgin Islands 00840
Fax: 340-773-7701

Index